Strike a Pose

And the dance began again. The same two people. The same twenty-five feet apart. But now there was new music, a fugue with a minor undertone.

"Perfect, Linda! Perfect!!"

With every bit of encouragement, Linda grew bolder. First her calves, then her knees, then her thighs emerged through the unbuttoned slit of her dress.

"Perfect!" Charlie moaned.

She whirled, she twisted, and she danced. Under the relentless desert sun, the sky a vivid blue behind her, she was not just a perfect woman, she was all women. She was the only woman on earth.

And then, achingly too soon for Charlie, it was over.

But, the last dance was about to begin...

FATAL
PHOTOGRAPHS

JACK R. NERAD

AVON BOOKS  NEW YORK

FATAL PHOTOGRAPHS is a journalistic account of the actual murder investigation of Charles Rathbun for the 1995 murder of Linda Sobek in El Mirage, California. The events recounted in this book are true. The scenes and dialogue have been reconstructed based on tape-recorded formal interviews, police department records, and published news stories. Quoted testimony has been taken from pre-trial transcripts and other sworn statements.

AVON BOOKS, INC.
1350 Avenue of the Americas
New York, New York 10019

Copyright © 1998 by Jack R. Nerad
Published by arrangement with the author
Visit our website at http://www.AvonBooks.com
Library of Congress Catalog Card Number: 98-93297
ISBN: 0-380-79770-4

First Avon Books Printing: December 1998

AVON TRADEMARK REG. U.S. PAT. OFF. AND IN OTHER COUNTRIES, MARCA REGISTRADA, HECHO EN U.S.A.

Printed in the U.S.A.

WCD   10 9 8 7 6 5 4 3 2 1

For my maternal grandmother, Esther Landsea,
who always wanted a writer in the family.
Thank you for your encouragement,
both here and there.

Acknowledgments

This book would not have been what it is save for the unselfish contributions of a large number of people. Most sources with whom I sought to speak gave unstintingly of their time, and I would like to thank them publicly, whether they felt comfortable with being quoted or preferred the cloak of anonymity.

I owe a great debt to both legal teams involved in the case. Charles Rathbun's defense attorney, Mark Werksman, was unfailingly accessible and remarkably candid, and for that I offer many thanks. On the prosecution side, Deputy District Attorney Stephen Kay and Assistant District Attorney Mary-Jean Bowman were also extremely forthcoming and helpful. Despite Charles Rathbun's protests to the contrary, Kay certainly rides a white horse as one of the best prosecutors in the country, and I for one am glad he is so zealous in both putting away murderers and keeping them put away.

While we are talking about good guys, I would also like to extend my profound thanks to Sergeant Mike Robinson of the Los Angeles County Sheriff's Department Homicide Division. This tenacious cop spent hour upon hour revealing nuances of the case to me, and his contributions made the narrative much richer. My sincere thanks also goes to Sheriff's Department Sergeant John Yarbrough, whose telling insight into the personality traits of various criminals was both fascinating and helpful in understanding what happened in this case.

As to interview subjects many spoke only under the condition of anonymity, and I have honored their requests. Many thanks to them and those who were willing to go on the record, among them Scott Killeen, Jim Nichols, Shannon Meyer, Trish Peterson and Phil Spangenberger. Each had a different perspective on the crime and on Charles Rathbun, and each proved extremely helpful in developing a true picture of this very complex case.

I would also be remiss if I didn't offer thanks to several people who helped make this book a reality: Robert McCord, my agent who supported this book from the beginning; Coates Bateman, the Avon Books editor who accepted the book proposal; and Yedida L. Soloff, the Avon Books editor who shepherded the manuscript through the entire process. Thanks to all three of you for your intelligent questions and comments. And for the same reasons, I would also like to thank my friends and colleagues Sheryl Goodrich and Michele Samit for their suggestions.

I thank Charles Rathbun for deciding to speak to me about the entire case and giving me carte blanche to tell it as I saw it. His brother, Robert Rathbun, also was helpful, particularly in delineating the Rathbun family history.

And finally, I must not only thank the family of Linda Sobek—her mother Elaine, her father Bob and her brother Steve—for their cooperation, but I also share in their grief. The loss of a daughter is a horrible prospect to contemplate, and it has taken a terrible toll on them. My hope for them is that they will some day find peace.

To all these acknowledgments, I add my heartfelt thanks to my darling wife, Sandi, and my daughter, Madeleine. For long periods of time this project left them on their own without my help, and I thank them for bearing with me to its completion.

Jack R. Nerad
June 2, 1998

Chapter 1

THE THREE towns of Manhattan Beach, Redondo Beach and Hermosa Beach cling to the southern crescent of Santa Monica Bay like barnacles on a piling. Not more than fifteen miles from downtown Los Angeles and a much shorter distance from the leviathan Los Angeles International airport, the trio of beach towns forms an insular community that seems much farther from the daily strife of the City of Angels than their distance might suggest.

Collectively, the towns are part of what is called locally the South Bay, but though they are often lumped together, each town has its own personality. Redondo, sprawling from the dreariness of the inland flats to the wooded hills of the Palos Verdes peninsula, is home to giant aerospace companies, suburban neighborhoods and high-rise apartment buildings. Its residents are mostly middle class, though the less desirable sections in its northern and eastern reaches harbor enough gang activity for its police department and longtime citizens who remember a kinder and gentler Redondo to have become more than a little concerned.

At the same time that its near neighbor has begun to suffer from the realities of urban Los Angeles in the nineties, Manhattan has emerged as a sanctuary for the upwardly mobile. Each day this formerly out-of-the-way beach town sees a little more of its history wiped away

1

as fifty-year-old cottages that went up by the dozen after World War II are ripped down to make way for grander houses that are quickly populated by six-figure-salaried professionals, their children and their nannies. Each bull-dozing and construction creates a minor windfall for the local developers, and if at the same time the heritage of the town is dealt another body blow, no one seems to care. Violent crime is a reasonably rare occurrence in Manhattan, although the murder of one of its policemen did gain national attention in 1993. The major reason for its news-worthiness: it was the first such death in the eighty-year history of the Manhattan Beach police force.

The final town of the trio is Hermosa Beach, a strange fit, jigsawed between Manhattan on the north and Redondo on the south and east. Hermosa is a town that shares neither Redondo's middle-class center nor its gang-inspired edginess, and it's a town that refuses to buy into Manhattan's accelerating snootiness. In some ways Hermosa Beach is as oddly off-center as it was in the twenties, when bootleggers landed cases of illegal booze on its wide beaches under the unseeing eyes of its local constabulary, which in those days was available to the highest bidder.

Today the town is epitomized by a former mayor who makes no bones about his former alcohol and drug use, a former mayor who collected his local following by hosting a cable access TV show. It is a town where million-dollar beachfront homes mix with peep-show porno shops, a town that hosts the annual Hermosa triathlon, which consists of swimming a mile, paddling a surfboard in heavy swells and then downing a six-pack of beer. The worthy contestant who can do all that in the shortest time—and keep the beer down for half an hour—is deemed the winner.

Obviously this is a town that doesn't take itself seriously. Today, just as when it was founded ninety-odd years ago, the beach is Hermosa Beach's reason for being. Because of this, Hermosa is a town that takes monumental pride in the perfection of the human form. With more than two hundred beach days a year, days when bikinis and baggies are the only acceptable attire, in Hermosa Beach comeliness is next to godliness. Its beach town culture worships beautiful people, and at the same time it's full of them. In fact, one saying in town is that beautiful girls are just like buses: if you miss one there will be another one along in just a couple of minutes.

On November 16, 1995, one of those beautiful women, a bathing suit model and hopeful actress named Linda Sobek, vanished from the funky beach town that was her adopted home. At about 10 o'clock that morning she left her beachfront apartment, climbed into her white Nissan 240SX and seemingly drove off the face of the earth.

Linda Sobek wasn't born in Hermosa Beach. In fact, she had lived there for a relatively short portion of her twenty-seven years. But she was definitely *of* Hermosa Beach. She filled out a bathing suit provocatively; she was a workout fanatic; and she loved to have fun. If the Beach Boys, who hailed from nearby Hawthorne, had started their careers thirty years later, she was just the type they would have been singing about.

Linda was certainly a California girl. She grew up in Lakewood, a tidy blue-collar section south of downtown Los Angeles, bisected by the 605 freeway. Her landlocked neighborhood was chock-full of tiny two- and three-bedroom bungalows owned and maintained by hard-working people who didn't seem to notice as some of the sections around their tiny enclave began to give in to decay and crime.

But Linda did notice, and she wanted out. She had bigger things in mind for herself than the confines of Lakewood would permit, and she loved the beach. So when she was twenty years old, she left the small bedroom that she loved so much in her parents' tidy little house and went out on her own. Over the next couple of years, she lived in Redondo Beach, Huntington Beach and Playa del Rey. Each town was a mecca for singles, and each time an expanse of sand was just steps from her apartment door.

Finally, after a live-in romance had fizzled, she moved again, this time into an apartment building bordering Hermosa's broad beach on the strip of concrete known as the Strand. A haven for bicyclists, joggers and Rollerbladers, the Strand was the perfect setting for her. Less than twenty feet from the sand, fifty yards from the surf, her shared apartment put her right in the middle of the action. Because she was a social person who made friends easily, she was in her element.

In an area packed with an abundance of attractive people, Linda stood out. Not only was she naturally attractive, with big eyes and a lovely smile, but also she approached her appearance the way others might approach their career—she worked it.

From the time she was in high school, drawing admiring glances from the boys, she knew she wanted to be a model. She attacked the challenge of breaking into that cruel and crowded field with her trademark tenacity. Coming of age in the midst of the hardbody craze, she fought her slight tendency to gain weight with an intense exercise program. She had her naturally light-brown hair colored blond. When that wasn't enough, she had her breasts enlarged and her nose retouched. In essence, she approached her body the way one might approach a home renovation project. Some areas she fixed herself. For others she required professional help. But one thing she could do nothing about was her height.

At five foot three, she knew it would be impossible to become the type of high-fashion model who struts European runways wearing Chanel, Lagerfeld or Versace. Pretty and fit as she was, there was no way she was ever going to be a willowy, six-two fashion stick with small, pouty breasts and a little boy's butt, so reaching the zenith of the modeling profession was beyond her.

Instead, it became obvious that her niche would be another, less prestigious area—bathing suit modeling. Bathing suit models are used like condiments on a hot dog. Their job is to improve the appeal of an otherwise mundane subject. They are more likely to pose next to a tricked-out pickup truck than appear in a New York couture debut. They are more likely to make figurative love to a socket wrench than they are to tout makeup on TV. And they are more likely to appear in a poster for an engine-oil additive than in a major motion picture. For those who model bathing suits, the "bod" is the thing, and in most instances, the more bodacious the body, the better. Large, full breasts and tight buttocks are de rigueur. A narrow waist and a pretty face are welcome but not always necessary additions.

In bathing suit modeling, it seems like there's always some guy—photographer, client, passerby—who's after the model to take off her scanty top so as better to see exactly what lies underneath. A woman has to work awfully hard to keep her dignity while wearing a bathing suit and high-heeled shoes in the first place. Imagine how hard it must be when seemingly every third guy or so wants to get a look at her breasts.

But Linda Sobek, unlike many in her profession, was always able to keep her dignity. In fact, she was as serious about it as she was about improving her body. When photographers got out of line with her, she'd let them know in no uncertain terms that she was a model, not a bimbo.

She approached her work seriously, kept appointments punctually and maintained constant contact with her friends in the business. If some blond bathing suit models deserve the description bubbleheaded, Linda Sobek was not one of them. She had purpose and direction in her life.

Which made it all the more frightening to her friends when she disappeared.

Chapter 2

THE THURSDAY before Thanksgiving, 1995, dawned gray and chilly in Hermosa Beach. Inland the day had begun bright and sunny, but in the South Bay strands of ocean fog hung low in the air like Spanish moss in a Louisiana oak tree, while a thick cloud cover, slate-colored and ominous, blotted out the sun. If you were from the Midwest, you might have expected the clouds to bring rain. But if you hailed from the beach towns, you knew better. The burn-off was inevitable, and soon the sun would again be pouring down on the wide, flat expanses of dirty-beige sand. Another beach day was brewing, just like the hundreds that had come before and the hundreds that would come after.

Linda Sobek, a veteran of the beach scene, took scant notice of the weather that morning. She wasn't the type simply to loll away languid afternoons on the beach. As always, she had things to do.

According to her many friends, she possessed a cheery disposition and a sweet, spiritual soul, but she was also a driven woman. She had an agenda for herself, things she wanted to accomplish, and she was always pushing herself to accomplish them. Amazingly, she was always able to do that while consistently making time for other people.

That morning, up at about eight, she prepared a pot of coffee and then shared it with one of her roommates, Betty Burgos. The two chatted for a few minutes, and

6

Linda seemed her usual happy, upbeat self. Dressed in workout gear, she was ready for the first of her twice-a-day trips from her home in Hermosa to hit the weights at Gold's Gym in neighboring Redondo Beach. She also mentioned she had a couple of errands to run that morning, including a stop at a Manhattan Beach photocopy shop where she was having some business fliers printed up, but the talk was as lightweight as a helium balloon. Linda never mentioned a modeling assignment, something she would very likely have brought up if she'd had one, and she didn't speak of boyfriend troubles, financial worries or other problems that might have led her to turn her back on her present life and disappear.

After finishing her cup of coffee, Linda called her boyfriend, a man she had met just the month before, and the two talked briefly. Again the conversation was mundane. Again she made no mention of a modeling assignment. Promising to phone him later that day, she hung up.

Betty Burgos knew that Linda wanted to get to the gym, so she went outside to move her car, enabling her roommate to get into her Nissan 240SX and be on her way. Linda's five-minute drive was uneventful, and she arrived at Gold's Gym around nine. She said a friendly hello to several of the familiar faces, both patrons and staff members, and then got into her workout routine, a strenuous ritual of weight work and stretching. She was straining at it, a sweat breaking through her leotard, when her ever present pager went off, signaling the prospect of work. She responded to the page immediately, since a two-hour photo shoot could net her as much as five hundred dollars, and the voice on the other end of the line, a voice she'd heard only a couple of times before, asked her if she could model for him that afternoon.

She knew she was free, but she hesitated for a moment, a good bargaining tactic, before telling the inquiring photographer that she was available. She asked what the assignment was. The photographer, whom she had worked with a couple of times and had last seen at an automotive trade show a few weeks before, told her that she would be posing with a new luxury sport utility that was soon to be introduced by Lexus. She liked the fact that it was an upscale product, because that could enhance her image, but she didn't agree to take the job until she had made certain of the amount of time the session would take and the rate of pay, something she did with meticulous precision before agreeing to any modeling session. It was the way she did business.

She agreed to meet the photographer at a nearby Denny's coffee shop. Looking up at the clock on the wall, she decided she could still get part of her workout in before she had to leave for the assignment. She returned to the weights, but instead of her normal hour-and-half stint at the gym, she only put in about forty-five minutes.

Departing the gym, she made a quick trip up the road to Manhattan Beach, not more than ten minutes away, where she picked up the materials she had left to be duplicated. Then she stopped back at her now empty apartment to pick up a pair of outfits that might prove useful on the photo shoot. At 10:45 that morning her mother Elaine called from her home in Lakewood, and Linda said that she was hurrying off on a last-minute photo assignment. In fact, she was in such a hurry that she didn't take the time to tell her mother who the photographer was or what the assignment was for, facts she usually would have shared.

Later that morning Linda phoned her own answering machine, a drill that she repeated umpteen times a day, and changed her outgoing message, telling callers that she was on a photo assignment and would not be reachable.

That phone message was the last her family and friends ever heard from Linda. Perfectly in character, she was taking care of business and thinking of others until the very end. And with that ethereal message, she was gone. After that, no one, save one man, can remember seeing her. After that, no one, save one man, can remember speaking to her. It was as if a swift tsunami had washed over her and carried her out to sea without a trace.

The cliché is to describe a disappearance as sudden, as in, "Suddenly, Linda Sobek was gone." But the fact of the matter is that the realization that a loved one has disappeared is rarely sudden. Instead it creeps up on those who care like a summer cold progressing into pneumonia.

Most often the realization that a disappearance has occurred begins with a vague question hanging in the back of a loved one's mind. "Wasn't she supposed to call me this afternoon?" That's what Linda Sobek's mother and boyfriend thought to themselves as the hours of November 16 droned on without a word from her.

From a vague, uncomfortable feeling the realization progresses to a more definite and obscurely ominous wonderment. "I wonder what happened to her? I really expected her to call by now." As day turned into night and Linda had still not been heard from, the wonderment grew in her mother, boyfriend and roommates. Linda was simply too considerate of others and too businesslike a person to go even four or five hours without phoning one or more of her confidantes, most especially her mother. By the time the early darkness of November had descended and dinnertime had come and gone without a word, Elaine Sobek's concern about her daughter had escalated to serious proportions.

She had reached the next step in the plodding progress of a disappearance—recognition that something might really be wrong, that the slight ache in the back of your mind and the pit of your stomach might actually mean that some harm has come to a person you care deeply about. At that point the question arises, "What should I do?"

What Elaine Sobek did was the same thing anybody might have done. She called Linda's apartment, but instead of reaching Linda, she spoke to one of her roommates. The answers she got were more unsettling than helpful. When it was all added up, the indications were ominous. Even in a short span of hours too many un-Lindalike things had happened.

The punctual career woman who phoned her mother several times a day hadn't called in more than twelve hours.

The aspiring actress who was working hard to establish a television career had missed a wardrobe fitting that might have led to her big break.

The reliable, responsible roommate who kept in nearly constant touch with her friends hadn't come home at night and, more troubling, hadn't let her apartment mates know where she was.

Heavily dependent upon her mother and her female friends, Linda just wasn't the type to take off on the spur of the moment. She certainly had friends who had the financial wherewithal to hop on a plane to Tahiti or Monaco at a moment's notice. And she was certainly fun-loving, with no real encumbrances. But impulsive? Not Linda.

Her absence without a phone call or a note left on the kitchen counter was so uncharacteristic of her that it immediately led those closest to her to jump to the direst conclusions. And when she didn't show up to a television audition the following day, those closest to her didn't just suspect but *knew* that something horrible had happened to Linda. But beyond a loathsome, heartsick worry, there was nothing much they could do, and though they reported her missing, there was nothing much the authorities would do.

The sad fact is that it's not unusual for people to go missing in Los Angeles. Each month more than a hundred men, women and children vanish in Los Angeles County, leaving their loved ones, if indeed they have loved ones, in the same uneasy state as Linda's parents and friends. The police jurisdictions in the Los Angeles area just don't have the resources to search for them, particularly when the authorities have so many more obvious and immediate needs staring them right in the face.

It's not that the police are unsympathetic to the mother of a missing daughter or the father of a missing son. It's simply that they know that the vast majority of the missing turn up a few hours or days later, perhaps somewhat the worse or the better for the experience, but most often alive. Sometimes the purported missing persons were staying at a friend's house down the street; other times they ran away from home; in still others they ran off with a boyfriend or girlfriend. But despite what the evening news would lead you to believe, it is very rare for the missing to turn up dead. Most often they are found quickly, safely and happily. On those occasions when they stay missing, it is usually because they want to stay missing, not because of that old bogey "foul play."

All of which provided no solace to Linda Sobek's frantic family and friends. They didn't care that others would run off without informing their families; they didn't care that others would pick up and leave town without so much as a see-ya-bye. All they cared about was Linda, and the fact that "she just wouldn't do this" scared them.

"How could a woman as centered and thoughtful as Linda just take off?" they asked themselves. The answers they got back did nothing to appease their worry.

Since the police found it impossible to help, the next source of possible help seemed to be the news media. Broad publicity surrounding Linda Sobek's disappearance might reach someone who had seen her recently and so shed light on where she might be. Or, if the unthinkable had happened and she had disappeared intentionally, it might prompt her to phone home.

Ninety-nine times out of a hundred, the news media are even more cynical about missing persons than are the authorities. They know from long experience that most missing person cases don't really amount to much, so they rarely cause a ripple on the five o'clock news. But those friends and family who wanted to publicize Sobek's disappearance had one weapon in their arsenal that most who seek publicity about their missing relative or friend don't have—Linda Sobek was a beautiful woman.

And so, over the weekend of November 18 to 19, 1995, a Los Angeles TV station aired Linda's story and then *Hard Copy,* a syndicated tabloid television show, broke it nationwide. To the most terminally cynical, it might have looked like a publicity stunt: video on national TV of attractive model who has vanished without a trace, likely to be followed by her joyful, tearful reunion with friends and family a day or so after the original airing.

But Linda Sobek's disappearance was certainly no stunt, and unlike the vast majority of missing persons cases, once it appeared on *Hard Copy,* her story drew a flurry of attention from the local Los Angeles television news operations. Jumping on the bandwagon started by *Hard Copy,* they grabbed the Sobek story and ran with it. Of course, there wasn't much to report—only that Sobek had left her Hermosa Beach home a few days before and hadn't been seen since—but the Los Angeles media made the most of a feeble storyline. Locked in the midst of a November sweeps month, a key television ratings period, Los Angeles TV stations treated her disappearance as they would a catastrophic fire or an impending storm, manufacturing every possible opportunity to splash her comely cheerleader face and ample chest across area TV screens.

Though she was a celebrity in only the broadest sense of that shopworn term, the story of Linda's sudden absence quickly grew into a media frenzy. Not the least of the reasons for the heavy media coverage was that to the delight of news directors across the LA metroplex, Sobek had left behind a legacy of video: fleeting shots of her bantering happily with a few fans in her Los Angeles Raiders cheerleading costume, complete with silver pompons, and a more serious Sobek striking provocative poses while draped over a manly motorcycle, her blond hair flowing in a fan-forced stream. "Model Missing" screamed the news teases supered over her exposed flesh, and who could resist the speculation about who or what had caused this quintessential California girl to suddenly drop from the face of the Golden State?

Yes, Linda Sobek was gone, but where?

Speculation ran rampant. Video showing Linda Sobek's surgically altered breasts ran rampant. But as to finding out what had happened to her, determining where Linda Sobek was, that task was as far from being accomplished as it ever had been.

One of the steps to accomplishing that was to determine where Linda had been up until the time she disappeared. Which begged the question: just who was Linda Sobek anyway?

Chapter 3

From the time she was a baby, Linda Sobek was outgoing and vivacious. Her mother, Elaine, fondly remembers the big smile she would always shine for her grandfather, a smile warm enough to melt hearts, and over the years she would smile that winning smile in many directions.

Described by her parents as a good baby, Linda grew up in the wake of her elder brother, Steve, who was a good-natured but boisterous child bent on doing what he wanted to do just to see what would happen. One of his regular habits was to take away Linda's pacifier, a stunt that sometimes sent her into a screaming fit at embarrassing times. One of those came at a drive-in movie, where the Sobeks had hoped to enjoy the big-screen version of *The Odd Couple*. Before the evening was over, Linda's wailing had driven away all the cars around them.

But that situation was more the exception than the rule. Most often the young Linda was very well behaved, and her mother had no qualms about enrolling her in ballet class at the ripe old age of three. Several times a week the bus operated by the Twin School of Dance would pick her up from the Sobek's home, and she would dive into her lessons.

"She was so intent on what she was doing," Elaine remembered. "She was kind of klutzy with her ballet, but

14

she tried real hard. She was even in dance recitals at the Pomona Fair.''

Her brother Steve recalled that the little ballet dancer also had a bit of tomboy in her.

''Up until she was about five years old, she used to hang out with me and try to do what I was doing,'' he said. ''She even used to try to dress like me.''

Quite early in her life, she began to develop an independent streak that would characterize her throughout her life.

''I remember when she started kindergarten, I walked her to school,'' Elaine said, ''and then at lunch I rode my bicycle over to get her, and she said to me, 'Mom, you don't need to pick me up any more.' I was devastated. She didn't need me.''

As she grew up, her little room in the cozy Sobek family home became her sanctuary. She spent a great deal of time there, doing things so private her family never knew quite what she was up to.

Of course, the family was privy to her collecting binges.

''She'd get into a hobby and then start collecting the things,'' her father, Bob, recalled. ''One time it would be horses, another time it would be teddy bears.''

''She redecorated that bedroom five or six times while she lived here,'' Elaine added.

Linda also developed a love for animals, and one day in her grammar school years she brought home a cat she called Bo. Her family remembers how deeply she loved that cat, often dressing him up and smothering him with affection. It was obvious she had a lot of affection to give, a trait that endeared her to many who came in contact with her.

By the time Linda reached junior high school, her tomboy days were over. She started to get interested in boys and became even fussier about the clothes she wore. She went on frequent excursions to the mall with her mother, trying to find just the right outfits while staying within the restraints of the family budget.

As a freshman in high school she was chosen to be a cheerleader, but in subsequent years she had to content herself with being in the flag section, doing routines at halftime. Though she had hoped to remain on the cheerleading squad, she was repeatedly passed over for that honor and instead waved a banner for much of her high school career.

Her parents described her as studious, and she usually brought home a B average on her report cards. At the same time she was involved in several extracurricular activities, including a mountain-climbing club, with which she went on several excursions.

Some of her other extracurricular activities in high school weren't nearly as benign. Like many teenagers, she sometimes hung around with the wrong guys, and she did her share of drinking.

"In fact, I think she did a lot more drinking in high school than after it," her brother Steve remembers.

Perhaps some of her bad behavior could be traced to the romance Elaine described as Linda's first love. As a freshman in high school, she started going out with a freshman named Greg Dally, and soon the couple was going steady.

"They really cared about each other," Elaine said.

For several months the young man became a part of the family, and Linda vacationed with Greg and his family on Catalina Island. Unfortunately, soon thereafter the young man developed symptoms of cancer, a disease that ran in his family. With Linda by his side, he underwent a series of rigorous treatments that left him confined to a hospital room. Linda often visited him there, but as the cancer spread, he finally asked her not to visit him any more, not wanting her to see how he had deteriorated.

He died at age sixteen, and, as her mother said, "It hit her hard."

In the wake of Greg's death, with Linda sinking into

depression and unwanted behavior, her parents looked for a positive outlet that might revitalize her, and they found it in Barbizon, a modeling school. Naturally attractive, Linda was eager to try modeling, and though Elaine thought the school was expensive, she decided that if it helped her daughter, it would be worth the money.

Linda dove into modeling with her characteristic energy. She ate up her classes at Barbizon, and friends she made in the school suggested that she get involved in outside modeling sessions. Before her seventeenth birthday she was modeling for photography students at Cerritos College, a school she would later attend, and she was participating in modeling days hosted by *Western Photographer* magazine.

The magazine-sponsored events were designed for amateur photographers, who paid a fee to shoot pictures of models hired for the occasion. Most often for these sessions Linda's costume, like those of the other girls, was a skimpy bikini, and her father had some difficulty with that. But Linda loved posing so much that he didn't have the heart to insist that she stop.

There is no doubt that Linda reveled in the attention and enjoyed the glamour of her new avocation. As her mother described it, "She used to kid us that we never took that many pictures of her, because she was the second one [child], so that's why she got into modeling."

She was named Junior Model of the Year by *Western Photographer* in 1986, the year she celebrated her eighteenth birthday, and that same year she entered the Miss Artesia beauty pageant. A series of other beauty pageants followed. She became a cover girl for Ujena, a swimsuit manufacturer, and became a contestant on the *All-New Dating Game* television program.

Many budding models are pushed into the business by their mother, but that was not the case with Linda.

"It wasn't our idea; it was hers," Elaine remembered. "She went and signed up for all these pageants, and we'd all go. And it was hard. We'd watch her and think she was the best, and when they didn't pick our daughter, we'd say, 'What's the matter with these fools?' ''

Win or lose, Linda enjoyed the competition, and she kept a neat scrapbook of clips and photos from her various modeling events and beauty pageants. Also included in the scrapbook were memorabilia from her high school graduation, but graduation received minor treatment compared to her modeling work. Along the way she held jobs at Burger King, Federated (a home electronics retailer), and Oshman's Sporting Goods, but those mundane jobs paled next to the excitement of modeling.

Linda entered Cerritos College and eventually graduated with an Associates Art degree, but she had already chosen her career path. Her stints with *Western Photographer* led to paying sessions, and her ability to fill out a bathing suit soon made her popular with many of the Southern California-based automotive photographers.

In 1987 she tried out against hundreds of other hopefuls for a spot on the Los Angeles Raiders cheerleading squad, the Raiderettes, and she had already made the team before she informed her family that she had auditioned. She performed for the team at every game that year, and the following season she thought she was a shoo-in for the squad again. She invited her entire family to the audition, but when the final names were called, hers wasn't among them. She was crushed and embarrassed.

That slap in the face might have stopped others with less spirit than Linda, but she had loved being a Raiderette, so she tried out for the squad again the following year and made it. Though she wasn't a sports fan, she enjoyed the spectacle of the games, and she invited her mother to every one of them. Often Linda would persuade one of her boyfriends to pick Elaine up and escort her to the Coliseum.

Being a member of the Raiderettes also offered Linda a swirl of social opportunities. She was invited to parties all over town, parties that were often filled with important people from various walks of life. But Linda was never starstruck, and according to her brother, who attended many of the parties with her, she often had no idea who the stars she was mingling with were.

"I remember at the SEMA [Specialty Equipment Marketing Association] show we all saw Reggie Jackson, and she didn't know who he was," Steve recalled. "Can you imagine not knowing who Reggie Jackson is?"

By the time she reached her twenties, men were coming into her life so thick and fast that her family members couldn't keep up with them. But while Linda was popular, she wasn't promiscuous. She did go from one boyfriend to another, but while she was with each one she treated him as something special.

Several of her boyfriends were bodybuilders, some of them professional. Others, like Fabio, with whom she had a brief relationship, were well-chiseled actor-models.

As her father, Bob, observed, "She seemed drawn to very buff men."

She met one of her boyfriends when, as a bouncer at a club, he tried to throw her brother out of the place. She came to Steve's aid, talked with the club employee, and the two hit it off. Ultimately the pair lived together for a time in the beach community of Playa del Rey.

Another boyfriend persuaded Linda to end her stint with the Raiderettes. A well-known name on the bodybuilding circuit, he told Linda he wanted to take her with him as he competed all over the world but that it would be impossible if she was still with the Raiderettes. Against her better judgment she quit the squad, but the relationship ended shortly thereafter, and when she asked for reinstatement, she was told she would have to try out for the team the following year.

Despite the ups and downs of her love life, Linda remained a devoted daughter. She visited her parents frequently, and without being asked, she'd start dusting, clean cupboards or sweep out the garage. She was extremely generous, often giving thoughtful gifts for no reason at all, and she couldn't wait for Christmas, starting her gift shopping very early each year.

While she was more than willing to spend her money on others, however, she was also hardworking and frugal.

"The only time she wasn't working was when she was sick," her brother recalled. "I asked her once why she was always working, and she told me she was doing all this for her family."

As Bob and Elaine explained, Linda wasn't talking about her father, mother and brother, though she loved them very much, but about her hoped-for husband and her dreamed-about kids. That's what Linda wanted most of all. And sadly, that's what Linda would never have.

Chapter 4

IT IS easy to think of beautiful people as happy people. On television, in the movies and in magazines, if you're attractive, you enjoy a pleasant, carefree existence, wallow in consumer products, and bask on the beach during fabulous vacations. The ugly, the overweight, the poorly dressed—those are the people who are having painful, miserable lives.

Yet although Linda Sobek was remarkably beautiful, she was also, at times, thoroughly unhappy. She gave much to others, but as the years went by, she began to wonder if she was getting back nearly as much as she gave. Cynicism was growing within her, a feeling that she was always being used. She was becoming convinced that to most people she was just boobs, blond ñair and nothing else. Sadly, too, at just twenty-seven, Linda had begun to fear age.

Though she may not have been scholarly, Linda Sobek was smart. She ran her career like a business and worked her body as her business's biggest asset. She knew only too well that a bathing suit model's days are numbered from the day she pulls on her first bikini. She was well aware there would always be younger, shapelier girls waiting in the wings, and after more than a half-dozen years in the business, working trade show after trade show, waving pom-pons on the sidelines at countless football games, she was wondering rather seriously, "Is this all there is?"

She was ready for the big break, ready to make the transition to the next level of her career. Would it be a guest shot on a network comedy? Would it be a continuing role on a syndicated show? Would it be a splashy layout in *Playboy*, something she had resisted up to that point?

She wasn't certain. On her confident days she felt she was getting close. On her less confident ones she was afraid that her big break was as far away as it had ever been.

Like many, she could be contradictory. She was happy-go-lucky yet serious, frivolous yet introspective, normally upbeat to a fault yet on rare occasions depressed nearly to the point of suicide. She made her living by looking sexy, yet many who knew her and worked with her felt she was one of the least sexual people they had ever met.

On the gray morning of November 16, 1995, Sobek had a number of conflicting thoughts running through her head. She was excited about the prospect of auditioning for *Married with Children*. She had a feeling a little TV exposure, even in a dumb-bimbo role, could propel her career ahead dramatically. In the back of her mind, she was hoping for a shot at a part on *Baywatch*. She certainly had the body for it, but she had recently seen new roles on the show go to women who had bared it all for one of the men's magazines. She didn't want to go that route, but . . .

She had recently posed seminude and nude for some test shots intended for submission to *Playboy*. Even so, she had her problems with posing for the magazine. On her twenty-seventh birthday she had acknowledged her born-again Christian status with a swimming pool baptism, and posing in the nude for a men's magazine struck her as being contradictory to her renewed religious faith.

Still, she thought, if it will advance my career, maybe I should do it.

Her growing cynicism about her career frequently did battle with her born-again vow. She still was a sincere helpmate to her many friends, but she was growing warier and warier of being used by people. In the early days of her career, she had found satisfaction in the work, some thrill at being the center of attention, but as her career progressed, the joy vanished, and modeling assignments became nothing but work for her. The money became the job's only justification.

A large part of her cynicism had also been spawned by the pain and loneliness of a series of failed relationships. Though Linda had a wide variety of close female friends, the closest being her mother, Elaine, her choices in boyfriends had been miserable. She usually found to her sorrow that the muscleman types she was drawn to were much more interested in having a babe than having a baby. And being part of a loving family was what she wanted most of all.

Linda dreamed of the day when she would have a strong, loving husband and several affectionate children. Picturing her family, she saw herself ensconced in a lovely home right out of a magazine layout. She would be the beautiful wife; her husband would be almost equally beautiful; and their children—well, of course, they would be the most beautiful of all. Several times Linda thought she was close to realizing this dream.

After meeting him at a party, Linda had become infatuated with Lorenzo Lamas, the internationally famous star of the syndicated television show *Renegade.* They began a romance, and she fell in love with the darkly handsome actor, partied with him in Hollywood, and hoped and prayed for the day when he would ask her to marry him. But the proposal never came, and Linda left the relationship, heartbroken.

Sobek also had a long-term affair with internationally famous bodybuilder Bill MacClure (not his real name), the one who had persuaded Linda to quit the Raiderettes. Again she fell for the muscleman heavily; again she waited for a proposal of marriage; and again she waited in vain.

There were other men along the way as well and other personal tragedies. Each breakup left her heartbroken, but with a strong will and a romantic heart, she got past them, hoping the next guy would be the one to make her dreams come true.

Of course, most of the time Linda curbed her growing bitterness and kept it well hidden. She enjoyed children immensely, and any kind of charity work left her feeling fulfilled. To her friends she was a happy person, much more considerate than most and always ready to lend a helping hand. It was sad that in her mind she felt she was growing old when in reality she was so vibrantly young.

As Sobek prepared herself for yet another photo session with yet another photographer on that dreary late-autumn morning, she wondered to herself what this shoot would be like. Then she quickly put the thought out of her mind. She knew what it would be like. It would be like all the others.

That was where she was very wrong.

Chapter 5

IT'S IMPOSSIBLE to know what Charles E. Rathbun (Charlie to his friends) had in mind when he climbed from his Hollywood Hills bed on the morning of November 16, 1995. The tall, slightly balding photographer will tell you that the nondescript Thursday was just another workday for him, another day filled with the minute details involved in shooting magazine-quality photographs of automobiles. Others, after the fact, insist there was a fire burning inside him that morning that had to be quenched.

What no one can deny is that on that gray morning Charlie, like Linda, was on the move. Three years before, he had left the comforting cocoon of a full-time paycheck to test the waters as a freelance photographer. Prior to that he had labored for nearly four years as an employee of Petersen Publishing Company, a Hollywood-based magazine industry powerhouse that publishes *Motor Trend, Hot Rod, Teen, Guns & Ammo* and a slew of other titles. Because of his contacts in the industry and the quality of his work, he had quickly established a career on his own after leaving Petersen, but like all freelancers, he knew he had to hustle to keep the work coming in. Aware of the constant pressure to produce, he rolled out of his rented Hollywood Hills home early and began to fight the thick weekday traffic.

As he worked his way south, Rathbun had some new positives in his life to contemplate. In the previous six

25

weeks he had met a woman named Glenda Elam, and their chance meeting had quickly led to romance. An attractive blond slightly older than Charlie, Glenda was a rather quiet, fragile-looking woman, who carried her years well. When the two met, she was working at Petersen Publishing, whose offices Charlie still visited often despite having left the company on less than pleasant terms. They had several mutual friends at Petersen, and according to Charlie, they immediately connected. In fact, their romance moved so rapidly that by November 16 they were thinking about marriage, and though no ring had been given, they considered themselves engaged.

Not only was Charlie involved in a new romance, he was also about to realize the dream of a lifetime—owning his own home. He had already signed a contract to buy a Hollywood Hills property not too distant from his current rental home, and as he wheeled his sport utility toward Lexus that morning, he smiled to himself, thinking how good it would be to have his own place. The home was more than a domicile to him; it was proof that he had not only survived the topsy-turvy world of freelance photography, he had thrived in it. His success was all the more fulfilling when he looked back at the difficult days he had endured as a second-banana staff photographer at Petersen.

The weather deteriorated a bit as he wended his way from the California-style bungalow that he shared with Bill Longo toward the coast, but Charlie had many reasons to feel fortunate that morning as he slugged along to Torrance. There, exiting the busy 405 freeway at Western Avenue, he pulled up in front of the shiny black marble United States headquarters of Lexus, Toyota's luxury car division.

In addition to the positive turns in his social life, Rathbun also felt fortunate about his assignment for the day, because the vehicle he was set to pick up from Lexus wasn't just any vehicle, it was a vehicle that promised to make him some serious cash. What the comely Joella

Lamm of the Lexus public relations department had for Charlie that day was a shiny-new prototype sport utility vehicle that hadn't yet been introduced to the marketplace, a Lexus LX 450.

Rathbun was on assignment to photograph the vehicle for Detroit-based *AutoWeek* magazine, a publication that had regularly given him work after his departure from Petersen. But the reason the photo assignment promised to be lucrative to Rathbun wasn't just the compensation from *AutoWeek*. As an independent contractor for the magazine, Rathbun was confident he could sell some of the photos to other publications, since the prototype entrusted to his care was still secret. In fact, it was just one of a handful of Lexus 450s then in existence, a prototype that had been meticulously hand-constructed, using a Toyota Landcruiser as its base. Including all the handwork that had gone into the creation of the vehicle, estimates are it was worth in excess of $100,000.

Technically, because Rathbun was getting the vehicle through an arrangement *AutoWeek* had struck with Lexus, all the photos from the assignment should have become the property of the Detroit publication. But freelancers frequently hold out some photos for sale elsewhere, usually using a second background or adding some elements to differentiate the photos from those they send to the publication that has made the assignment. This type of double-dipping is fairly routine in the industry, and the art directors who give the photo assignments most often look the other way as long as they get what they need for their own publications. The rare LX 450 promised to be rich fodder for this mildly unethical but lucrative practice, and Rathbun had already sounded out at least one other publication about buying some photos of the vehicle.

In the pristine Lexus corporate headquarters, Rathbun and Joella Lamm chatted amiably for a few minutes, and he promised her that he would have the vehicle back in her hands by the end of business the following day, Friday, November 17. When they are assigned to photograph a run-of-the-mill production car, photographers usually get substantially more time to do their work, often as much as a week, but because the LX 450 was so rare, Lexus could only afford to have it out of their hands for forty-eight hours. Lamm explained to Rathbun that Lexus wanted to have the weekend to go over the vehicle before it went out to another publication early the following Monday morning. Rathbun told her he understood, wrote down his Michigan driver's license number and signed the formal borrower's agreement.

Before he left the building, he stopped in the lobby to telephone Linda Sobek, and he was mildly upset when he got her answering machine instead. He proceeded to dial her pager and keyed in the phone number where he could be reached. Ever the businesswoman, Sobek called him almost immediately. Their conversation was relatively brief.

"Hello, this is Linda Sobek. You paged me?"

"Yes, this is Charlie Rathbun. Remember, we saw each other at the SEMA show a couple of weeks ago."

"Oh, yeah. How are you?"

"Fine. Say, I was wondering if you might be able to do a job with me today."

"Today?"

"Yeah."

"For how long?"

"Well, it won't be too long. I've got a prototype sport utility vehicle from Lexus, and I have to get it back to them fairly soon."

"Lexus builds a sport utility?"

"Yeah, like I said, it's a prototype. It won't be out till next year. Do you think you can do it?"

"Maybe. How much time will it take?"

"Shouldn't take more than a few hours. I want to shoot some beauties, and I have to do some action, too, but it shouldn't take too long."

"Who are you shooting for?"

"*AutoWeek* and probably a couple of others."

"And how much?"

"I don't know. Say three hundred bucks?"

"Just three hundred?"

"That's all I've got for this shoot. I'll only be using you for about fifteen minutes."

"Well, all right, I think I can do it, but I absolutely have to be back by six o'clock. I've got a fitting tonight at eight, and I can't miss it."

"Oh, no problem. The light's gone by five o'clock. I'll have you back by six easy."

"Okay. Where should I meet you?"

"Why don't we meet at Denny's by the 405 at Crenshaw, say eleven o'clock? Then we can ride to the location together."

"Where are we shooting?"

"Depends on the weather, but it shouldn't be too far."

"All right. I'll see you at eleven at Denny's."

"Great. And bring a couple of dresses, okay? This is a luxury vehicle, so I want an upscale look."

"Okay," she concluded.

Satisfied that he had someone who could drive the vehicle for action photography, Rathbun put the handset into its cradle, walked out the front door of the Lexus building and started to move his photo equipment from his sport utility vehicle into the larger LX 450 prototype. Because of the amount of gear—camera bags, a tripod, materials to clean the vehicle—this process took him several minutes. Then he drove off in the substantial and very costly prototype.

At the other end of the phone, Linda Sobek was left wondering. Her financial picture was a little dim at the moment, so the prospect of a quick three hundred dollars was very appealing to her. But she also felt the tiniest bit uneasy about the familiarity in the photographer's voice.

She only had a vague recollection of seeing Rathbun just a few weeks before at the Specialty Equipment Marketing Association, or SEMA, show in Las Vegas. (The show is a trade convention for buyers and sellers of automotive performance equipment.) She had attended the show to keep up her contacts in the auto industry, a good source of work for advertising, calendar shots and personal appearances. Several times in years past she had appeared at a booth at the show as a sort of human traffic-builder, grinning for pictures and signing autographs for auto parts buyers, mechanics and other attendees. Keeping one's dignity while being the object of leers, whistles and gropes was a difficult task, but the money was good, so Sobek put up with what were oftentimes uncomfortable situations.

Although the photographer who had called her seemed to remember their encounter in detail, there was a reason Sobek's memory of her meeting with Rathbun was dim: it wasn't much of a meeting. Charlie had noticed her on the floor of the show, but as was often the case, Linda was surrounded by several people, so Charlie stood off to the side for a few minutes until the crush around her eased up a bit. Then he walked over, said "Hi," and the two exchanged awkward small talk for a minute or so. Rathbun mentioned the possible opportunity of work in the future, so she wrote down her telephone and pager numbers for him, and he jotted down his name and phone number in her DayPlanner. That was it. Charlie went on his way, and Sobek was quickly surrounded by another group of admiring males.

When Sobek and Rathbun next met, on the morning of November 16, 1995, in the parking lot of Denny's, a pistol shot from the 405 freeway, the scene was far less crowded than the SEMA show. That morning, dressed in a skin-tight white workout suit unzipped down to the top of her breasts, Linda was a picture that might have just stepped out of a male adolescent's dream. Despite the fact that she was wearing very little makeup and her blond hair was in curlers under a hastily tied scarf, she could have stopped traffic simply with her figure and her friendly yet sexy smile. Beauties like Linda don't walk by every day, but no one caught a glimpse of her as she hopped out of her white Nissan, reached into the back for two dresses on hangers and then climbed into the imposing Lexus sport utility in which the bespectacled Rathbun had been waiting.

"Do you think it's okay to park here?" she asked him, directing his attention to the signs on the lampposts warning "Parking for Customers Only All Others Will Be Towed."

"Oh, sure it's okay," Rathbun replied, jamming the gearshift into reverse and starting to back out of the parking spot. "I use this lot all the time, and I've never had a problem."

Mildly reassured, she sat back into the leather-covered front seat as Rathbun turned right out of the parking lot and almost immediately right again up the ramp onto the freeway.

Chapter 6

As Rathbun negotiated the freeway ramp that morning, he was at a stage of his life many men would have envied. At thirty-eight, he had put a difficult childhood behind him, survived an encounter with the law as he passed into adulthood and worked his way to a respected status as one of the best automotive editorial photographers in the country. He'd come a very long way from a childhood spent hopscotching around the country, following the path of his father's career.

From the outside, many would look at Rathbun's upbringing and express surprise that it was in any way troubled. On the surface, Charlie had enjoyed advantages that most children lack.

One of those advantages had been a solidly upper-middle-class lifestyle. Charlie's father, Horace Robert Rathbun, had made a good living as a management consultant for Arthur Young and Company, Door Oliver, and a selection of other respectably mundane concerns. Toting a master's degree in business administration, his career had required the family to make several jarring cross-country moves as he weaved his way through corporate America, but there was no denying that the money was good.

Charlie was born the youngest of four children on October 2, 1957, in Encino, California. Then, as now, Encino was an upscale suburb of Los Angeles located along the foothills of the southern reaches of the San Fernando Valley. But unlike now, in Rathbun's first years in California, the Valley was largely unspoiled and still almost rural. Rathbun's homesite was a plot of hillside land carved out of what had been Clark Gable's ranch.

Charlie's birth had been preceded by those of three other siblings—Louise Ellen, Robert Grant and Maryanne. His mother, Shirley Annette Hahn Rathbun, was a well-organized, college-educated woman, who dropped her ambitious career goals to concentrate on raising the family and on her husband's career.

It was in Encino that the young Charles Edgar Rathbun learned to walk and talk, and it was there that he had his first brush with mortality. Just two years old, he was playing in his backyard one day when his brother, Robert, about five at the time, found a snake slithering through the dry grass. Thinking it was a snail, one of the few words in Charlie's toddler vocabulary, he ran over to look at what was in actuality a fair-sized rattlesnake. Robert grabbed his brother before the snake could bite and dragged him into the house. A short time later a neighbor came by and cut off the snake's head with a shovel, giving the rattle to Robert as a souvenir of the incident. Recalling the incident thirty-five years later, Charlie remembered that his mother got very upset when he put the rattle in his mouth but doesn't recall her being upset about learning that her son had almost touched a live rattlesnake.

After less than two years in Encino, the Rathbuns moved again in 1959, this time to Del Mar, California, an elite enclave on the Pacific Ocean just north of San Diego. Their neighborhood was so tony that Lucille Ball was one of their neighbors, but the family's brief stay in Del Mar didn't leave many memories with Charlie—only the bridge over the estuary, the look of the Rathbun house and the fact that he referred to the kelp in the cold ocean water as "zorch."

By the time little Charlie was four years old, his family had changed addresses again, this time from upscale Del

Mar to considerably less wealthy Tulsa, Oklahoma. If the
lifestyle wasn't exactly the same as the one offered in
exclusive Del Mar, well, that was the lot of the management consultant—the corporate world's version of a gun
for hire.

Though Tulsa was a rough and ready oil town, Horace
Rathbun was maverick enough to drive a red MG instead
of a big Cadillac, Lincoln or Buick. Charlie often sat in
the small well behind the bucket seats when his dad tooled
around town.

Enrolled in pre-school in Tulsa, Charlie attended with
two neighbor girls. A Christmas pageant put on by his
sisters' elementary school made a vivid impression on
him. It was the first time he had ever seen angels or a
choir.

Less beatific but perhaps more emblematic of the adult
Charles Rathbun was another Tulsa incident. The three-
year-old Charlie was swinging a golf club one day when
suddenly he felt a thud. He looked behind him to discover
that his best friend, Ronnie Bishop, also three, was bleeding from a huge cut on his forehead.

The trauma of unintentionally injuring his friend panicked the young Rathbun. Instead of calling his parents
or his friend's parents, Charlie took off running without
even checking to see if his friend would be okay. He
finally ended up in his room, where he hid behind his bed
for a couple of hours until his mother came home and
found him there. His only punishment was his own terror.

Considerably less traumatic for Charlie was the family's move from Tulsa to Weston, Connecticut, in 1960.
The journey made a profound impression upon him.

In Tulsa the family boarded a three-tailed Lockheed
Constellation for the trip to New York. Charlie was
dressed for the occasion in a suit, cowboy boots and string
tie—a westerner set to take on the more sophisticated
East.

Aboard the huge, propeller-driven plane, Charlie was
sipping on a hot chocolate when the aircraft tumbled into

an air pocket and bounced crazily through the sky, spilling the hot drink on young Rathbun in the process. Crying, he was trying to wipe himself off when a stewardess took pity on him.

Approaching him with a big smile, she invited him to come to the cockpit to meet the pilot. A little shy, he was reluctant at first, but she took him in tow and introduced him to the captain, who chatted with the enthralled youngster and then presented him with a set of Pan Am wings. Those wings became a treasured souvenir. Charlie later wrote, "When I'd go to New York City I'd recognize the Pan Am building because of those wings."

After the family stayed in a Connecticut hotel overnight, Horace Rathbun announced that he was going to pick up the family car. Charlie asked how they got the big blue station wagon onto the plane, which brought derisive laughter from his siblings, something that was fairly common in the Rathbun household.

As he tells it, "I was always the baby of the family— the youngest. I used to get told that I was too small, too young, always too something. In the pecking order I was always at the bottom."

When Horace picked up the car—a new gold-colored Oldsmobile station wagon that replaced the car they had owned in Tulsa—the family set off on the trek to their new house amid a winter snowfall. As they made their way cautiously down the narrow roads of rural Connecticut with Horace a bit nervous behind the wheel, the trees became filled with fresh snow, and it was an awe-inspiring sight to young Charlie.

He recalled later, "As we drove down the road to our new house, the headlights of the new car lit up what seemed to be an ice tunnel with a million sparkles of light. I'd been to Disneyland; this was better."

From that night on, Charlie was in love with the snow. He built snowmen, snow forts and had innumerable snowball fights with the neighborhood kids. After a long day in the snow, his cheeks red in the fading light of an early winter sunset, Charlie would try to ignore his mother's calls to come inside until they became so insistent he couldn't disregard them.

Weston represented the happiest point in Charlie's childhood. There was always something to do; there were always places to explore. Behind the Rathbun property was a farm owned by the Andersen family, and Charlie, his brother and the other neighborhood kids used it as their playground. In summer they would run for hours in the grassy meadows, fly kites and when haying time came and farmer Andersen pressed the hay into bales, Charlie and brother Robert would make forts out of the bales and engage in childish warfare. In winter they would get their Flexible Flyer sleds down from the rafters in the garage, wax the iron runners and drag them to the crest of Andersen's hill. From the top it seemed like the ride down took forever, the sleds steadily gathering speed, sending ice crystals careening into their riders' enthralled faces. And at the bottom of the hill was a frozen-over pond that always sent the runners skidding crazily after they hit that final bump which would send them flying for a heart-stopping moment.

A wealthy town of only seventy-five hundred souls when Charlie lived there, Weston offered its newest resident a wide variety of activities suitable to his adventurous, athletic nature. One of the highlights each year was the Memorial Day parade, complete with homemade floats, marching bands and the surviving veterans of World War I, World War II and the Korean War.

Charlie excelled at Little League baseball, but as with most things in the Rathbun household, he had to wait his turn. His elder brother, Robert, became a Little Leaguer first, and Charlie was so anxious to play that he served as batboy for the team a year before he was eligible to join. When he finally got his chance, he made the most of it. Hours spent throwing rocks at trees while waiting for the school bus or killing time in the yard paid off quickly, and Charlie became the star pitcher for his team. Over the course of several years his teams, first the Yankees and then the Indians, won championship after championship largely on the strength of Charlie's pitching.

"I can't remember a year we didn't win the pennant," he said later.

But baseball wasn't the only sport the growing Charlie Rathbun played. He joined the local swim team, and the coach soon remarked that he had flippers for feet. Big for his age, he was strong on the basketball court, a good football player and a reliable soccer player.

Charlie also played a lot of tennis, one of the most popular summer sports in well-to-do Weston. He spent what seemed like one whole summer batting a tennis ball up against a backboard while waiting for the pool to clear from his sisters' and brother's swimming lessons. He said later that boredom was the inspiration for his dedication to tennis practice and as a result of it he "almost got good."

While Charlie seemed to be in the midst of a dizzying whirl of sports and other activities that spoke of a happy childhood, there was one nagging problem that was always in the back of his mind. Even in his own family he felt like someone outside looking in.

Unlike many families, where the youngest child seems to get more than his or her share of nurturing from parents and older siblings, in the Rathbun clan there didn't seem to be quite enough time for Charlie. For instance, instead of helping his son with his math homework by walking him through the problems and helping him solve them, Horace did the homework for him. Some children might have found this a pleasant surprise, but to Charlie it was belittling and frustrating.

"I got treated like a baby and I didn't like it," he wrote years later. "I hated making mistakes because invariably someone would tease me about it."

In the face of teasing at the hands of his own family, Charlie became further and further withdrawn. And in addition to teasing, his brother and sisters often excluded him from their games with other neighborhood children, telling him he was too young to participate in their activities.

"Instead of playing with the other kids I often felt like an outsider, like I was observing others play instead of playing with them," he said. "In fact, I think that's why I became a photographer. I was so used to observing rather than being a part of things."

When confronted with this type of rejection, many children respond with violent and destructive behavior. But Charlie's reaction was different. Often unaccepted by his family, he sought out acceptance where he could find it.

One place was in the home of Terry Griffiths, a child of about Charlie's age who was afflicted with Down's Syndrome. Because children can be very cruel, little Terry led a fairly solitary existence with the exception of the support of his parents. Solitary, that is, until Charlie Rathbun entered the picture.

Charlie took an immediate liking to Terry and often came over to his house to play. In fact, he came over so often that Terry's mother grew suspicious of his motives. The Griffiths had filled Terry's room with expensive toys, trying to compensate in some small way for the conspicuous absence of friends his own age. When Charlie started coming around as a regular visitor, Terry's mother wondered why.

One day when Charlie appeared again at their front door to play with Terry, his mother confronted him.

"You're just coming over here to play with Terry's toys, aren't you?" she screamed at him. "Admit it! You don't care about Terry at all!"

Her unexpected tirade scared the young Charlie into silence. He didn't know what to say.

"Admit it!" she continued, her wrath growing harsher. "I'm tired of kids coming over here to play with Terry's toys and then making fun of him behind his back! I'm just sick of it! It's not his fault he's different! It's not his fault he has Down's Syndrome!"

Charlie was crushed by her onslaught, but he still managed to squeak out a short reply.

"Mrs. Griffiths," he said, "I like Terry. I don't know what Down's Syndrome is, and I have plenty of my own toys, but I like Terry. He's a nice guy, and I like to play with him."

Sensing Charlie's sincerity, the woman pulled him into a long hug as her eyes filled with tears.

A couple of years later, with Charlie growing into one of the biggest kids his age, he befriended a boy named Robin White, who had a palsied right side, the result of polio. Like Terry Griffiths, Robin was often the target of cruel taunts from his classmates, but Charlie Rathbun always stood up for him, always had a kind word for him.

Another of Charlie's friends was Peter Motavoli, a child who didn't quite fit into the WASPish Weston milieu because of his Iranian ancestry. He and Charlie became fast friends and played endless games of chess against each other.

Despite the fact that Charlie often felt estranged from his family while growing up, he had what from an outside observer's point of view seems like a very typical middle-class upbringing. He went fishing with the neighborhood kids in several of the innumerable streams that flowed through Weston. He went on bicycle trips with his friend Jimmy Phipps, often to visit the house of Helen Keller, the famous blind social advocate. And he went to summer camp.

Summer camp was an especially pleasant time for Charlie Rathbun. He went on hikes with the other kids and got the chance to shoot .22-caliber rifles, which reminded him of the Old West. He was on the camp swim team, where his flipperlike feet stood him in good stead, and he spent a lot of time boating on the lake. His only regret was that the camp didn't have a rowing team, because he got so much practice he was certain he'd be good at it.

Charlie grew up so active and so attuned to the outdoors that being confined in a classroom was a struggle for him. His IQ tests confirmed that he was a bright child with significantly better than average intelligence, but he found it hard to apply himself to his studies.

As he told it, ''I just couldn't sit still when the sun was up. I wanted to be outside. And once the sun was down I was too tired.''

The result was that Charlie Rathbun became a student who put in just enough effort to get by, a student many of his teachers labeled an underachiever. As someone who always did his homework on the bus ride to school, Charlie was remarkable not because of his mediocre grades but because of how well he did on so little effort. But externally, at least, Charlie had a childhood that most would envy. And none of his friends, relatives or neighbors would have expected his adult life to be any different.

Chapter 7

THE 405 freeway at lunchtime on a weekday is not a place for those who want to get anywhere in a hurry, and so it was as morning collided with afternoon on Thursday, November 16, 1995. The irritating flashes of brake lights first appeared south of Century Boulevard and created variegated, glimmering puddles of red all the way to Sunset.

"Where are we going?" Linda Sobek asked absently as the Lexus sport utility vehicle inched its way along in the thick of the traffic.

Charlie looked over at her and smiled.

"I was thinking about a couple of places in the Valley, but I'm a little worried about the weather," he said.

A quick scan out the tall windshield showed a thick overcast, a cloud cover not likely to burn off any time soon.

"I don't care where we're going, but I absolutely have to be back by six o'clock," she replied curtly.

Charlie smiled again.

"That won't be a problem," he said. "It should be clear in the Valley, and even if it isn't, we'll run out of light long before six o'clock. I'll get you back in time."

Linda turned away from him, settled back in her seat and gazed out the window. She didn't like the way the day was going. The lack of a definite course of action was an affront to her orderly nature. But she reminded herself

41

that every photo shoot offered at least a grain of aggravation; none of them ever went exactly as planned. In her seven years of modeling she had seen it all, from horny photographers who offered her an extra hundred bucks to show them everything she had to gay photographers who were more interested in her shoes than she was. This was just another day, she told herself, just another simple photo shoot, and in just a few hours it, like all the others, would be over.

At the wheel of the big Lexus truck, Charlie was in a considerably better mood. In fact, he couldn't help grinning to himself. Here he was all alone in a very expensive vehicle with a startlingly beautiful woman, and he was getting paid for it. As his own boss, he could come or go as he pleased, hire the assistants he wanted to hire and work for the clients he wanted to work for. Against fairly sizable odds, his dreams were coming true.

Noting the traffic coming to a standstill again, he sneaked another glance at Linda, who was still drowsily looking out the window. He noticed with approval her huge blue eyes, high cheekbones and well-formed lips. And he couldn't help but notice the shapeliness of her body.

He exhaled deeply as he looked away and peered down the road again. Even the snarl of traffic and dismal gray weather couldn't dim his positive spirits. He was making it in Hollywood, just as he'd dreamed he would. And he was doing it on his own terms. He chuckled inside when he thought how many people had said he wouldn't be able to do it.

From his days as a chronic underachiever in grade school, a wide variety of people who encountered Charlie over the years felt he wouldn't amount to much. They considered him too boisterous, too unmotivated, too self-centered or just plain too weird to become a truly successful adult.

By the sixth grade Charlie had become something of a

class clown. Eager for attention, he told jokes, tossed paper airplanes, shot spitwads and generally made a nuisance of himself at school to the endless aggravation of his teachers. Early on, he learned that if he made fun of other people, it hurt their feelings, making him even less popular than he already was, so he usually turned the jokes on himself. This philosophy won him considerable amounts of attention if not lifelong friends.

One afternoon in geography class Charlie was typically engaged in the sixth graders' version of snappy patter when the teacher of the class, one Mr. Bowditch, called on him to answer a question. Of course, Charlie couldn't answer, since he hadn't even heard the question, so intent was he on entertaining the class.

Many teachers would have simply called on another student, but instead Bowditch gave Charlie a withering lecture that left the class absolutely hushed. Charlie responded to the embarrassment by spending the following night studying his geography feverishly.

The next day a chastened Charlie volunteered to go to the map at the front of the room and point out the geographical features requested by his teacher. Bowditch threw a variety of questions at Rathbun, but the sudden scholar had all the answers, and when he sat down, he felt he had earned the admiration of his class.

Amazingly, Charlie's newfound quest for excellence didn't stop there either. Bowditch used the unexpected situation to create a competition between Charlie's class and another sixth-grade class with Charlie and another student as the key gladiators. When the competition concluded, Charlie's class was the winner, which gave him a warm sense of pride. It also brought him much closer to Mr. Bowditch, who became a mentor to the impressionable youth. Every day Charlie would spend an hour or two with Bowditch after class, and the staid New England-bred teacher instilled in his young protégé a deep interest in history and geography that has never been sated.

Unfortunately Bowditch's influence didn't last long. In the summer between Charlie's sixth- and seventh-grade years, the entire Rathbun clan moved again, this time to Worthington, Ohio.

The move to Ohio was a jarring one for Charlie. After bouncing through three towns in the first three years of his life, the young Rathbun had grown to feel at home in Weston. He liked the area, had a select smattering of friends and had experienced some success both in school and on the baseball field. But suddenly that was all over, and Charlie would have to establish himself again in a strange town.

Sadly, Charlie's relocation to Ohio got off to a painful start. Two weeks before he was to begin attending his new school, he broke his arm while jousting on bicycles with another kid. His arm plastered all the way to his shoulder, Charlie couldn't participate in sports or do much of anything for the first couple of months in Ohio.

While certainly a pleasant community, Worthington didn't have the appeal to Charlie that Weston had. It was significantly less rural than Weston, tucked into a corner of the state capital, Columbus, and home to the gargantuan Ohio State University. Whereas in Weston Charlie could head out into the wide-open spaces, in Worthington he was considerably more constrained. And the Ohio landscape was considerably less appealing to an outdoor boy like Charlie.

As he described it, "The rivers in Connecticut were cold, clear and rapid. The rivers in Ohio were slow and brown."

Still, Charlie took up the requisite upscale sports, satisfying both his own desires and those of his status-conscious parents. He swam at the local swim club and got involved in another round of tennis lessons. He also played baseball, but though he continued to experience success, the joy of the game was gone for him. The way he saw it, Connecticut kids played baseball because they wanted to, Ohio kids played baseball because their parents forced them to. Behind his pitching, his Ohio team won the championship, but he was so disheartened that he never bothered to pick up his trophy.

Souring on team sports, Charlie got off more and more on his own. Though he didn't like the overall topography of mid-state Ohio, he did appreciate one thing about it: it was flat, which meant he could ride his bicycle all over the place.

By the time he was sixteen, he was riding his bike twenty to forty miles a day. Each day presented a new adventure; each road offered somewhere new to explore.

Bicycling and Charlie's interest in the outdoors led him to join the high school field studies group, which investigated natural history. As a ninth-grader, Charlie traveled to the Northwest in the summer of 1972, a trip that he said changed his life.

Riding a bike through the suburbs of Columbus was one thing, but sliding down a glacier in Estes Park, Colorado, was quite another. He spied on sheep in Wyoming, gazed at moose in Yellowstone and stood on the silent battlefield of the Little Big Horn. For a teenager who already had a strong interest in history and geography, it was the perfect adventure.

It was an adventure that also sparked Charlie's interest in photography. His grandfather on his mother's side was an amateur photographer who had already exposed Charlie to the fine points of shutter speeds and f-stops, but the trip to the Northwest opened his eyes to the breathtaking art of photography.

With a camera and lens lent to him by his brother, Charlie chronicled the entire trip. In his determination to get the perfect picture, he almost got himself killed in the Tetons when a bull moose that had been bedded down for the night suddenly rose up and charged him as he tried to creep close enough to it for a good picture. He learned at that moment the usefulness of a telephoto lens.

The trip out West seemed to connect with a lonesome,

spiritual side of Charlie that was largely untouched in Worthington.

As he wrote, ''There is nothing as wondrous as watching an eagle float above you, twelve thousand feet above sea level in the tundra of the Rockies, while you're sitting on a lichen-covered rock and eating 'gorp,' a chocolate-raisin-nut mix.''

The following year the Worthington Field Studies group took another long trip, this time to the Southwest, and Charlie became the designated photographer for the journey. Again the majesty of the West enthralled him, and he began to think that a career in photography was something he should pursue.

He was captivated by the work of Ansel Adams and began to hope that someday he could do similar work, putting on film the grandeur of his beloved outdoors. In his room at night he pored over the pages of *National Geographic* magazine, dreaming of the time he would be traveling to exotic locales, snapping pictures of the local flora and fauna.

Back at high school in Worthington, he got a job as a photographer for the school newspaper, and he also took a variety of pictures for the school yearbook. Those assignments also introduced him to one of the hidden benefits of a photography career: he got into all the events for free.

Charlie's father and mother encouraged their son's interest in photography. When it came to careers, Horace Rathbun's only advice was that Charlie should pursue something he liked, because then he would be motivated to succeed. Shirley had more definite ideas for her son. She wanted him to get involved in a creative field, because she thought he was both bright and gifted creatively. Her first choice for him was architecture, a path she considered more respectable than photography, but she in no way discouraged her son's pursuit of a photographic career.

As Charlie neared his senior year in high school, it seemed as if his plan for the future was set. Except for one thing: his parents were about to go through a divorce that would throw his world upside down.

Chapter 8

THE TRAFFIC began to loosen up at Sunset Boulevard, and Charlie pressed his foot down on the accelerator. The big Lexus moved forward with the authority of a railroad train as it started up the twisting grade of the Sepulveda Pass through the Santa Monica mountains about fifteen miles northwest of downtown Los Angeles. He peered over at Linda again, and she looked back at him, saying nothing.

"Still a lot of clouds," Charlie said awkwardly.

Linda moved forward in her seat to look up through the windshield, but maintained her indifferent silence.

"It should clear up when we get to the Valley," Charlie gamely continued. "It usually does."

"Well, I hope so," Linda replied. "I'd hate to have you pay me for nothing."

Actually, Linda thought, she wouldn't hate it at all. In fact, in this particular instance, getting paid for nothing might be the best possible outcome, because she absolutely did not want to miss her costume fitting that evening.

"Oh, I'm sure we'll be able to shoot something," Charlie said, trying to ignore her obvious indifference to the project at hand. "You did bring the wardrobe I asked for, didn't you?"

She pointed to a couple of dresses she had hung from one of the vehicle's coathooks.

"Right behind you," she said.

Sensing this line of conversation wasn't going anywhere, Charlie took another tack.

"It was sure lucky I saw you at the SEMA show," he said.

Yeah, she thought, lucky like contracting the flu. But ever the businesswoman, she replied aloud, "Yeah, it was lucky."

"We haven't worked together in a long time, have we?"

"No, we haven't."

"Well, it's going to be good to have the opportunity to work with you again."

"Thanks."

Linda let the word hang there as she stared out the window again.

Charlie had always had difficulty communicating with women. The problem went back to the first time he fell in love in the middle of the fifth grade.

The girl's name was Gail Pope, and she moved to Weston from a small town in Ohio, a town Charlie had never heard of. The first time he saw her he was smitten. He thought she was incredibly pretty, despite an overbite that some might have uncharitably described as buck teeth. Charlie's problem was he didn't know how to get to know her.

Gail quickly made friends with Karen Witherspoon, which made her all the more desirable to Charlie since Charlie's pal Brad Johnston had a case for Karen. But none of the four was ready to make the first move.

The fifth grade school year ended and summer began with nothing more than an occasional smile between Charlie and the object of his affection. His friend Brad was having a similar lack of success getting together with his sweetheart.

By the time the sixth grade began, Charlie and Brad were getting a bit desperate to make at least verbal contact, but still neither of them had produced enough courage to approach his potential girlfriend, nor had either one bowed to the simple expedient of having his buddy go up to his potential girlfriend and say, "Charlie (or Brad) really likes you."

It was hard to reconcile Charlie's nearly terminal shyness concerning Gail with his complete lack of inhibition in school. He was such a show-off that he was always getting in trouble and always trying to talk his way out of it. Visits to the principal's office were almost routine with him. But when it came to a girl he was interested in, he was all but mute.

Despite this, though, Charlie wouldn't let the idea of the romance die. Day after day he stood in front of Gail's house, hoping to catch a glimpse of her, hoping to find some excuse to talk to her. This gambit proved less than successful, however, because Charlie finally discovered he was hanging out in front of the wrong house.

Eventually Charlie chanced to meet Gail's brother on the school bus. He was Robert Rathbun's age and turned out to be a nice enough guy. Charlie struck up a friendship with him, and one thing led to another until Charlie was introduced to Gail near the end of sixth grade. To his surprise Charlie found the girl he had been seeking to meet for the better part of two years had similar feelings about him. In fact, she admitted to him, she had often loitered near the Rathbun house, endeavoring to run into the strapping sixth-grader. If only he hadn't been standing around a third party's house, he might have seen her. Despite its stumbling beginnings, romance blossomed quickly between them, and for the next few weeks Charlie and Gail were inseparable. But before the summer was over, the Rathbun clan had abandoned Weston for Worthington, leaving the hard-won relationship in the dust.

In Ohio Charlie's luck in love wasn't much better. While he was beginning to pursue photography as a career, he was also pursuing Laurie Binghampton, an attractive, athletic girl his age. Eventually the gangling high school sophomore not only caught her but also lost his virginity to her. However, the experience was so disappointing, bordering on embarrassing, that he didn't try intercourse again until two years later. It wasn't till he met Cherie Albus that, in his words, he "found out what the to do was about."

Usually senior year of high school is a year of triumph. It is a year of being top dog, an object of envy by the underclassmen. It is a year of fateful decisions on college and career. And it is a year when relationships grow more serious or fall apart.

For Charles Edgar Rathbun, senior year was a year of abandonment. Of course, by that time his sisters and brother were off at college. That kind of abandonment was both temporary and expected, even though it was painful for the "baby" of the household. But beyond the absence of the siblings, there was more trouble brewing in the Rathbun household. Charlie became aware in those small, rumbling, unspoken but undeniable ways that his parents' marriage was coming apart. Shirley, who had abandoned her career goals for marriage and children, was getting ever more shrill in pushing Horace to higher levels on the professional ladder, and Horace, after some two decades of not quite measuring up in his wife's eyes, was getting tired of it. The two argued, then patched things up, then argued some more.

For days there would be an uneasy truce in the house. Then an explosion would come, and his parents would be at it again. Finally, one day in the middle of Charlie's last year in high school, his father moved out of the house to live with his secretary, and he never came back.

Years later Charlie tried to rationalize the event.

"The biggest difference for me was that suddenly everyone was gone. My brothers *[sic]* and sisters were all away at school, mom was now working and dad had moved out. I wanted to get out and get on with it, too.

"It wasn't the fact that my parents weren't married all of a sudden. I saw that coming for a couple of years. It didn't bother me. I didn't blame my dad. I didn't blame my mom. They got married when men worked and women stayed home. I knew my mom had a college education, was intelligent and was bored at home. She was unhappy so dad was unhappy. By 1975 society had changed. My parents needed to go do whatever would make them happy. I realized all this even back then. No bull.''

While the older Charlie Rathbun puts a brave face on it, the fact was that his parents' divorce hit him at a very bad time, and he resented it. His older siblings had all had the advantage of a college education paid for by their parents. But when Charlie's turn came, there was just no money. The divorce had taken care of that.

In spite of the hardship, Charlie was determined to become a photographer, and he did all he could to move himself onto that career path. But while the path to becoming a CPA or an auto mechanic or a history teacher is pretty clear-cut, the path to becoming a professional photographer is murky at best. All the photographers that Charlie ran into were either professors at the local university or professional students. And he didn't want to be either.

After his parents' divorce, his first bold effort to embark on a career in photography was to move across the country. He had heard that his idol, Ansel Adams, was teaching workshops at a community college in Cupertino, California, so he finagled an invitation to stay with an aunt and uncle in nearby San Jose.

Charlie immediately responded to the challenge of college by buckling down and getting good grades. He liked the fact that in college the students were treated as adults and felt that college was more thought-oriented than high school, which seemed to him to emphasize memorization rather than learning. Even though he never got to take a course with Ansel Adams, he did turn in a solid record of As and Bs. But then the money ran out, and Charlie's resentment grew.

Horace Rathbun's response to the breakup of his marriage was a common one. After twenty-five years in the salt mine, he simply stopped working. At the same time, Shirley was struggling to reestablish a career that had been on hold for two decades. She was making more money than Horace, but not enough to send Charlie through school.

Lacking the resources to continue his education in California, Charlie returned to Worthington, Ohio, where, still a resident, he could afford the fees at Ohio State University. He turned the trip back into a long vacation in the company of Beverly Barton, a girl on whom he'd had a "huge crush" in high school. The journey was a pleasant one, and his camera clicked nonstop, but he couldn't escape the fact that his return to Ohio was caused by what he considered abandonment by his parents, not his own desire.

Back in Worthington he got a job as a stock boy in the building materials department of a local Kmart. The substantial Rathbun home had gone up for sale as a result of the divorce, so Charlie took a tiny apartment sparsely furnished with hand-me-down furniture.

It took him several months to earn enough money to continue his education, but as soon as he could afford it, he enrolled in a Fine Arts program at OSU, specializing in photography. The schedule he set for himself was a killer. Each weekday he had a full day of classes followed by his job at Kmart until nine or ten o'clock. He worked on the weekends as well, trying to find time to squeeze in the assignments for his photography classes. He often thought to himself how much easier life would be if he simply quit school and concentrated on his job, but the drive to become a professional photographer wouldn't let him.

There was one other factor that kept Charlie in school—his mother.

As he tells it, "I had to work my ass off to afford college. My mom in particular stayed on me to get through school, which annoyed me to death at the time, since she wasn't supporting me. But if she hadn't, I think I would have gotten lazy and comfortable and ended up a Kmart manager.''

It was difficult for Charlie to avoid reflecting on how much more difficult it was for him in comparison to his brother and sisters, who got a free ride through college before the money woes of the divorce set in. Charlie doggedly stuck to his work-plus-college schedule, but the grueling hours took their toll on him.

He left his job at Kmart and took another at a Kroger supermarket. At first he liked the change. His coworkers were more interesting than the crowd at Kmart, and because his hours were longer, he made more money. Over the course of the following few weeks he befriended a Kroger employee named Erica Ellis. At the time he thought the move was a good one, but one night, when he invited her to his place, it turned into disaster.

Chapter 9

THE 405 freeway drops headlong out of the Santa Monica Mountains into what has become the busiest intersection in the world. A little before noon on November 16, 1995, one of the vehicles approaching that intersection was the Lexus LX 450 prototype driven by Charles Edgar Rathbun accompanied by a now very bored Linda Sobek.

At the top of the grade Charlie looked down into the Valley and sighed. Instead of the clear weather he had expected, he was confronted by a thick, dark overcast, and his well-trained weather eye told him the clouds would not clear quickly, if at all.

"Looks like we might have a problem," he said to Linda.

She shook her head from side to side almost imperceptibly.

Now what? she thought, and she gave the driver of the vehicle a dark, questioning look.

"I think we might have some weather problems," he said, responding to her inquiring eyes. "I thought the clouds were going to burn off, but it looks pretty thick."

She shook her head again.

"Where are we going, anyway?" she asked.

"Well, I was thinking of going to a ranch I know near Santa Barbara, but now with the weather . . ."

"Near Santa Barbara?" she shot back. "Don't you remember I need to be back by six o'clock?"

"We could have made it," Charlie said defensively, "but with the weather the way it is, that's not even an option now."

"Well, where are we going to go?"

"Looks to me like El Mirage is our only choice."

"You mean the dry lake?" Linda asked, and her expression made it plain she didn't like the idea.

"Yeah, we're almost guaranteed to have sun there, no matter what the weather is here."

"And if we don't get sun?"

"Then I guess I pay you for your time, and we go home," he replied, his tone resigned. "But I think we'll be all right. Seems like it's always sunny out there, and we don't have too much to shoot."

"How long will it take to get out there?"

"Not more than an hour. It's up the 14 and then down Pearblossom. We should have it all wrapped up by ten minutes after the sun sets—four-thirty or so. And then I'll get you back by six."

"I just can't afford to miss that fitting tonight," she said, trying to take a bit of the edge off the conversation.

"I understand," he said. "We'll just get the shots we need and be on our way."

Unconsciously, he pushed his foot down a bit harder on the accelerator as the sport utility sped under the 101 and emerged on the other side. The two were racing the clock now, and the outcome of that race was still very much in doubt.

By 1981 Charlie knew all about racing the clock. His life had become a study in delayed gratification. After spending nearly half a dozen years going to college, he felt no closer to getting a degree than when he first started. Part of the problem was that the Fine Arts program in which he had enrolled was designed more as a continuing education course than a degree curriculum. His education was continuing all right—six years and counting.

But the bigger part of the problem was Charlie himself. He loved photography, but he wasn't interested in photography strictly for art's sake. He wanted to make it a paying career. Because of that, the theoretical side of his studies at Ohio State left him cold. Frequently he simply ignored it, to the detriment of his grades and his success in the program.

Of course, this lack of advancement did not sit well at all with his mother. Shirley was a demanding woman who expected success, so she kept after her younger son to finish school and amount to something. Charlie's problem was he knew what he didn't want to be, but he wasn't sure what he did want to be. He was certain he didn't want to work in a camera store. He was already working retail and liked it about as much as a rapper likes melody. And he was certain he didn't want to do portraits, the get-a-grin-and-flash school of photography. He had already done some, and he felt that people were never happy with pictures of themselves. But knowing what he didn't want to do wasn't getting him any closer to what he did want to do.

By that time Shirley had moved to Michigan, where her interior design career was flourishing, and one weekend Charlie came up for a visit. What started as impulse proved to be a turning point in his life. While there he met Bill Jauss, a professional photographer who wasn't an academic. Instead he was making a living as a product photographer, shooting mostly cars, trailers and motor homes.

Jauss did not only encourage Charlie; he became the young photographer's role model. Newly energized, with a course of action that promised to lead him out of his going-nowhere combination of work and school, Charlie vowed to follow in Jauss's footsteps. He quickly finished up the courses he was taking in Columbus and somehow got enough money together to embark on a three-week trip to Ireland, his final adventure before moving to Michigan and going to work as a photographer's assistant full-time.

Soon after, Charlie settled in Detroit, convinced that his

decision to pursue a job in automotive photography was a good one. In fact, the more he thought about it, the more he liked the idea. He knew that commercial product photography paid well. While other photographers might be content to win artists' medals for their work, Charlie wanted to feel the cold, hard cash. But he hated the idea of spending his life in a studio. That was too static, too boring.

What he found in the automobile was the perfect combination of product and scale. Certainly automobiles are a commercial product, and their manufacturers pay handsomely to obtain high-quality photographs that capture their essence, as do the magazines that cover the automotive world for their millions of readers. Cars are also substantial in size, which means that it is often easier to bring the photographer to them than to bring them to the photographer. The result of that is travel, often to some of the most pleasant locations in the world. In the chance meeting with Bill Jauss, Charlie had stumbled on a job that perfectly matched the lifestyle he had envisioned for himself.

He quickly found, however, that one doesn't simply show up at *Car and Driver* magazine with a Nikon bag slung over one's arm and get photo assignments. There were dues to be paid, an apprenticeship to be served. For Charlie the apprenticeship began with Jauss and then continued with Jim Haefner, a Troy, Michigan-based photographer specializing in the high-quality images that end up in magazine ads.

Rathbun worked hard for Haefner, and for the most part the two got along well, but Haefner did note a volatile side to his young protégé. When a shoot wasn't going well, Charlie would sometimes burst into a rage, throwing equipment around the studio until he cooled down. On those occasions Haefner chided Charlie for his lack of professionalism and proper schooling. Often those discussions bordered on lectures.

Rathbun remembered years later, "He used to tell me

I would never make it, because I wasn't motivated enough. If I was *[sic]* truly motivated I would have found a way to go to the right school, like he did. I would find a way to finance my portfolio pieces, my photo gear.''

Haefner's derision used to get under Charlie's skin, but he was able to brush it off until one night at a cocktail party, when his eyes were opened.

As Charlie recalls it, ''Jim's mother had a few too many and told us all about Jim. Seems he was painting houses in New Mexico when she told him one day, 'Jim, pick whatever school you want to go to; we'll pay, but go to college.' So that's his way of finding the money. His grandmother, one of the Dodges, gave him twenty thousand dollars to get going. His parents gave him the down payment on his house.''

That news disillusioned the young photographer, who, despite their occasional rows, had come to look on Haefner as a mentor.

Over the course of a half-dozen years in the Detroit area, Rathbun graduated from raw apprentice to journeyman assistant. His work record was good, the list of clients he had served impressive; but by 1988 he was ready for a change. Though he had established a small circle of friends and dated occasionally, he began to feel his life was going nowhere. So he did what hundreds of thousands have done before him. He moved to California.

Chapter 10

As the big black sport utility slipped through the narrow slit in the hills that connected the 405 freeway to Interstate 5, Linda Sobek was peering into her Day-Planner.

"I've gotta make a phone call," she told Rathbun brusquely.

He gazed over at her for a moment before he replied.

"Sure, no problem," he said, trying to ignore the edge on her voice. "I'm gonna need some gas pretty soon, and you can make a phone call then. It'll take us maybe twenty minutes to get to Acton."

He'd driven the route so often that he knew the mile markers by heart, so he had no difficulty in making the mental calculation of how long it would take to get to the nearest pay telephone. Traveling on photo assignments, it seemed like he had used every pay phone from San Diego to Santa Barbara.

By now it was nearing noon, but Rathbun wasn't especially hungry. Because automotive photographers' schedules revolve around sunrise and sunset, the "golden hours," when the outdoor light is most favorable for their craft, keeping anything like a normal eating schedule is impossible. A large percentage of their meals consist of 7-Eleven soft drinks and packaged snacks bought on the way to or from a photo location.

At the moment Linda wasn't particularly hungry either.

A model who lived by her appearance, she watched what she ate with the intensity of a hawk spying a brook trout. Her five-foot-three, one-hundred-five-pound body was testimony to that. And the last thing on her mind right then was food. She just wanted to get the pictures taken and get home. She'd been on some ill-planned photo excursions in her time, but this one was right down there with the worst of them.

"How's your love life?"

Rathbun tossed off the question without even looking at her, and for a moment Linda wasn't sure she could believe her ears, it was such a non sequitur.

"How's your love life?" Charlie tried again, this time turning a little to look at her and smile.

Oh, my God, Linda thought to herself, now I have to play this game, too? She forced a grin onto her face and said, "Fine," about as noncommittal an answer as she could imagine.

"Someone told me you were going out with Fabio."

"I never went out with him. I was just on a shoot with him."

"Oh, yeah?"

"Yeah, in Hawaii. But aside from the time we were shooting, I hardly even saw him."

"That's not the way I heard it."

"Well, you heard wrong then."

"If I was in Hawaii with you . . ."

Not again, she thought. How often am I going to have to go through this?

"Have you ever been to Hawaii?" she interjected, trying to move the conversation she didn't want to have in a more neutral direction.

"No, I haven't, but I've always wanted to go," he said. "I hear it's beautiful."

"Yeah, it's beautiful. Really beautiful."

"Say, do you have a boyfriend?"

Linda exhaled audibly and stared out the side window.

"Yeah, I've got a boyfriend," she said. "How long did you say it would be until we get to a phone?"

When Charles Edgar Rathbun came to work in the photo department of Petersen Publishing Company in February, 1989, he was a golden boy. After nearly seven years working with and learning from Jim Haefner, one of the auto industry's top pros, he had a great deal to bring to the overworked crew that was creating the photography for some twenty monthly magazines at the West Hollywood-based publishing behemoth. During the course of his apprenticeship with Haefner, he had become an expert in automotive studio work, a tedious process that requires an artist's eye for light and shape, and he was an excellent outdoor shooter with a good sense of composition. If he had one weakness, it was photographing vehicles in motion, but that was a weakness shared by many car photographers, including some well-established pros. With time, he was convinced he could develop that skill, too.

At first Bob D'Olivo, the legendary automotive lensman who headed up the department, thought his new hire was a gem. Unlike many photographers working in the comfortable hammock of full-time employment, Charlie wasn't content to do the simple minimum. He worked hard, and the photos he turned in showed it. He even assembled his own checklist of shots and angles so that he would be certain to turn in a complete package of photographs after every shoot. But before long it became clear that Charlie had some problems being a team player.

Early on in his tenure at Petersen, Charlie was called into a meeting that included a number of company bigwigs, including the editorial director and art director of *Motor Trend*, the organization's cash cow, and key members of the photo department, including D'Olivo. At issue was the fact that instead of using the photo department, *Motor Trend* was relying almost entirely on freelance photographers. When asked why, Bill Claxton, the *Motor*

Trend art director, said that Petersen staff photographers often forgot to provide certain important shots of the vehicles being photographed, while freelancers didn't. D'Olivo countered by exhibiting Charlie's personal checklist and claiming that all of his photographers worked from a checklist given to them by the department. Upon hearing that, Charlie didn't back up his boss; he laughed out loud. It was a performance that started him on his way to the photo department blacklist.

Another time Charlie and Margie Dickinson, a longtime photo department secretary, got into a row when she accused several of the photographers of just hanging around in one of the studios on a day she, ironically enough, had arrived late. While the other photographers were content to let her blow off steam, Charlie fired some verbal salvos back at her, and the two ended up in a shouting match. Later that day, when Charlie heard a rumor that Dickinson was badmouthing him, he went to confront her, but not finding her, he left a note, saying, "Please stop this. Either come to me or I'm going to Personnel." All that got Charlie was a lecture in D'Olivo's office.

One day Charlie walked into Petersen's Studio II to hear fellow photography-department staffer Scott Killeen complaining about his immediate boss, Jim Brown, to D'Olivo. According to Killeen, Brown had been incompetent in setting up a piece of equipment in the studio the day before, and Killeen was giving D'Olivo an earful about how stupid Brown was. Charlie had no special attachment to Brown, but he resented the way Killeen was talking, and he was especially bothered because Killeen had been laughing and joking with Brown all the previous afternoon as the equipment was being installed. When Killeen asked, "Isn't that right, Charlie?" Rathbun exploded at him, telling him what a backstabber he was. And if that wasn't enough, Charlie then asked D'Olivo how he could sit there and encourage one employee to badmouth another without the second employee being in the room to defend himself.

As Charlie remembers it, "I made two enemies that day. I didn't raise my voice to them or insult them, but I raised a moral tone to them that put them on the defensive."

Rathbun knew he was creating problems for himself, but he found it impossible to change his behavior. Unconsciously, perhaps, he preferred having negative attention to no attention at all.

"That's been the story of my life since then," he said. "A high regard for my own abilities, a pathological dislike for what some people would call politics. That's why I loved being a freelance photographer. I got to work with clients *I* liked and who liked me. When someone would b.s. me or try to blame me for *their* mistakes, I'd drop 'em like a hot potato."

From an early zenith Rathbun's star at Petersen quickly went on the wane. Certainly he didn't help himself by embarrassing his boss, but he also brought some other liabilities with him. For one thing, many of the other photographers in the department found him forbiddingly egotistical.

Scott has a vivid recollection of the first time he saw Charlie Rathbun.

"When I first walked in [to the photo department office], I held out my hand and said something like, 'Hi, I'm Scott,'" Killeen remembers, "and he didn't even look up from his desk, which was right across from mine; he just said, 'I'm Charlie and I'm busy.'"

Of course, not everyone at Petersen developed the same level of distaste for Charlie. He also built several strong friendships, most especially with Trish Peterson and Phil Spangenberger, both of whom worked in Petersen's Outdoor division, which included *Hunting, Guns & Ammo*, and *Fishing* among its titles.

Peterson and Rathbun got along so well that eventually she became a roommate in his Hollywood Hills home for a time. Often they'd get together for lunch and talk about their romantic involvements, office politics and any other topic that might come up.

"I thought he was wonderful," Peterson said. "Maybe sometimes he didn't give the quote-unquote bimbos what they needed, but I can tell you one thing—older women adored Charlie."

Rathbun and Spangenberger hit it off because of their shared enthusiasm for history and particularly the Old West. Spangenberger is a writer and weapons expert who has established himself as one of the leading authorities on the Civil War and the saga of the western United States. Like Bowditch and later Haefner, Spangenberger assumed a mentor's role in Charlie's life. Though Spangenberger and Charlie became very close friends, the older man offered a two-sided portrait of his protégé.

"Charlie's basically a pretty good guy," he said. "He's sincere, and he cares about his friends. I always found him to be an honest person, but he is a bit stubborn and finds it difficult dealing with stupidity and foolishness."

Over the years of their friendship Spangenberger became quite aware that Charlie was having his ups and downs in the Petersen photo department. It was obvious that Charlie had no feel for corporate politics, and at Petersen Publishing Company that often spelled eventual doom.

"It was a problem for him when he was confronted with things that were foolish," Spangenberger said, picking his words carefully. "He wasn't a yes-man. People were talking behind his back, but there were no angels without any tarnish in the photo lab."

Though Charlie lacked a feel for the Machiavellian machinations of corporate politics, he did embark on his own brand of personal public relations. Feeling that the staffs of the various magazines at Petersen didn't know one another very well, he decided to host an impromptu lunchtime barbecue on the back patio of the high-rise office building on Sunset Boulevard. The object: creating a little intra-office camaraderie. He bought several pounds of hamburger meat, commandeered a grill, lit up some charcoal and invited the whole company to join him. To his delight, scores of people showed up.

The first event drew such a warm response that Charlie decided to throw the barbecues on a regular basis. Over the course of the next few months, Charlie manned the grill, scorched the burgers, and the barbecues became a monthly occurrence, but though they continued to be well attended, Charlie grew more and more disillusioned with the whole thing.

"What bothered me most about them was that nobody ever helped me with them," he said. "Nobody ever helped me do the work and nobody ever helped me pay for them. After a while I started to feel like I was being used."

And that was that. Like Gatsby in West Egg, he shut the parties down, never to resume.

As it turned out, lack of recognition for his parties should have been the least of his worries. Charlie was about to get fired.

Chapter 11

WHEN THE big Lexus sport utility came to a stop next to a gas pump, Linda Sobek was out the door as though the upholstery under her bottom were in flames. Her friends always kidded her about being addicted to the telephone, and now she made a beeline to the pay phone almost as if it had reached out and grabbed her. She had several calls to make, and she was trying to decide which one she should place first.

Charlie took much longer to swing out of the driver's-side door of the Lexus. He noted Linda's headlong dash with a dismissing shake of his head.

Dumb blond bitch, he thought, and then he corrected himself—the "dumb" part was redundant.

He pulled the gas nozzle from the pump, pried open the Lexus's fuel filler cap and slammed the nozzle into the receptacle. He paid little attention as the electronic display flashed out its rapidly changing totals behind him.

Over at the greasy pay phone attached to a hefty steel post, Linda was having trouble getting a dial tone. She kept punching in numbers on Chiclet-sized silver keys, but nothing seemed to be happening.

"Oh, Christ," she muttered under her breath. She had recently become a born-again Christian, but she occasionally reverted when under pressure, and she felt the pressure now. The telephone was her lifeline, and it wasn't working.

She redialed and then keyed in her credit card number, but again she was unable to get a connection. She groaned, shook her head and slammed the receiver into its cradle. Stalking off, she looked up to hear Charlie calling to her as he strode from the gas pumps toward the convenience store.

"You want something to drink?"

What I really need is a telephone that works, she said to herself.

"Yeah, sure, get me a bottled water."

"Anything else?"

"No, that will be fine."

"Okay," he smiled, pulling the door open and stepping in.

She walked back to the black vehicle and leaned up against it. Her pose would have made an excellent photograph, but that certainly wasn't on her mind. She wanted to check in with her mom, a ritual she performed several times daily, and check her answering machine, something she did at least as often, and she was upset that she hadn't been able to do either.

I'll have to call about my phone card when I get back, she made a mental note to herself. Maybe that was the problem.

"Here's your water," Charlie said, emerging from the store and pushing the bottle toward her.

"Thanks," she said as she took it from his hand.

The two climbed into the vehicle, and Linda immediately reached for her purse.

"Oh, no," Charlie said, noticing what she was up to. "It's on me."

Linda Sobek wasn't always averse to taking things from men. But most often she was very choosy about the men from whom she took them. And she was particularly careful about separating her private life from her modeling business.

Despite her bombshell looks, and contrary to Charlie's

crude assessment of her, Linda was a sweet, almost demure woman, who had a strong motherly side. Once, when it became obvious that a friend of hers had become an alcoholic, Linda not only sought counseling for her but also went to the counseling sessions with her. Each step along the way Linda was always there to lend a sympathetic ear or offer encouragement, even in the depths, when the struggle wasn't going very well. On the day her friend finally graduated from the program, Linda was right there to celebrate with her. Some said that Linda seemed to get much more fulfillment from the triumphs of her friends than from her own successes.

Considerate to a fault, she could have assembled a forest of trees from the birthday cards, thank-you notes and just-thinking-of-you greetings she had sent to others over the years. No matter how trivial the kindness shown her, Linda responded with a warm thank-you, which to her was both a symbol of good breeding and a genuine expression of her feelings.

Because of her nurturing, caring nature, Linda developed a large number of very close friends, the vast majority of them women. From her teen years, she had always been much more comfortable with females, perhaps because males always seemed interested in her sexually. In a community of transients where so many people were on the make so much of the time, Linda's personality seemed a throwback to an earlier, gentler era. There was no doubt that she had an iron will about getting where she wanted to go, but her actions made it clear she didn't intend to do so at the expense of others.

An obvious example of that was her experience as a Raiderette, one of the attractive sideline cheerleaders for what was then the Los Angeles Raiders football team. In Los Angeles, making the cheerleading squad is in some ways more competitive than making the football team. In a city filled with pretty women drawn from all over the country by the allure of the beach, the climate and their show-business dreams, hundreds of hopefuls try out each year. Many of them aren't looking to cheer for the local jocks nearly as much as they are looking for the visibility that will break them through into modeling, television or even the movies. Beauty alone is not nearly enough to assure them a place on the squad. In Southern California, pretty girls are as common as palm trees and about as distinctive.

To become a Raiderette, each woman must not only be very attractive but also have the physical and mental skills to perform intricate dance routines. Each must pass an arduous combination of auditions and interviews before she is ever offered the chance to wear the skimpy silver and black uniform and ruffle the silver pom-pons. Each woman must have the maturity and dignity to perform her work while so dressed in front of thousands of slobbering males who toss vulgarity at her team as if it were confetti. And unlike the football players for whom the women cheer, none of them is doing it for the money. The per-game stipend is little more than carfare, and even a heavy schedule of personal appearances booked through the team adds little extra money to the pot.

Given all these demands, Linda did not only survive; she prospered. Within weeks of making the squad for the first time in 1989, she became one of its most popular members both with leering male football fans and with her fellow Raiderettes, a difficult feat amidst a bevy of high-maintenance egos. Though she enjoyed the color and scale of the football games, her favorite appearances were at charity events. There her inner warmth could really glow as she posed for a picture with a crippled little boy or showed an abused little girl how to wave the pom-pons.

After just a couple of years on the squad she was named Raiderette of the Year, and she was featured on the cover of the Raider calendar. Though the schedule was hectic and the money rewards low, she stayed with the Raiderettes for five seasons. Along the way she got to know several of the football players, including star running back Marcus Allen. Though the Raiderettes were officially forbidden to date the players, that rule was routinely ignored, and she went out with several of them. Through Allen, she met Los Angeles Laker basketball star Erwin "Magic" Johnson and attended her share of parties with basketball players as well. But Linda wasn't a hard-core partier in the Hollywood sense. She drank very little and steered away from drugs. But she did like the glitter and action connected with the big-time sports scene.

Linda's personal life never intruded into her career. The photographers who worked with her agreed that Linda gave them exactly what they needed. On a shoot she was strictly business.

"She was just good," one photographer remembered. "She had the look. Of course, to me in real life she was way too skinny and her boobs were way too big, but on film she looked great. And I never had to hear about her boyfriend or her family."

Unlike some models whose lives are open books, Linda kept her personal life well in the background when she was working. It was one way she could maintain her dignity.

"Let's face it, some girls would do anything for a guy with a camera," said a full-time automotive photographer who often used Linda as an adornment for a hot rod or a pickup truck he was shooting. "And a lot of guys use the camera to get laid. I mean very slimy. Some girls would fuck you for a shoot."

Linda never stooped to that level. She just wanted to do her job and get out.

"She was very business-driven," the photographer continued, "and she'd often do more than one shoot in a day. I remember for one particular shoot I didn't have much budget, just a hundred and fifty dollars, and when I offered her the job she said, 'Okay, you have half an hour.' And the shoot came out fine. There was no horseplay, no fooling around; she was very professional."

Because of her no-nonsense approach, some photographers didn't get along with her. She could pull some attitude, get feisty or even fiery at times, and this turned a few photographers off.

"Some of the guys thought she was very bitchy," the photographer added. "She sure pushed my buttons at times. I remember one shoot where she just stopped posing for a second and announced to me, 'You've got fifteen more minutes.' "

Another car shooter remembers a particularly difficult location shoot with a rare Chevrolet Nomad station wagon on the beach at San Onofre between Los Angeles and San Diego. After a great deal of effort, Linda's makeup and bathing suit were right, the car was positioned right, and the light was right and getting better. But twenty minutes into the session Linda said she wanted to go home. The photographer thought she was playing a bit of financial gamesmanship, and when he took her aside and offered her more money, she stayed till the end.

"It wasn't a great memory," the photographer said later. "I've got a temper and she's got a temper, but when all was said and done, it worked out great. We got great pictures, and that was the bottom line."

Great pictures, that's what kept photographers coming back to her, despite an occasionally difficult attitude.

One photographer said about her, "Linda made it very, very easy. She was spot on all the time. She had the poses down. She had the smile down. She had the whole California girl thing down."

A Petersen staff photographer agreed.

"I shot her once for *Car Craft* magazine," he recalled, "and she was a total professional. On time. Looked great. Pleasant to work with. After that I recommended her to Wieder Publications [the publishers of several fitness monthlies.]"

In between photographic assignments, Linda made personal appearances at events like the SEMA show, and eventually she put together a group of women to act as hostesses at special gatherings.

"I hired her to hostess for the Safari Club," said a

business acquaintance of hers. "She walked around in khaki shorts, a sports shirt and hiking boots all night, and she hired some of her friends to do the same thing. She was a real hustler, and I liked that about her. She had her own little impromptu agency."

But one thing Linda did not want to be doing for the next twenty years of her life was attending cocktail parties as a paid human ornament.

"Linda had another agenda, and it was not about swimsuits and cars," said a photographer who knew her professionally. "She was really driven and real smart."

Smart enough, it is certain, to know that the days of a swimsuit model are numbered from the first time she steps in front of a camera lens.

"When you're thirty-five, it's over," said a longtime professional. "It's a brutal profession. If you try to hang on longer, it gets pretty pathetic. I would hope my daughter wouldn't want to do it."

That afternoon, as she sat in her Lakewood home, waiting for the phone to ring, Linda's mother, Elaine, began to think the same thing.

Chapter 12

SOME OLD-TIMERS say that the good Lord created California on a day when He was confused. There can be no other explanation for the state's bizarre topography of burnt clay hills, rock-strewn granite mountains and wide plains so starved for water that often the ground itself puckers from thirst.

Leaving the town of Acton, which in reality is little more than an exit from the highway and a couple of gas stations that also sell soda pop, Charlie and Linda found themselves heading east through hills pockmarked with long-abandoned mines. It is land so drab, so barren, that all but the most hardy plants refuse to grow in it. And those plants that do spend most of their lives parched to the edge of extinction.

Given the forbidding nature of this land, most travelers do not tarry long or take much note of what they see, and so it was with Charles Edgar Rathbun and Linda Sobek at about twelve-thirty in the afternoon on November 16, 1995. Each was thinking private thoughts as the huge black Lexus roared up the Highway 14 grade toward Palmdale.

"Have you seen Cherie Michaels lately?" Charlie asked, breaking the lull with a question about a model Linda knew.

"No, not lately," Linda replied.

"Well, I saw her the other day, and we had a long talk."

"Oh, yeah," Linda said warily. "What about?"

"A lot of things. We were on a drive to a shoot, so we had a lot of time to talk. Did you know she's broken up with Robbie?"

"She broke up with Robbie a long time ago."

"Yeah, but I didn't know she was dating some other guy before they broke up. She told me the guy was an underwear model."

"An underwear model?"

"Yeah, and she said he was really smart. I'm not sure I ever met a really smart underwear model."

"Well, he could be."

"She said he had an engineering degree."

"See."

"Well, maybe he is smart. Possible, I guess. She also told me about her part in the vampire movie."

"What did she say about it?"

"She said she had a nude scene. That kind of surprised me."

"It did?"

"Yeah, she always talks about how she won't do *Playboy*, then she does this nude scene in some stupid low-budget horror video. What sense does that make?"

"I'm sure it made sense to her."

"Maybe. Then she told me about her and Stella."

"Stella Henderson?"

"Yeah. She said she was driving her car one day, and Stella reached over and tweaked her nipple. Just grabbed her. Said to her, 'You're turning me on.' "

Linda let out a long sigh and turned away. Again she was hearing things she didn't want to hear.

Charlie, his eyes on the twisting road ahead, didn't notice her disdain and kept on talking.

"She also told me she had tried anal sex," he said, smirking.

God, don't guys ever think about anything else? she asked herself.

She didn't bother to reply aloud. Instead she sat silently, staring out the windshield as the green sign announcing the Pearblossom Road exit came in view.

From being a golden boy when he started in the photo department at Petersen Publishing, Charlie's career had quickly spiraled downward. Though Charlie made some friends among the staff photographers, notably Mike Banks and Lynn McCready, a significant majority of the department had difficulty warming up to him. Many of them found him cold and distant, unwilling to share much about himself.

"He never mentioned his father, so I always assumed his father was dead," remembered a photo department staffer. "And when he talked about his mother, he just mentioned that he was going to visit her. She lives in Detroit, I think, and the way he talked about her wasn't positive or negative. There was just no emotion. And in contrast, there was no mention of his father at all."

Charlie would occasionally bring girlfriends to work, but they rarely created much stir in the heavily male-dominated department, which had grown used to seeing models parade in on casting calls. While some photographers used their camera to date women who otherwise would have been out of their league, Charlie didn't have much success in that regard.

"His girlfriends looked just like dishwater," one co-worker remembers. "They wore no makeup, and they were all wimpy or wiped out, completely unadorned."

Nobody in the department really cared whom he dated. But Charlie began to develop a reputation as a prima donna, a reputation that manifested itself in ever greater proportions the longer he worked for the company. His special nemesis was fellow photographer Scott Killeen, who joined the company after Charlie and quickly became his rival for the choice assignments.

One of his superiors in the department saw it this way: "He and Scott were in opposition to each other, and the more I thought about it, the more I thought Scott was in the right. More often Scott's intentions were right. It wasn't any one thing that made me feel that way. It was just a slow accumulation of observations."

Charlie didn't help his cause by displaying a violent and easily provoked temper. He was often confined to the photo studio to photograph handguns or fishing rods for the Outdoor group, and when something went wrong, he would suddenly erupt in rage.

"He'd throw stuff around all the time," a coworker said. "He'd say it was my fault that a light fell down, and he'd start throwing light stands around. Another time he got mad and started throwing camera stuff around in the photo van."

Rathbun didn't win any points for himself with his superiors at Petersen when he started to display what has been described as a know-it-all attitude on major assignments.

"I battled D'Olivo because they kept trying to tell me I was doing things wrong, and I was sure I was doing things right," Charlie said later. "I'd spent ten years assisting the best in the country, and I wasn't about to forget everything I'd learned to do it Bob's way."

On January 5, 1992, Charlie got a citation from a California Highway Patrol officer that was to become a special thorn in his side and may well have been one of the hidden reasons for his eventual termination by Petersen Publishing Company. That afternoon he was on assignment to do a simple one-car shoot in the high desert near Palmdale. Needing only one or two angles, he had positioned the car off the side of a lightly traveled road when a Highway Patrolman rolled up, the lights on his big sedan rotating ominously.

"Where's your permit?" the neatly groomed patrolman asked from behind his dark glasses.

The short answer was: Charlie didn't have a permit.

Technically he was in violation of a Los Angeles County law that requires a permit, payment of a fee and often hiring off-duty police officers to direct traffic whenever a commercial film or photo session takes place on public roads. Because Los Angeles County is the hotbed of the film industry, shoots of one sort or another go on all the time, and the law helps the county both regulate them and derive some revenue from them. But many Southern California-based photographers resent the law and routinely ignore it, taking their chances that they won't be cited. Over the years it had become fairly standard practice at Petersen to forego the permit process on simple assignments when time was of the essence and the chance of interrupting normal traffic flow was minimal or nonexistent.

With this in the back of his mind, Rathbun tried to explain to the officer that the vehicle he was photographing and his equipment vehicle were completely off the highway, presenting no possibility of disrupting what little traffic came by, but the officer was unmoved. He began to issue Charlie a ticket, and the discussion grew more heated. Finally, with tempers flaring on both sides, Charlie was hauled into the local station, where he was forced to post bond before he was released.

Back at work the following day, Rathbun told his superiors about the incident, and he says they assured him they would pay for the fine and in other ways back him up. A month or so later, Rathbun went to Lancaster court, hoping to put the whole incident to rest, but the fine was significantly more than he had anticipated—almost five thousand dollars. When word got back to his superiors how steep the fine was, Charlie says, they rolled over on him, refusing to pay it. Eventually he had to eat the cost himself or risk a jail term for a warrant violation.

While Rathbun took the brunt of the incident financially, in his superiors' eyes it was simply another instance that showed that trouble followed Charlie Rathbun around like a yapping puppy. From golden child he was becoming the problem child.

To hear him tell it, one of Charlie's difficulties in the auto-oriented world of Petersen Publishing was his lack of enthusiasm for the mechanical side of automobiles. Very often he would photograph a set of headers or a turbocharger for one of the car books, but he had no idea what they were for or why anybody would care about them. He was far more likely to cook a gourmet meal than rebuild a carburetor, that was sure. In a company full of "gearheads," who often have difficulty making conversation on subjects other than automobiles, this left Charlie at a distinct disadvantage. His only recourse, he said, was to revert to the other surefire male topic: girls.

"He would talk about his interest in women incessantly," recalls one of his fellow photo-department staff members. "Every new female that came on the radar screen, he was immediately on her. Any female was a target."

When left to themselves, men are often prone to banter salaciously about women, frequently describing in rich detail the things they would like to do with them sexually, and in the conservative, male-dominated world of Petersen Publishing (veterans of the place describe its company political orientation as feudalism), Charlie was often plunged into the midst of male-only assignments in which half a dozen guys in half a dozen cars drove off somewhere to put a story together. In those circumstances, the conversation frequently turned blatantly vulgar, often just for comic effect. But several of Charlie's coworkers noted an almost maniacal level of intensity in his discussion of females and in his pursuit of them.

"He was the biggest hound dog in the world," one of his superiors said. "I never knew of any other guy who was so constantly sniffing after girls."

In these days of workplace lawsuits, Petersen management began to fear Rathbun's relentless pursuit of women might slip over the line into sexual harassment. The last thing they wanted was an expensive-to-defend lawsuit, so they began to keep a weather eye on Charlie.

"His behavior was always on the edge of inappropriate," said one of his supervisors, "and as his manager, I was afraid I could be held liable, so I tried to document what he was doing, but no one at Petersen decided to come forward and point the finger at him. I'd talk to some women about behavior I had witnessed, and they'd say, 'Oh, it wasn't that big of a deal.' "

Some forms of harassment are physical—inappropriate touching, rubbing up against women in crowded places, fondling of breasts or buttocks—but no coworkers reported that Charlie was ever that blatant. Looking at it from one point of view, he simply asked a lot of women to go out with him. Unfortunately for Charlie, he often had difficulty discerning when the objects of his advances just weren't interested, and he continued to toss out invitations well past the point where others would have found it embarrassing and slightly pathetic.

"He was very verbal," one Petersen employee remembered. "He was always ready to offer invitations, ask suggestive questions. It was always verbal pursuit."

Though his pursuit of women became almost legendary within the walls of Petersen, there was another rumored facet of Charlie's character that drew far less notice. One staffer who watched him closely had this assessment:

"My own theory is that Charlie's gay, a closet gay," he said. "That's why he was such a sexual animal. It was overcompensation."

To back up his theory, the Petersen employee cited an instance of being told by an art director who had long been rumored to be bisexual that Charlie had propositioned him.

"Looking at that and his constant interest in women, I think that Charlie was either trying to compensate for his inner feelings of gayness or he was just sexually omnivorous," the coworker said. "He was always on, never off."

One might guess that these types of behaviors would have been enough for Charlie's employers to send him packing, with sexual harassment as the reason for termination. But like many companies in this era, Petersen is as wary of lawsuits from its terminated employees as it is from its current employees who allege sexual harassment in the workplace. When Charlie's employment at Petersen Publishing finally ended on June 5, 1992, he was told it was due to budget cuts in the photo department that necessitated the layoff of one photographer. The photographer chosen to walk the plank—Charles Edgar Rathbun.

Hardly a stupid person, Charlie saw it coming and was prepared for it.

"I knew they were putting it to me, hoping I would quit," he said. "I wasn't going to quit. They'd win. But I especially wanted to collect unemployment while I gathered my wits and found clients."

Instead of being upset by the firing, Charlie said he celebrated his dismissal from Petersen by taking his friend Shannon Meyer to dinner. An attractive, auburn-haired woman with a fit, outdoor look, Meyer had been his frequent lunch partner and confidante for a couple of years.

According to Charlie, the dismissal came at a good time. He claimed he had been only planning to work at Petersen for about a year to build credibility and contacts, but then the recession of 1991 or so had persuaded him to stay. What he liked most about the layoff was it provided him with unemployment benefits.

"That two hundred thirty dollars a month was the working wife I never had," he said.

While Rathbun was celebrating his dismissal with Shannon Meyer, there was a celebration of sorts going on in the Petersen photo department. Scott Killeen, in particular, was not very sorry to see his old rival go. But there was also a little wariness.

"There was a joke going around the photo department after he left," Killeen said later, "that if Charlie came back, everybody should run and duck. We were afraid it would be a postal kind of thing."

Chapter 13

JUST AS Route 14 begins to turn north toward Palmdale, Lancaster and Mojave, the Pearblossom Highway swings off east toward the little ramshackle villages of Pearland, Little Rock and Longview, which stretch out in a crooked line toward the San Bernadino County border. Not so long ago these out-of-the-way places were more than a half-day's drive from downtown Los Angeles and a great deal farther removed in terms of mentality. But since the construction of the Antelope Valley Freeway, as one stretch of Highway 14 is now known, access to the city and the city's access to these tiny rural outposts have increased exponentially. And the wickedness of the city now frequently comes calling.

At a little after one-fifteen on the afternoon of November 16, 1995, the imposing black truck carrying Linda Sobek and Charlie Rathbun swept hurriedly through those unknowing towns, past the weed-choked yards strewn with decaying cars set gingerly on concrete blocks, past the shuttered filling stations, their paint fading from neglect, past the hand-painted signs offering "Puppies for sale" or the simpler, more direct "RaBBiTS."

"Looks like we're going to get some sun," Charlie piped up out of the silence, a statement of the obvious, since bright sunshine had been pouring down on them almost from the moment they exited Highway 14.

"Yeah, I guess you're right," Linda replied. "That's

good." She reached into her purse, rummaged through for a minute, and continued, "Do you think my pager will work out here?"

"I'm not sure," Charlie replied. "It's pretty desolate, but it might."

"When we're finished, I've got to get to a phone as soon as I can."

"Oh, no problem. This shouldn't take long."

"Good."

"Just a few shots to do, and we should be able to get some for your portfolio, too. Did I tell you that I saw Stella at the SEMA show?"

"No."

"Yeah, I ran into her right before I talked to you. She asked me if I had seen Cherie."

"Had you?"

"Not for a while, but the last time I talked with her, she told me a funny story."

"Oh, yeah?"

"Yeah, she said the first time she had her breasts done she had them done by a doctor in Florida who specialized in doing them for topless dancers, and it turned out they were too big."

"She told me that, too."

"She had to have them done all over again," said Charlie, laughing.

Linda didn't think the story was all that funny, but she tried to laugh along anyway.

"Say, you were with the Raiderettes, weren't you?" Charlie asked after a moment had elapsed.

"Yeah."

"How long?"

"Through 1993. I'd had enough of it by then, and the team was moving back to Oakland, anyway."

"Did you like it? Being with the Raiderettes?"

"I liked it a lot. I mean some of it was hard, but there were a lot of good things about it, too."

"Like what?"

"Well, the parties were great. Always a lot of celebrities."

"And you like that?"

"Don't you?"

"Well, I've photographed quite a few celebrities, and a lot of them are assholes."

"I know what you mean, but most of the time it was fun. I got to know Marcus Allen and Magic Johnson and Denzel Washington, and they were great."

"I never worked with any sports people, but some of these actors . . . shit."

"Like who?"

"Sly Stallone. What a jerk!"

"No kidding?"

"Yeah. On the other hand, Charlie Sheen was a great guy. Very cool. And Lisa Kudrow—you know, from *Friends*—I shot her when she was just getting started. She was going to a comedy workshop right across the street from my house. She came over a couple of times."

"How did you like her?"

"I thought she was great. Pretty girl, but no boobs."

"Not any more."

"Yeah, that was a few years ago. I think it was her first comedy class. We talked for a while, and she told me I had great comic timing."

"That's quite a compliment."

"I guess it is."

"Well, being with the Raiderettes was a lot of fun, especially Magic Johnson, he's very cool."

"Oh, yeah?"

"Yeah, very cool, and his doctor is a genius."

"Why do you say that?"

"Because he cured Magic of AIDS."

Hmm, Charlie thought to himself, I didn't think anybody had found a cure for AIDS. But he didn't challenge her on it. Now that the sun had appeared, she seemed to be in a better mood, not nearly as bitchy as earlier, and he didn't want to spoil it.

*   *   *

When Charlie Rathbun's career at Petersen Publishing crashed and burned around him, he was lucky enough to have several friends he could fall back on for support. Phil Spangenberger, the western expert, was one friend who stuck with him through the bad times, and Trish Peterson, another Petersen employee, was another staunch supporter. But Charlie had also assembled a small coterie of friends outside the Petersen orbit.

One of them was Jim Nichols, a successful lawyer who has spent his career defending doctors in medical malpractice cases. Like Spangenberger, the rail-thin, spectacle-wearing Nichols is an Old West aficionado, and it was through Spangenberger that Nichols met Charlie.

A member of an equestrian group called The Spirit of the West Riders, a band of horsemen and horsewomen who dress in traditional western garb and ride in events like the Rose Parade, Nichols first ran into Charlie at a photo shoot. At the suggestion of Spangenberger, Rathbun was there to photograph the group, something he proceeded to do with what Nichols considered to be uncommon care and sensitivity.

"He was just an exquisite photographer," Nichols enthused later. "First he took pictures of us as a group, and then he took pictures of every one of us individually. He was affable, professional and had a good sense of humor."

After the photo session, several members of the group retired to Viva's, a Mexican restaurant in Burbank, and Charlie joined them. They all enjoyed a pleasant lunch, much of it spent talking about the history of the western United States, one of Charlie's favorite subjects, and when lunch was over, Charlie picked up the tab.

The next time the group met, there was Charlie with what Nichols describes as outstanding photographs. He distributed them to the members of the group, and he absolutely refused any payment for his work. From that point on, Charles Edgar Rathbun was the unofficial photographer of The Spirit of the West Riders. He attended virtually all of their gatherings, including several at the Gene Autry Museum of Western History in Glendale, and photographed them again and again—all simply for the love of it.

"I remember one time the group got together at the Autry Museum and after the shoot we decided to have a little impromptu picnic, so Charlie and I went over to Pavilions [a supermarket] in Burbank to get lunch for everyone," Nichols said. "We picked out lunch for about twenty or twenty-five people, and when we got to the cash register, he wouldn't let me pay. I told him, 'Charlie, I'm lucky enough to be making a good living; I don't mind paying for this or at least splitting it with you.' But he refused. And that's been my experience with him. I found him to be generous to a fault."

Another time Rathbun took a photograph that Nichols especially liked. The two chatted about it before or after another photo session, and very quickly Charlie said, "I'm going to send it to you." Soon after, Nichols received an enlargement of the photo, and typically, Rathbun refused any compensation.

Over the years Nichols invited Charlie to several big get-togethers at his home, and he found the photographer to be a very pleasant guest.

"He'd show up with a girlfriend, and he would always be a gentleman," Nichols recalls. "I never saw him get drunk, nothing like that. I was always very comfortable with him."

In the later years of their relationship Nichols also got to know the woman who would become Charlie's fiancée.

"I thought Glenda was one of the sweetest, nicest, most comfortable-to-be-around people I've ever met," Nichols said.

Jim Nichols wasn't the only member of The Spirit of the West Riders who befriended Charlie. Shannon Meyer, a pretty, fresh-faced freelance animation cell painter who happens to live next door to the Nichols family home in

Burbank's equestrian neighborhood, was another rider who developed a relationship with the tall, hulking photographer.

Like Nichols, she was very impressed by how hard Charlie worked.

"It seemed like he was earnestly trying to get the best shot," she recalls. "And that made a favorable impression."

Apparently Meyer made an equally favorable impression on Rathbun.

"One day Charlie called, and we talked on the phone for a long time," Meyer said. "He told me how his grandfather influenced him to become a photographer, and he seemed like a genuinely nice person. Finally, at the end of the conversation, he said to me, 'Do you want to go out?' "

The only problem was that Shannon was married, though she had recently separated from her husband, Andy.

"At first I was reluctant," she recalls, "but then I decided I'll go out; maybe it will help me stop feeling sorry for myself."

She agreed to a date with Rathbun, and the two had dinner together, but for Meyer there were no sparks.

"I felt comfortable talking to him," she continued, "but there was no physical attraction. He asked me out again, and when he came to the door to pick me up, I told him I was comfortable with him as a friend, but I did not want a relationship with him. He said, 'Okay, no problem,' and we still went out, but that was pretty much it. The way I describe it, I had one and a half dates with him."

Though shut down romantically by Shannon Meyer, Charlie continued to seek her company. He would call her frequently, ask her to join him for lunch, and the two would meet at Dalt's Grill in the Burbank media district, a stone's throw from Warner Brothers Studios.

With a tiny salad in front of her and a plate of meatloaf

in front of him, the two would discuss people they knew in common, movies they'd seen and their shared enthusiasm for mountain biking. The lunches continued well after Shannon reconciled with her husband as pleasant get-togethers that helped her break the monotony of her home-based business.

One topic that frequently surfaced during the lunches was the pair's romantic aspirations.

"I remember he liked a woman named Pam in Colorado," Shannon recalls. "He told me that he really liked her and that she had stayed with him at his house when she visited California, but she had a boyfriend back in Colorado. He felt very romantic toward her and would send her cards and flowers all the time, but she would never leave her boyfriend."

That instance and others like it sent Meyer a message.

"I thought he was naïve," she said. "He was all over the map with women, and with Pam he was always wishing it would develop into something."

Since Charlie's occupation put him in the middle of the fast-paced world of automotive photography, one might have expected that he dated models on a regular basis. But according to Meyer, that was far from the case.

"He didn't go out a lot," Shannon recalls. "He didn't talk about models much, but he'd say some were nice, some were hard to work with. He wasn't seeking out models per se, but I don't think he was opposed to going out with models, either. He was just kind of flippant about it, but I think he was covering up. He would have loved to go out with a model."

Though Shannon had resumed her marriage and was committed to sticking with her husband, like nearly any wife, she occasionally let loose a mild complaint about her spouse. Charlie didn't want to hear it.

"It seemed like if I complained about Andy, he wasn't comfortable with that," she said.

In fact, to hear Meyer tell it, Rathbun might have been a disciple of Benjamin Disraeli, the man who said,

"Never complain, never explain." He seemed to have a deep-rooted dislike for complaints.

"I remember once I said something negative about something my dad did," Shannon said, "and Charlie got real serious and said to me, 'You shouldn't complain about your dad; you should be glad you have a parent who loves and cares about you.' He couldn't tolerate complaints about life in general. He'd get really mad and tell you you weren't trying hard enough to make things better."

When it came to his family, though, Charlie made an exception to his never-complain philosophy.

"He was really disappointed that his parents didn't insist on seeing the last child out the door in proper fashion," she recalled from a rare conversation in which Charlie discussed his family. "He told me his mother drove his dad out; she was highly critical."

In contrast to his family, whom he felt had betrayed him, Rathbun valued his friends very highly.

"One time we were talking about a friend who had been arrested for drunk driving, and I told him I was unsympathetic," Shannon remembered. "Charlie got upset. He told me friendship is very important."

Over the course of a two-year period, Shannon not only went to frequent lunches with Rathbun but also rode mountain bikes with him, most often in Griffith Park. (Despite Charlie's association with The Spirit of the West Riders, he wasn't a horseman himself.)

Though his coworkers in the Petersen photo department remember him as constantly on the make, Rathbun seemed to be a totally different person when he was with Shannon Meyer.

"I never got an uncomfortable feeling when I was exercising with him on our bikes in Griffith Park," she said. "I never felt any danger, never said to myself, 'He's thinking something I don't like.' "

In her company he was the consummate gentleman.

"He absolutely never used foul language, never made

innuendoes that made me feel uncomfortable," she continued. "In fact, one time he told me about a photo shoot he'd been on where some of the models were getting dressed in the open near the car, and he couldn't believe that. It appalled him."

During the course of her friendship with Charlie, Shannon recalls only one dose of the noted Rathbun temper. The two were driving together, and when they arrived at their destination, the seatbelt hit Charlie in the head as he was trying to get out. It wasn't much of a blow, but he went ballistic.

"He got really mad, really, really mad, and it scared me," Shannon remembers. "When he calmed down, he said to me, 'I get really mad when I get hit in the head.' "

Shannon and Charlie remained friendly for a couple of years, but as time went on, the lunches became less frequent. If she thought about it at all, Meyer believed it was a natural result of their going their separate ways. She was happily reunited with her husband, and Charlie had expressed interest in several other women.

"We hadn't been going to lunch as much, and he seemed okay with that," Shannon recalls. "But one day we were at lunch at Dalt's, and I said to him, 'Andy's not into mountain biking, so if you want to go with me sometime,' and I was stunned at how the conversation went."

What shocked Shannon was Charlie's reaction. He shouted at her like a wronged lover, telling her he was sick of playing second fiddle to her husband and making it clear that he was tired of being used. Their argument continued out of the restaurant and into the car.

"It became obvious to me he had this strong feeling that he was carrying around with him," Shannon recalls.

In the car she made it clear to him that while she considered him a friend, she had no romantic thoughts about him at all.

"He said, 'Well, fine, if you feel that way,' " Shannon

continued. "I got out, shut the door, and that's the last time I saw him."

At least, it was the last time she saw him until many months later, when she attended a party that included among its guests Charlie and his new girlfriend, Glenda Elam. Shannon and Glenda immediately hit it off, but Charlie was little more than civil.

"Glenda was really outgoing, friendly, well centered," Shannon recalled about the meeting. "She fit well in her skin."

In fact, Shannon got along so well with Glenda that she hoped for a good future for the new couple, but she couldn't help having misgivings.

"I thought she was really neat," Shannon recalls, "and I said to myself, 'I hope he doesn't screw this up.' "

In her own relationship with Charlie and in the lunchtime tales he had told of his amorous hopes and dreams, Shannon had already seen her photographer "screw it up" more than once. Charlie seemed to have an uncanny knack for missing subtle signals and for expecting alternately too much or too little.

"He was immature in his relationships," Shannon said. "He put women on a pedestal, and if they screwed up, then that was it. They were either great or not for him."

Though their relationship had experienced ups and downs, Meyer still wished the best for her mountain-biking pal. She hoped that Glenda would be the woman who could finally give Charlie a sense of happiness.

"I know he wanted to be married," Shannon recalls. "One time he said that to me in just so many words and then he added, 'And I'm going to work on that.' I just think he was lonely."

As the Lexus rolled inexorably toward its destination at El Mirage dry lake, the lonely photographer was in the company of one of the most beautiful women he had ever met.

Chapter 14

A S THE Lexus charged eastward on Pearblossom Highway, Charlie was feeling much better about the proceedings than he had as recently as one hour before. The
brightening of the skies and the accompanying brightening of his vehicle partner's mood was responsible for the
change.

The way he saw it, his model and traveling companion
for the day had been a little out of sorts, if not downright
cold, from the moment she climbed into the vehicle with
him. Was it his fault, he asked himself, that the weather
was cloudy? Was it his fault that they had to scrub their
original photo location? Was it his fault that he had to
come up with a new concept on the spur of the moment?

But he had to congratulate himself on his quick thinking. In a matter of seconds he had shifted his sights from
Santa Barbara County to El Mirage dry lake because his
experience had told him he could find sun there, and sure
enough, he was right. The rays that were beaming down
on his massive black vehicle were further testimony to his
intelligence.

Better yet, his decisive thinking seemed to have had a
positive effect on his passenger. Sure, her original attitude
had been chilly. In fact, before she had been so friendly
to him at the SEMA show, he had always felt she carried
around a lot of attitude—she could be very demanding
and difficult to get along with. But after they had talked

for a while, he could tell she was warming up to him.

He sneaked a quick look at her and again, for what must have been the hundredth time during their drive, he was dazzled by her attractiveness.

What a piece of ass, he thought, and he exhaled a deep sigh.

He stayed within his reverie for a moment as the vehicle zoomed onward down the lonesome road. Finally the novelty of a passing car loping along in the opposite direction brought him out of it.

"We're getting pretty close now," he said, knowing the report would be welcome news to his passenger.

"Great," Linda replied, looking over at him, her blue eyes under thick lashes sending a little jolt down his spine.

I wish goddamned D'Olivo could see me now, Charlie thought, and goddamned Haefner, too. On this fine afternoon, beautiful model in tow, he was a successful Hollywood photographer making it on his own terms. Anyone who didn't think so could go fuck himself.

Of course, the road to successful freelancedom after his enforced departure hadn't been easy. There is something about a regular paycheck that eases the pain in the gut that many freelancers experience every day. But Charlie had cultivated some friendships with editors and art directors over the years, so when he was forced to go out on his own, he wasn't starting at ground zero. And ironically, given his very recent past, Petersen Publishing Company, with its dozens of magazines, loomed as one of the most fertile fields for freelance assignments. While Petersen had its own photo department, the work of that department was not held in universally high esteem by the art directors of the various publications. Often they opted to work with freelancers rather than battle the bureaucracy of the photo department.

Not only that, but in many circles at Petersen, Charlie had gained a reputation as a photographer who went above and beyond the call. While the average ex-photo-department staffer might have had a hell of a time getting photo shoots from cynical Petersen art directors, Charlie's reputation for good work put him in a different category. He had several supporters at Petersen, some of whom had the authority to hire him themselves; others, including Phil Spangenberger, could alert him to possible assignments.

One thing an aspiring freelance photographer has to do is press the flesh a lot. Without making a pest of himself, he must show up, telephone, meet for lunch and otherwise make and keep himself visible in editors' and art directors' eyes. This fact was not lost on Charles Edgar Rathbun. Virtually the day after he was terminated, he was back at Petersen Publishing, this time soliciting freelance work.

Of course, the prospect of losing intra-company work to a newly terminated former staffer was about as palatable to the photo department management as a turd on their dinner plate. Charlie believes they immediately started a whispering campaign of disinformation about him, designed to prevent him from getting freelance assignments.

In one incident that he recalls, Charlie was in the office of an automotive performance group editor, about to close a sale on some freelance work, when a member of the photo department chanced to walk in. Seeing Charlie there, the staffer scoffed, "You're not thinking of hiring *him*, are you?" and the editor, fearing a political brouhaha, immediately backpedaled on the deal Charlie was convinced he would have made with him.

According to Charlie, his old nemesis Scott Killeen was one photo department employee who went out of his way to make it difficult for him to get freelance assignments from Petersen Publications. After a month or two of trying to gain assignments from art directors at Petersen with no notable success, the situation got so bad that Charlie asked his brother, an attorney living on the East Coast, what he should do about it. After discussing the situation at length,

Robert sent Petersen legal counsel Robert Gottlieb a letter requesting that Petersen employees refrain from bad-mouthing Charlie and blackballing him. The letter threatened legal action if the harassment and restraint of trade didn't cease. According to Charlie, Gottlieb agreed with the Rathbuns' premise and promised a halt to the whispering campaign. But even if Gottlieb had the noblest intentions, it proved impossible to stop rumor and innuendo. Charlie decided that he would be well advised to spend most of his efforts seeking work elsewhere.

Over a period of time, largely through perseverance, Charlie built up a reasonably impressive clientele. He did a great deal of photo work for magazine editor Dan Sanchez. He won very lucrative press kit assignments from Volkswagen and Oldsmobile. And he began to get assignment after assignment from Larry Saavedra of *Sport Compact Car*.

When Charlie began working for Saavedra, the two had a positive rapport, but after a couple of years the relationship began to deteriorate. If it hadn't been a financial necessity to continue working with him, Charlie almost certainly would have quit. But after years of rootlessness, which began when his parents divorced, he had the dream of buying a house for himself, so he continued to toil for Saavedra, even though he found it increasingly distasteful.

"Larry was someone who was the worst," Charlie said later. "He would call up and leave a message one day at 10 A.M. When you'd call back the next day at 9 A.M., he'd act like I was out avoiding his call."

Even more vexing to Rathbun was Saavedra's failure to heed his counsel.

"He wouldn't listen to my advice, so I'd do it his way. Then he wouldn't like it, so I would do it my way, and it would be exactly what he wanted in the first place," Charlie continued. "And the problem was I was doing two to three days' work for a one-day rate. He always had last-minute shots he needed yesterday, and he whined about his company and his job. I used to tell him to quit."

If Rathbun's work with Saavedra was sometimes frustrating, he had no such problems when he was on assignment for *AutoWeek*. As a key West Coast freelance photographer for the venerable Detroit-based publication, he really found a home.

Charlie got his first assignment for *AutoWeek* by showing then art director Charles Krasner his portfolio work, a great deal of it shot during his Petersen days. Krasner immediately saw that Charlie knew how to shoot cars, and a lengthy relationship began, a relationship that continued when Marilee Bowles took over the helm as art director.

According to an *AutoWeek* staff editor who worked with Rathbun, "Charlie was always adding little nuances to his photos. He wouldn't just send in pictures of cars; in some of the shots there might be ducks on a lake or a horse galloping by."

Rathbun's extra effort was appreciated by the *Auto-Week* crew. Occasionally Charlie hired a model to appear at the wheel of a vehicle in some of his photos, and that was appreciated, too, even though *AutoWeek's* official stance was "No models—the cars are the stars."

"We would usually get some fat, sloppy staff editor to drive the vehicles for the pictures," said an *AutoWeek* staffer who prefers anonymity. "So if Charlie showed up with a model, nobody was going to complain about it."

It was fulfilling enough for Rathbun to turn in good work to a magazine staff that seemed to appreciate it, but Charlie also found fulfillment in the camaraderie he developed with *AutoWeek's* West Coast crew. The group he fell in with seemed genuinely to like him and his off-beat sense of humor.

"We would all joke around, and it was a lot of fun," the *AutoWeek* staff member continued. "I remember some shoots in Azuza Canyon where we'd make a game of walking along the side of the road and finding condoms in the dirt. Just stupid little things like that, joking along to help the time pass."

Another popular addition Charlie occasionally brought

to photo sessions was his sometime assistant CeCe Berglund. A vivacious brunette who also did some modeling work, CeCe was from Denver and had a boyfriend there, but when she came to California, which was fairly often, she would stay with Charlie.

"She was like a little ray of sunshine," recalls the anonymous *AutoWeek* staffer. "I remember one time we were on a shoot, and we wanted to use this big fire hose to wet down the skidpad, but we couldn't get the water to come out of the thing. Well, she came up and said, 'Hey, Pete, why don't you suck on it?' and that broke everybody up."

Though the humor was sophomoric, the *AutoWeek* staff member didn't find anything offensive or unusual in it. He never noted an inappropriate "edge" in the banter, and found Rathbun to be among the most benign participants, at least most of the time. But there were a few instances that were unusual enough to stick in his mind.

"There was one time near the end [of the period I worked with him], he had a model with him, a tall blond, just a little heavyset," the *AutoWeek* staffer continued, "and then the next time I saw him, Charlie said to me, 'She wants to do you bad, man. She really wants to do you bad!' I said, "Yeah, right, sure she does,' but he was really insistent about it. Of course, that's the kind of stuff guys will say sometimes. Most of the time it was like a big group of friends having a fun time."

Perhaps the oddest and most disturbing instance the *AutoWeek* employee remembers is Rathbun's off-hand description of CeCe Berglund's sex life.

"He used to say that she liked being raped," the source said. "He told us that the only way her boyfriend could have sex with her was to rape her."

By 1995, Rathbun was so well established as a top automotive freelancer that he was invited to Italy as part of a journalist group covering the introduction of a new Pirelli tire. Also traveling as part of the group were Lisa

Barrow and Pat Stalionis, both of the *MotorWeek* television show.

Producer and cameraman Stalionis remembered, "At first we didn't like him. He seemed a little strange. But pretty soon he was offering to help us carry our gear around—you know when you're in TV, you've got a lot of equipment—and after that we kind of warmed up to him. He turned out to be very helpful. And he really seemed to like Lisa."

A tall, attractive brunette with the diction of a practiced television personality, Barrow smiles when she talks about Rathbun.

"We didn't really like him initially, but he ended up hanging out with us a lot," she remembers. "One thing about him: he could certainly eat cookies. I remember one night in Italy he must have eaten at least three bowlsful of cookies, you know, biscotti. The waiters kept bringing them out and he kept eating them. I couldn't believe anyone could eat that many."

On the trip Rathbun's demeanor toward Barrow was one of helpful friend, but when the group returned home, scattering to various parts of the country, he began to pursue her romantically. He called frequently, sent her flowers and though they lived on opposite coasts, he invited her to attend *The Phantom of the Opera* with him. That invitation drew little more than a laugh from Barrow.

Because the auto journalist and auto public relations community is so small, rumors make the rounds rapidly. Barrow got a chortle out of the *Phantom* invitation because she knew through the grapevine that there was hardly a woman in the whole of that community whom Charlie *hadn't* invited to see *The Phantom of the Opera*. Like the flowers he bestowed on virtually every woman who caught his eye, tickets to *Phantom* were one of his calling cards.

Though many of the women he tried to court thought his attentions were strange, awkward or even the slightest bit spooky, there is no law against a man inviting a woman to see a play. The flowers he routinely sent may have been unwanted, but they weren't viewed as a symptom of psychosis either.

As his friend Shannon Meyer put it, "Charlie didn't seem any more or any less clueless about women than a lot of other guys I've met."

Despite Lisa Barrow's lack of interest, Charlie tried to keep the long-distance relationship alive.

"One day he called out of the blue and said he was coming to Washington, D.C., and asked me if I'd like to go out to dinner with him," Barrow remembers. "I told him I wasn't sure what I was doing and that I'd have to think about it, and it turned out that he wasn't going to Washington at all. He was going to some place like The Greenbriar in West Virginia, but he told me he would drive into Washington if I wanted to have dinner with him. I couldn't make it, but I've always wondered what would've happened if I had."

Stalionis had another observation about Rathbun: "Charlie was always following us around with his cameras on the bus when we were going from place to place, and he took a lot of pictures of Lisa. The odd thing about it was, he took most of them of her while she was asleep."

Chapter 15

EL MIRAGE dry lake is so off the beaten track, you might say that it is on the edge of nowhere, beyond which there is nothing at all. Turning off the main road, Rathbun left the blacktop behind as he approached the vast flatland from the south, maneuvering up one heavily rutted dirt road, then veering off onto another under the unabating late-autumn sun.

Back in the mists of history, when the climate of Southern California was far different from what it is in these rain-starved decades, the place was a substantially sized landlocked lake, teeming with water creatures. But hundreds if not thousands of years ago, the water evaporated, leaving behind an unremittingly level surface several miles around.

Startlingly enough, viewed at the right time from the faded-brown hills that surround it, the bone-dry lake bed can still appear to be brimming with water. Peering down into the valley, you can picture graceful sailboats reaching toward the far shore and an idle fisherman, line in the water, nearly asleep in his anchored skiff. But with a blink it all fades away. This heartbreaking aspect of the eerie place—the false vision of a cool, clear lake in the midst of a cruel and uncompromising desert—led the Spainards who first charted it to name it El Mirage—the illusion.

Yet despite its otherworldly isolation, the dry lake does have its share of visitors. The area is most popular in early fall, when the diehard hot rodders of the Southern California Timing Association descend upon it for their top-speed runs. They are attracted not by the dry lake's beauty but by its immense flatness. The parched clay, rent in innumerable cracks for lack of water, provides the perfect surface for their tests of men and machinery. It affords them miles to bring their modified vehicles up to speed and further miles to slow them down again, all without anything to obstruct their progress or send them careening toward disaster.

One weekend it happens like clockwork. Suddenly the hot rodders appear, towing their handbuilt, homebuilt contraptions behind battered pickup trucks. They set up their tents, break out their coolers, split open beers and "shoot the shit" while individuals of their number climb into their vehicles and get them up to speed. Then, just as suddenly, they fold their tents, push their now dust-laden contraptions back onto their trailers and silently steal off for home.

While the SCTA speed demons bring the largest influx of visitors to El Mirage, even on a mundane midweek day there is the chance of seeing some activity on the dry lake. All-terrain-vehicle riders in helmets, gloves and body padding occasionally blast across its broad reaches, the odd itinerant will set up camp, and sometimes a pilot, mesmerized by the sight of its vastness, can't resist the temptation to touch his light plane down, lingering in the emptiness for a moment before lunging skyward again.

But though the dry lake attracts more human activity than one would first guess, its immense size, its incredible vastness, swallows everything up like a whale gulping plankton. The scale of its flatness dwarfs all who enter, making them self-consciously aware of their minuteness in the overall scheme. More than any, it is a lonely place.

As he entered the forbidding lonely place, Charlie Rathbun wasn't feeling lonely at all. Accompanied as he was by a beautiful woman, he was feeling pretty good about himself, certain that he had broken through the initial coldness she had shown. Now he attributed that crankiness to the fact that he had called her at the last minute. She was a little flustered by that and worried about keeping her appointment, he told himself, but after they'd gossiped a little about the industry and some mutual acquaintances, she had warmed up considerably.

As the sport utility made its way carefully over the pockmarked corduroy of the dirt road, Charlie resisted the temptation to step on the gas. He wanted to get to his destination as quickly as he could, but he knew that more speed would cover the vehicle in dust and leave him a lengthy and onerous cleanup chore. Better, he thought, to go a little slower now and have more time later.

Charlie was also pleased at the serendipitous circumstances that had brought him to the dry lake. His original plan, shooting at a horse ranch in Santa Barbara County, was properly upscale for the vehicle, but the trek to and from the potential photo site had promised to make for a lengthy ordeal. How much better it was, he mused, to be at the dry lake, not necessarily because it was the optimum photo location for the vehicle, but because the shorter trip promised to make a much more leisurely day.

We would have really had to hump it to get to Santa Barbara and back by six o'clock, he laughed inwardly. And if he had been honest with himself, he would have additionally acknowledged that if the two of them had tried to shoot in Santa Barbara, there was no possible way he could have had Linda back at her car in Torrance by early evening.

No, Charlie thought, it's much better things worked out this way.

The Lexus bounced along the road a mile or two more and then emerged onto the awesome immensity of the dry lake bed. No matter how often one has seen it, and by that time Charlie had seen it very often, there is still a majesty about the place, a kind of unearthly presence, that can suck your breath away.

Involuntarily he slowed down, drinking in a view that seemed to be pulled intact from another planet in another galaxy. Even the no-nonsense Linda, getting ready to punch the clock for her day's pay, couldn't help but be a little moved by it. The lake's vastness could make anyone feel small.

Charlie pulled the vehicle to a halt and looked at his watch. It was 1:15.

"Well, here we are," he announced jovially. "This should give us plenty of time to do what we need to do."

"That's good," she replied, eager to get on with the proceedings. "What do you want to do first?"

"I don't know," he replied, smiling at her. "Why don't you relax for a minute, and I'll get out my camera gear? Then we can get started."

"Okay."

Charlie pushed open the door and swung down onto the mottled clay surface of the lake bed.

"Boy, it feels good to stand up," he said, stretching his six-foot-two-inch frame. "I feel like I've been sitting for weeks.

Following his example, Linda clambered out of her side of the vehicle, her Ugg lambskin boots causing small eddies in the dust.

"You're right. It does feel good," she agreed.

She, too, stretched her back, her tight white leotard pulled tauter across her chiseled shoulders.

Charlie opened the rear hatch of the vehicle and wrestled his big camera bag to the edge of the cargo space near the bumper. Before he opened it, he squinted up toward the sky and shook his head.

"The light's pretty hot right now," he said. "I think we're going to have to wait for a while."

He had known that from the second the sun had appeared as they left Route 14 more than forty-five minutes before, but in the interest of diplomacy he hadn't mentioned the possible delay until now. Why spoil the mood unnecessarily? he had thought.

Linda sighed and stretched some more. Wait for a while—she had heard that refrain from just about every photographer she'd ever worked with. But she was a professional, and she reminded herself that bright overhead sunlight makes for deep shadows, not very flattering to any woman and especially unflattering to her with her pronounced cheekbones.

From experience she knew that intense sunlight didn't show off vehicles well either, although to her a car was a car and who really cared? But she had looked through enough camera lenses to recognize hotspots and flares when she saw them, and with the sun almost directly overhead, its rays heating the clay under her feet, she realized that those lighting imperfections were very likely to occur, given the current conditions.

Of course, she had worked with many photographers who didn't seem to care. Midday? Hot sun? Deep shadows? What, me worry? Those camera jockeys would park the pickup truck in the corner of the parking lot, tell her to take her T-shirt off to reveal the bitty bikini underneath and then shoot away to their heart's content. A couple of rolls run through the camera in twenty minutes, and they called it a photo shoot. But Linda recognized Rathbun wasn't like that. As strange as he sometimes seemed, he was an artist.

Charlie had a camera body in his hand as he walked toward her.

"I've got an idea," he told her. "You said you brought your portfolio with you, didn't you?"

"Yeah, I've got it right here," she replied, pulling it from underneath her leopard-print curler bag.

"Well, why don't we do this? Why don't we look over your portfolio, and then we can shoot a few rolls for it? You've brought some wardrobe with you, and I think this background might make for some pretty cool stuff."

"Okay," she said, offering the book to Rathbun.

She wasn't happy about the delay, but she was always interested in improving her career. If her companion for the day could give her some helpful advice, or better yet, provide her with photos that would enhance her portfolio, she was all for it.

The two climbed back into the Lexus, and Charlie moved his seat back from the big steering wheel so that he could have more room to look at the book. As Linda watched his reaction from the passenger seat, he turned the pages slowly, taking a lengthy period of time to examine each photograph.

He was at once struck by her nearly perfect beauty and by the silly imperfections of the photos that presented it. Even though he wasn't a portrait photographer, he was convinced that he could do better.

"This one isn't bad," he said, pointing to a photo that showed Linda smiling demurely, her head cocked in an innocent way that only made her look sexier.

Linda silently pouted at the faint praise.

"You know, I'm sorry that that pickup truck shoot didn't work out," he said, referring to an earlier shoot which had fallen through. "I wanted to use you, but those guys flake out on me all the time."

"That's okay," she reassured him.

"If I didn't need the money, I'd never work with those idiots again."

"I know what it's like to need money," she replied. "It's okay."

"Well, I'm glad we're getting the opportunity to work together now. Thanks for coming along at the last moment."

"It's not a problem," she said.

"You know, usually I'd give you more notice, but when I picked up the vehicle this morning, they told me it had to be back tomorrow afternoon. That didn't leave much time."

"Oh."

"I was originally going to have someone else drive for me, but she wasn't available today."

What Charlie didn't tell her was that "someone else"

was his steady girlfriend, Glenda Elam, who had found it impossible to get out of work.

"Huh," Linda replied, a little perturbed that Charlie had stopped eyeballing her portfolio for a minute.

"Really, I only needed somebody who could drive the car without running into me," he laughed. "I mostly need action stuff. But then I thought of you, and when you said you could do it, I knew there was more we could do. And now we have enough time."

"Well, I'm glad I could do it," she replied, though she was not at all convinced of what she was saying.

"It all worked out for the best," he continued. "I'm glad you're here."

He began leafing through the photos again. When he had looked at the last one, he handed the book to her, saying, "There's some good stuff here. You look terrific in a lot of these photos, but some of them don't do you justice."

"Do you have any suggestions?"

"Well, one thing I suggest is get rid of every photo where you don't look absolutely great. Don't settle for second best. Only include pictures where you look terrific. You're better off showing just a few pictures where you look great than a lot of pictures where you look great in some and only so-so in others."

"I see what you mean. Anything else?"

"Yeah, you also have to be very careful with lighting. When you smile, you get lines down your face, probably because you're so thin, and if you're not lighted correctly, those lines make you look hard."

"I really want to get past this bathing suit thing," she said.

"Well, then you have to get rid of some of these pinup shots. You know, it's not hard to figure out you've got a great body. I think you should add more pictures where you're wearing dresses, more fashion stuff. You know, hint at your body, don't just lay it out there."

"That makes sense," she said, grateful for the advice.

"Would you like to shoot a roll or two?" he asked, smiling. "You know this light is pretty intense, so they won't be perfect, but they'll at least show you what I mean."

"Sure," she replied. "Should I wear this or . . ."

"Why don't you put on one of the dresses you brought with you?" he said to her, sliding out of the driver's seat and heading back to retrieve his camera gear. "I'll load up and then we'll be ready to go."

As Charlie loaded the Fuji film in his Nikon, Linda clambered into the backseat of the Lexus and reached for the two dresses she had chosen to bring with her. One was a beige earth tone; the other was bone-white. She held them up for Charlie to look at.

"Do you have a preference?" she asked.

"Why don't you try the brown one first?" Charlie replied. "Then we'll try the white one."

"All right," she agreed, excited by the prospect of enhancing her portfolio. "I'm going to change now, so don't look."

"I wouldn't think of looking." Charlie laughed. But then he averted his gaze so that she wouldn't feel uncomfortable.

In just a few seconds she had pulled off her workout suit and slipped on the brown dress. It had a single row of buttons down the front, and she left the two top buttons and the two bottom ones open.

When she had the dress on, she pulled the curlers out of her hair one by one and shoved them into the leopard-print curler bag. As she began to brush her hair, she called out, "Hey, do you have anything to drink? I'm thirsty."

Usually photographers on the go pack as if they're leaving on a safari, with a cooler full of drinks and enough snack food to send Richard Simmons to an eating-disorder clinic, so she was surprised when Rathbun answered back, "Not really. I think I might have one Diet Coke, but that's about it."

"I don't want to take your last one," she said.

He left his camera equipment, walked to the side of the vehicle and started to rummage around in the backseat.

"Yeah, one Diet Coke is all I got," he said, "but you're welcome to it."

"It's your last one," she repeated.

"Oh, that's okay. We won't be here that long. Why don't you take it?"

"You sure you don't have anything else?"

"The only other thing I have is this half-bottle of tequila."

He opened up a fabric bag emblazoned with the logo MacUser and pulled the bottle out to show her.

"Oh, right," she said. "That's thirst-quenching."

"It's all I got. The Diet Coke and the tequila. Take your pick."

"Are *you* going to have some tequila?" she asked mockingly.

"I don't drink that much," he said, smiling and extending the bottle toward her. "I bet you twenty dollars you won't have a drink of tequila."

"What? You're betting me now?"

"Listen to me," he said with a slight bit of impatience, "I bet you twenty dollars you won't have a drink of tequila."

She pulled the bottle from his hand and took the tiniest little taste from it, the amount you'd give a baby, hardly enough for her to taste it.

"Okay," she smirked, "you owe me twenty bucks."

"You think so?" he smirked back.

She stood beside the open front passenger-side door and pulled the visor toward her so that she could see herself in the vanity mirror. After running a hairbrush several times through her long, blond tresses, emphasizing the wave, she checked her eye makeup and lipstick, repairing the slight imperfections that had developed during the drive.

"How do I look?" she asked, striking a mock pose.

"You look absolutely terrific," Charlie said, cocking

his camera. "Why don't you go over there?" he asked, gesturing with his free hand. "That's it, about twenty-five feet away. That's great. And now stand still for a minute and let me focus on you."

She had moved some distance from him, but as he looked through the telephoto lens, she was closer again, her form filling the frame under the white-hot light of the unimpeded sun.

"There. That's it," he ordered. "Okay, now move."

And in a practiced but unselfconscious way, Linda did move, bringing all of her years of experience to bear as Rathbun clicked off shot after shot after shot. She so much wanted to be something more than a bathing suit model; she so much wanted to be respected for her work and for her business sense; she so much wanted to be recognized for her talent and not her body. And all of that came together as Rathbun continued to shoot and shoot.

"Great. Great. Great. That's great!" he kept encouraging her. "Turn your face a little to the left. That's right. Now lift your chin. Just an inch. Perfect. Perfect. You look great. Great. This is great!"

It was a dance in the desert. Two people all alone in a lonely place, moving in harmony two dozen feet apart.

"You look great, Linda!" Charlie called. "Turn your head to the right more. Just a touch more. That's it. Now jump! Jump up in the air. That's perfect! Perfect! Now move your right leg forward. Six inches more! Give me another button. Come on, Linda, give me another button. That's it. One more! I want to see your thigh. I want to see your perfect thigh. Great."

When the first roll had been completed, Charlie rewound it and pulled it from the camera as quickly as he could, desperate not to lose the mood. Reloading just as quickly, he asked Linda to begin posing again, and she complied willingly.

"Great, Linda! Perfect! Perfect! Now turn you head toward me a little more! That's it! That's it! Now more teeth! More teeth! Beautiful! Beautiful!"

In a matter of minutes he had clicked off another roll and reloaded the camera with the swift, deft touch of an expert.

The dance continued, the desert sun sending its radiance over the scene.

"Perfect, Linda! Perfect! Perfect! Perfect!"

Then, too quickly, he was out of film again. He waved the camera at her.

"Reloading!" he shouted. Then, as she came closer, he said in a lower voice, "Maybe we should try the other dress."

"All right! I'll go change," Linda said, exhilarated by what she was doing, thrilled that in this shoot at least she wasn't just tits and ass.

She hurried over to the Lexus, climbed into the backseat and ripped off the beige outfit. Pulling the white lace dress from its hanger, she threw it on and climbed out of the vehicle again. After checking her hair in the mirror, she walked slowly toward Rathbun, gauging his reaction.

"Do I look all right?" she asked, knowing that the lace of the dress accentuated every one of her voluptuous curves, hiding everything but concealing nothing.

Beholding this vision, backlit in the desert sun, Charlie could barely choke out an answer. For a second he thought he was having a heart attack. Then he realized his breath had been knocked from his lungs by what seemed to him the sheer perfection of the moment.

"You . . . you look . . . fabulous," he groaned. "I . . . I can't tell you how good you look."

"Should we get started?" she asked eagerly.

"Yeah, yeah, sure," Charlie choked out the words. And when it came time to change the film, he did it with trembling hands.

"Same position?"

"Yeah, same position. You look great! Great!"

And the dance began again. The same two people. The same twenty-five feet apart. But now there was new music, a fugue with a minor undertone.

"Perfect, Linda! Perfect! Move your leg! A little more! A little more. One more inch! Perfect! Perfect! Dance for me! Dance! Dance! Dance! Perfect! Perfect! Perfect!"

With every bit of encouragement, Linda grew bolder. First her calves, then her knees, then her thighs emerged through the unbuttoned slit of her dress.

"Perfect! Perfect!" Charlie moaned.

She whirled, she twisted and she danced. He shouted out commands, and she obeyed. Willingly. Happily. Under the relentless desert sun, the sky a vivid blue behind her, she wasn't just a perfect woman, she was all women. She was the only woman on earth. In the solar system. In the universe.

And then, achingly too soon for Charlie, it was over.

Perfection lasted only as long as four rolls of Fuji Fujichrome 100 ASA film. One hundred forty-four exposures. One hundred forty-four impressions of index finger on shutter release. One hundred forty-four one-thousandths of a second.

After that the magic ended. The uptempo music faded. And all that was left was the variation in a minor key.

"Wow! That was great!" Linda said, walking past Charlie on her way to the Lexus. "That was fabulous."

Charlie could do nothing but gaze at her as she passed.

She continued to stride back toward the Lexus, calling out behind her, "God, I'm thirsty. Are you sure we don't have anything to drink?"

"I bet you twenty dollars you won't have a drink of tequila," he called after her.

She ran ahead, grabbed the tequila bottle from the floor of the truck and took a healthy drink.

"There," she said, triumphant. "Now you owe me *forty* dollars."

"No, I don't," Charlie intoned. "No, I don't."

"What do you mean you don't?" she threw back at him. "You saw me take two drinks."

"That means *you* owe *me* forty dollars," Charlie replied flatly. "Listen to what I said to you. I said, 'I bet you twenty dollars you *won't* take a drink of tequila.' I said won't, not would.''

"That's not fair!" she shouted.

"Life isn't fair, Linda."

"I'm going to change my clothes," she said, turning on her heel and walking away from him.

She was in the backseat, her dress off and barely covering her, the workout suit in her hand, when Charlie came up to the opened car door from behind her.

"Charlie!" she shouted. "I'm not dressed yet!"

He came closer.

"Charlie!" she screamed. "Go away!"

Closer still.

"No, Charlie, no!"

He pushed the tequila bottle toward her face.

"I think you should have another drink," he said dully.

"I don't want another drink!" she shrieked, shoving the bottle away.

He moved even closer to her, his six-foot-two-inch frame looking even larger and more menacing as he hulked over her.

"No, you don't understand," he said, extending the bottle again, "I said, 'I think you should have another drink.' "

She stared at him, hate radiating from her eyes.

"You don't understand," he repeated, "I think you should have another drink."

He shoved the bottle into her face, and again she tried to push it away, but looking in his smoldering eyes, she realized resistance was impossible. She took a gulp from the bottle. Then another.

Chapter 16

ON THE morning of Friday, November 17, 1995, Charlie Rathbun pulled up at the home of his girlfriend, Glenda Elam, in the freshly washed Lexus LX 450 he had taken to El Mirage the day before. By 10 A.M., when Charlie arrived at Glenda's house, he'd already been busy, and one of his chores had been cleaning the vehicle. The previous day's activities had left its shiny black paint covered with dust—there was just no way to avoid it when you drove on the sun-baked mud of the dry lake bed—and he had arrived at his house far too late on Thursday night even to consider having it washed then.

The following morning, though, he wanted a clean vehicle because part of his agenda for the day was to do a photo shoot of the big Lexus, using his girlfriend, Glenda, as driver-model. He had planned the shoot when he first learned that he would be taking possession of the expensive prototype, and he knew Glenda was looking forward to a lengthy ride in the luxury vehicle. Their goal was to drive from Hollywood to the Danish community of Solvang in Santa Barbara County, and since he knew the trip would be a long one, he didn't want to waste time trying to find a car wash on the run.

As he expected, Glenda was ready for him when he arrived. She had recently become quite attached to Charlie, though she hadn't been sure what to make of him when they first met. She had worked at Petersen, and she knew his reputation there was mixed at best. She was aware that some of the old Petersen hands who had worked with him liked him immensely but a substantial proportion thought he was weird or even creepy. Yet when she met Charlie by chance at a local auto show, she was immediately taken by his manners. He was always the gentleman, and she could tell that he was very intelligent, with a wide range of interests.

Of course, she also liked the fact that her age didn't seem to be an issue with him. She was far from over the hill, and most would describe her as attractive, with well-coifed blond hair and a trim figure, but she was several years older than Charlie. She had to admit that his attentions flattered her. She didn't realize that her new boyfriend had a history of dating older women. In fact, he had recently concluded a long affair with a fifty-ish auto show model, a cross-country liaison that had lasted several years. All Glenda knew was that he treated her wonderfully well, and that was enough for her.

Charlie might have been a little quieter than usual when he arrived on her doorstep that morning, but Glenda attributed it to the fact that he was obviously tired. She knew he kept an unusual schedule and guessed he might have been up at all hours of the night retouching a photo on his computer or fooling around with one of his collection of antique guns.

Though the trip to Solvang and back promised to be a time-consuming affair, Charlie told Glenda he had some stops to make in Hollywood before they could leave town. Jumping into the imposing sport utility vehicle, they proceeded to a couple of nearby business meetings, because Charlie, as a freelancer, always had to be hustling. At one of their stops, an acquaintance took a look at the big Lexus and said to Charlie, "That's really a great-looking truck."

"Yeah," Charlie replied, "And this one comes with a great-looking blonde."

It had come with a great-looking blonde the previous day, too.

After making the calls he had to make in Hollywood, Charlie and Glenda immediately set out for Solvang. They hopped on the 101 freeway and soon they were headed west as the mid-autumn sun, so regular in Southern California, beat down around them.

With his ambitious travel plans in mind, Charlie had become convinced that it would be impossible for him to return the vehicle when he had promised—late that same afternoon—so he had phoned Tracy Underwood, a co-worker of Joella Lamm at Lexus public relations, and told her that he had experienced some difficulties on the photo shoot the previous day, so he was still in the process of photographing the vehicle. Underwood hadn't been too happy about his report, but it was certainly not a story she hadn't heard before. She got him to promise to return the vehicle first thing on the upcoming Monday morning and left him to enjoy the remainder of the day with his girlfriend.

Charlie and Glenda reached the quaint community of Solvang not too long after one o'clock, and they spent the rest of the afternoon doing a leisurely photo session with the vehicle. For the action shots Glenda was at the wheel making pass after pass on a lightly traveled road outside town as Charlie caught the vehicle in his viewfinder. Later they moved on to another location, where Charlie set up his tripod to photograph a ''beauty shot'' of the vehicle as the last rays of sun turned the haze in the sky scarlet.

After the shoot was over, Charlie and Glenda made their way back into Hollywood at a very relaxed pace, stopping for a lengthy dinner along the way. Back at Glenda's, they enjoyed each other's company until about six-thirty the following morning, when Charlie kissed her good-bye and went home. As he walked out the door, she asked him, ''Is anything wrong?'' because he looked so subdued, but all he did in reply was shrug his shoulders.

That Saturday morning the house Rathbun shared with

Bill Longo, 1937 Canyon Drive in Hollywood, had more than its share of visitors. A little after nine one of the roommates' mutual friends came by, and the three chatted for a while. Charlie was excited about his imminent move to his new house on Cheramoya, only about three blocks west, and he couldn't help talking about it. But the visitor also noted that Charlie seemed tired, a little down.

Later in the morning Glenda phoned, asking Charlie if it was all right if she came over. She told him she hadn't liked the way he had looked when he left her earlier in the day when they'd parted. He said sure, and pretty soon she arrived.

Then Barry Klyckzck, a friend of Charlie's who worked at McMullen and Yee Publishing, dropped by. Klyckzck had recently turned in his notice to his employer and was planning to move to Detroit soon. Hearing that, Charlie invited him to an impromptu farewell get-together.

With Klyckzck in tow, Charlie and Glenda embarked on a sightseeing trip around Hollywood in the Lexus LX 450. They toured several of the local landmarks, then cruised up to the famous Hollywood sign in the hills above the city. Of course, cameras came out, and several photographs were taken showing a fun-loving, exuberant crew having a good time on their day off.

Later the gang retired to Charlie's new house on Cheramoya, where Charlie and the group continued to clown around for the camera. In one shot taken on the porch of the new house, Charlie was captured sticking his thumb out through his fly to make a mock penile erection, an idiot's grin plastered on his face. When the clowning was over, Charlie took Klyckzck to dinner and of course he picked up the check.

The next day, Sunday, was filled with computer work. Over the last couple of years, Charlie had become a master of computerized photo enhancement. He could manipulate colors, lighting effects, road surfaces and even make a car that was standing still appear to be moving by blurring the wheels and tweaking the background. That Sunday he spent most of the day in front of the cathode ray tube of his Macintosh. There was a big project for Oldsmobile that he had been working on for several weeks that he wanted to get out of the way before the photos of the Lexus LX 450 he had taken for *AutoWeek* came back from the lab. As always, *AutoWeek* was working on a very short deadline, so he was eager to clear the decks so that he could get the photos to art director Marilee Bowles as quickly as possible.

That evening, eager to spend a night in his new house, Charlie went over to the Cheramoya residence, but he was surprised and disappointed to find Bill Longo there, painting some of the walls. Crestfallen, Charlie returned to the Canyon Drive home, where he had one more chore to do: he washed the Lexus LX 450 again thoroughly inside and out. A neighbor who saw him at work remarked to himself how careful Charlie was with other people's cars.

Charlie had reason to be careful. The following morning he was due to return the vehicle to Lexus, and he wanted to make certain it was as close to the condition in which he had borrowed it as was humanly possible. That task completed, he turned in for the night.

And so the weekend that had started with a road trip to Solvang with his girlfriend, Glenda, and had then progressed to a half-day party with Barry Klyckzck came to a quiet close.

Fifteen miles south in Hermosa Beach, the weekend was closing quietly as well. But there the quiet wasn't welcome. There the quiet harbored secret dread. Linda Sobek had not been seen or heard from in over seventy-two hours.

Chapter 17

AFTER CLOSING the weekend on a quiet note, Charlie Rathbun hit the ground running on Monday, November 20, 1995. First thing in the morning he rounded up a friend to help him return the Lexus LX 450 in which he had had such an eventful four-day weekend.

Looking back on it, Charlie had put a lot of miles on the rare prototype. On Friday there had been some business appointments in Hollywood and then of course the trip to Solvang in the company of his girlfriend. He shot a wide variety of photos of the vehicle for *AutoWeek* on that trip, too, many with Glenda driving. After that had come the rolling party for Barry Klyckzck, Charlie's friend who was about to leave the Los Angeles area for Detroit. The fun-filled Saturday had included a tour of many Hollywood hotspots, highlighted by a behind-the-scenes look at the fabled Hollywood sign. It featured some photographic clowning on the porch of Charlie's new Cheramoya home, and it ended with a trip to dinner at a Hollywood nightspot.

And of course there was one other event—the lengthy Thursday trek to El Mirage dry lake for a photo shoot with Linda Sobek. By then Linda's name was on the lips of every newscaster in Los Angeles. Everybody from the host of *Hard Copy* to the guy at Starbucks Coffee was talking about the fact she had disappeared. But one person in Los Angeles wasn't talking about Linda Sobek, and his name was Charlie Rathbun.

When he returned the big black Lexus to Joella Lamm that Monday morning, Charlie didn't mention Linda Sobek's name once. But he did mention to Joella that "he had been thinking about her all weekend." He asked the attractive public relations woman if she'd like to go bike riding with him one of these days. Lamm was hardly certain that she would enjoy a biking adventure with the bulky photographer, so she diplomatically declined, wording her turndown in a way that wouldn't offend him.

While Charlie Rathbun was going about his business life that Monday, detectives in the Hermosa Beach Police Department were busily trying to track down the whereabouts of one of their town's citizens. After speaking to her roommates and her parents, detectives Mark Wright and Raul Saldana found Linda's disappearance very troubling.

The detectives were well aware that statistics show that the vast majority of missing persons vanish of their own volition. But given the information the veteran policeman had gathered, the prospects for a happy ending to the case looked rather grim. Linda didn't seem like a person who might run away without telling anyone, and though she had suffered a disappointment or two recently, she didn't seem like a candidate to kill herself either. Though she was in a bit of a money crunch at the time of her disappearance, the situation wasn't grave enough to warrant flight or suicide. And though her love life hadn't been devoid of ups and downs, she had a current boyfriend, and she gave no sign of having a secret lover (an indicator of possible flight) or of pining away for a man she couldn't have (an indicator of possible suicide).

From all the available evidence, Linda Sobek's life was in order. She had a supportive group of friends, and her relationships with her mother, father and brother were for the most part very good. Detectives did discover that

Linda had been a bit troubled by the recent decision of her brother and sister-in-law not to make her godmother to their new baby girl, but she seemed to be weathering that disappointment. In any case, it seemed too weak a reason for a disappearance or worse.

The natural conclusion of the preliminary investigation was that Linda Sobek might have met with foul play. But since very few people had seen her on the day she vanished and no one had seen her in anything resembling threatening circumstances, there were precious few leads the detectives could investigate. Starting with the obvious, they interviewed her roommates, her parents and her boyfriend and tried to run down a rumor or two, but there wasn't much to go by. There was no likely suspect in a foul play scenario and no real reason, except maybe intuition, to believe foul play was involved.

There were many loose ends dangling, however. One of them, though the detectives didn't necessarily consider it a primary concern, was the identity of the photographer with whom Linda had planned to do the last-minute photo assignment on the Thursday she disappeared. The mystery photographer had yet to come forward, but of course there were hundreds of innocent explanations for that. Perhaps he had immediately gone on assignment out of state. Perhaps he thought he had nothing to contribute to the search. Perhaps he didn't watch television news and was unaware that Linda Sobek was missing. The photographer's identity was just one of dozens of possible leads the detectives would need to track down.

Even though foul play was only a possibility in the Sobek case, there was already a great deal of heat on the investigation, much more heat than the relatively small Hermosa Beach Police Department was used to. Largely because of that department's efforts, the small beach community is virtually free of violent crime. A murder investigation within its borders is a rarity. But with television news and the tabloid shows shouting out the name of "missing model Linda Sobek" on a regular basis, there was uncommon pressure to make something happen. With few real leads and limited resources, the Hermosa Beach PD was in a tough spot.

It wasn't that the media was deliberately trying to pressure the small-town police force. Their only concern was the news, and the case was certainly news. But it wasn't unique. As the media quickly reported, Linda Sobek wasn't the only blond-haired model who had gone missing in the Los Angeles area in recent years. Soon the media was heralding the similarities between the Sobek case and the case of another missing model, Kimberley Pandelios, who had disappeared in February, 1992.

Like Linda Sobek, Kimberley Pandelios had wanted to be a model. And like Linda Sobek, Kimberley Pandelios didn't have the body type to go into high fashion. In police vernacular, she was short and built, just as Linda was—the perfect type to be photographed in a bathing suit next to a modified pickup truck or a chopped and channeled '32 Ford roadster. But compared to Linda Sobek, Pandelios was a rank amateur.

At the time of her disappearance, Sobek had been modeling professionally for more than half a dozen years. She had appeared as a paid model at a substantial number of industry events, and her image had graced the covers of several national magazines. Among photographers who served the automotive enthusiast magazines Linda was a well-regarded professional.

Pandelios, on the other hand, was almost completely unknown. Ask photographers in the business about her, and they will reply with shrugs. Her list of paid assignments was very short, her reputation nonexistent. Pandelios aspired to be what Sobek already was, and the sad fact is that her aspirations are probably what got her killed.

In late 1991, Kimberley Pandelios brought her aspirations with her from her home in Florida to a new residence in the San Fernando Valley. Just twenty years old, she was already married and had a baby, but she wasn't about to let her family get in the way of her dream of a modeling career. Her husband, trying to please his new spouse, supported his wife's ambitions, but he felt she was very naïve about the difficulties involved in making it in a career as competitive as modeling, and that naïveté was compounded by her youth and upbringing.

Her mother, Magaly Spector, agreed. As she later told the *Los Angeles Times*, "[Kimberley] grew up in a small city and she was very trusting, and I was always afraid she wouldn't recognize the danger around her. I didn't want to make her feel scared every time she went outside, but deep in my heart I was always afraid she would be kidnapped, because she was so beautiful and so trusting." Her mother's instinct proved sound.

Pandelios was naïve and trusting enough to have interviewed to do a seminude pictorial for a men's magazine, but there is no record that she ever completed the shoot. She also scanned the ads in local newspapers and shoppers, looking for local freelance modeling jobs.

On the morning in February, 1992, when she disappeared, she was responding to just such an ad. Earlier in the week she had called a photographer she knew only as Paul, who had run an ad in one of the many Los Angeles giveaway papers, looking for a model. The two had talked on the phone for several minutes. The man calling himself Paul sounded both nice and professional, and Kimberley agreed to meet him at an unspecified time a couple of days later for some photo work.

The morning of her appointment, amidst the cries of their baby, Kimberley and her husband exchanged some hurried words about what she was planning to do during the day. Like many husbands, he caught only part of it, but he got the impression that his wife was going to meet Paul for one photo shoot and then meet another, unnamed photographer for a second photo shoot later in the day. In retrospect, her husband thinks that the second photo shoot was going to be outside and that there was going to be a vehicle involved, but his memories are nebulous.

It turned out to be a busy morning for Kimberley Pandelios. She left her baby with her usual babysitter when she walked out of the house about nine o'clock, and she proceeded to run several errands around town. Then she stopped for a special session at her beauty shop. She was excited about what was in store for her during the rest of the day, and she wanted to look her best. She insisted that her hairdresser take extra care with her curly blond hair, which was so pale that it almost looked white.

At around one in the afternoon she phoned her baby-sitter and told her, ''If Paul calls, tell him that I'm on my way.''

About half an hour later Paul did call the Pandelios house, reached the babysitter and asked, ''Where's Kim?''

The babysitter assured him that she was on her way.

Paul said, ''Well, here's a phone number to reach me at, if she needs directions,'' and he gave her a local number.

Kimberley Pandelios never called for those directions. In fact, after her message to her babysitter, she was never heard from again.

But the mysterious Paul was heard from again, that same evening.

At about seven-thirty a man identifying himself as Paul called the Pandelios residence and spoke to Kim's husband, who at that point was a little concerned about his wife's prolonged absence but figured it was because the second photo shoot had run long.

Paul asked, ''Is Kim there?'' and when her husband answered no, he continued, ''Well, she left my house about four or four-thirty, and she left her DayPlanner. Have her call me.''

When Kimberley Pandelios failed to return home that night, her husband got scared. They had had their tiffs, but staying out all night wasn't like her. And when her car was discovered a day or so later, a burned-out hulk in a rustic campground in the Angeles National Forest, he feared the worst.

The case immediately went to the Los Angeles Police Department, where it eventually wound up on the desks of Detectives Tom Lang and Phil Van Adder, who would later gain a great deal of fame as the lead detectives in the Nicole Simpson murder case. An obvious lead was the telephone number Paul had left with the babysitter.

Los Angeles police tracked down the number and found that it had been rented for a week, much as a postal mail drop can be rented, by a man calling himself Edgar. On the application, Edgar had written that he lived at an address on Franklin Street in Hollywood. Detectives visited that address and interviewed an elderly man who had lived there for twenty years, and he told them, "There's never been anybody named Edgar living here."

Not only did that lead die, but the other feeble leads the detectives had perished as well. No one ever found Paul, though a composite of the supposed photographer was drawn up, based on the feeble recollections of the person who had rented him the phone line, and eventually got wide circulation. Of course, that the mysterious Paul was actually a photographer was just a supposition. Anyone with a camera can claim to be a photographer, and one might guess that innocent, good-looking potential victims from out of state are more likely to respond to a *Pennysaver* ad placed by "a photographer" than by, say, "a serial rapist."

The Pandelios case took another turn when a visitor to the Angeles National Forest claimed to have seen Pandelios on or about the date she disappeared with two men in the campground where her burned car was eventually found. The men were described as rough characters, possibly biker types, certainly a common sight on Angeles Crest, and though the woman wasn't bound or restrained, she seemed somehow lost or perhaps drugged. Alarmed by the rough-looking men, the visitor didn't stick around long enough to exchange business cards with them. He claimed that they threatened him with bodily harm if he didn't get the hell out of there.

With a beautiful model as its subject, the case drew the attention of the *Unsolved Mysteries* television program, which eventually ran reenactments of the case several times over the course of a couple of years, updated as more information became available. The television show's treatment dwelled on the two-men-in-the-camp theory, touching on the photography angle in only the lightest fashion.

Finally in March, 1993, a little over a year after Pandelios first went missing, a hiker out for a little constitutional in the Angeles National Forest stumbled across a skull that turned out to be that of Kimberley Pandelios. The crime scene investigation resulting from that discovery uncovered several of her bones scattered over an area half the size of a football field. She apparently had been buried in or near a creek bed, and twelve months' worth of precipitation and erosion not only had helped fully decompose her flesh but also had made it impossible to determine the original burial site or if she had been buried at all.

The skeletal remains were transported to the office of the Los Angeles County Medical Examiner for study, but they revealed no cause of death. Instead of answering questions, the coroner's examination seemed only to ask more. Had she gone into the forest, got lost and died of exposure? Had she been abducted, raped, murdered and buried? Had she committed suicide?

The possibilities were endless and are endless. The disappearance of Kimberley Pandelios is still an unsolved case.

But its similarities to the Sobek case were too much for the press to ignore. Each victim was a very attractive blond model, and each disappeared after hurrying off to a photo assignment with an unidentified photographer. And that was only the tip of the iceberg. In a matter of hours the similarities between the two cases were destined to increase.

Chapter 18

MONDAY, NOVEMBER 20, 1995, didn't start out as an especially important day for a Glendale, California, resident named Bill Bartling. At the time the forty-nine-year-old former maintenance worker was unemployed, so Mondays had no special meaning for him, and as he sat in his apartment and considered his prospects, he recalled the previous two days as one of the dreariest weekends of his life. Of course, he had volunteered for it, but that didn't make the work he had been doing any more pleasant.

The week prior, on Wednesday, November 15, the day before Charlie Rathbun drove with Linda Sobek to El Mirage dry lake, Bartling had been in court. He wasn't a criminal offender, but he did have about five hundred dollars' worth of outstanding traffic tickets. He was unemployed, and his girlfriend was seriously ill. He didn't have the five hundred bucks to clear up the tickets, and he was worried the court might soon put out a warrant for his arrest.

A matter-of-fact kind of person, he laid his predicament before the court and asked if it would be possible to work off his tickets by doing community service. The judge on the bench said the legal equivalent of okay, and Bartling was ordered to report to a forestry crew cleaning up trash in the Angeles National Forest.

The following Saturday morning, not long after Charlie

and Glenda Elam parted after their trip to Solvang, Bartling checked in for his community service work at Elk Grove Ranger Station high in the mountains above the eastern Los Angeles suburbs. He was assigned to help a forestry worker pick up trash from garbage cans along the Angeles Crest Highway.

Not exactly cerebral work, the job consisted of pulling the plastic liner and its contents from each can and replacing the liner with a fresh one. Each time, the garbage-filled liner was tossed into the back of the truck for later disposal.

For the better part of the morning the two men worked their way up Angeles Crest, pulling out effluvia-filled garbage bags and replacing them with empty ones. Then they turned around and started working their way back toward Elk Grove.

The only relief in the monotony of the job came from the forestry worker's profitable little sideline: he checked each of the bags for aluminum cans and then separated the cans for recycling. Bartling amused himself by eyeballing the contents of the trash container as his partner sorted cans.

The two amateur garbagemen were nearly back to Elk Grove Ranger Station, with just two or three stops to go, when Bartling's idle time-filler suddenly gained importance, though he didn't know it at the time. As his forestry worker teammate was separating cans from yet another trash bag, the unemployed maintenance worker noticed some photographs of a very attractive woman. He lifted the photos from the trash, brushed the detritus from them and scrutinized them carefully.

They were photographs of a blue-eyed blond woman in her twenties, and they had obviously been professionally taken. Some were Polaroids (which, though Bartling was unaware of it, are often used by photographers to test the composition before they shoot transparencies), and others were large, color portfolio photos. Struck by the woman's beauty, he decided to keep four of the pictures for himself, and he stuffed them into his backpack. Later he told the *Los Angeles Times* that he stashed them there "to make sure my girlfriend didn't see them."

Thinking there might be more treasure in the can, he looked into it again, but the most interesting thing he saw was a DayPlanner, and his first thought was that somebody had purse-snatched it and then dumped it in the garbage miles from the theft. He left the DayPlanner where it was in the garbage sack and then threw the sack into the back of the truck with the others.

A half-hour later the two-man crew finished its appointed rounds, gave each other a hearty good-bye and headed down out of the mountains. For the remainder of the weekend and into Monday night those photos stayed in Bartling's backpack, and they might have stayed in there even longer if Bartling hadn't done what we've all done: he lost the remote control to his television set.

On Monday evening, November 20, 1995, Bartling was sitting in his Glendale apartment, idly watching the eight o'clock news on Los Angeles television station KCAL, when a stock market report came on. Since he was unemployed, he didn't care how the day's business news had affected his portfolio, so he decided to change the channel, but he couldn't find the remote control. As he went through the time-worn ritual of rummaging through the sofa cushions, the stock report ended and was replaced on the screen by the image of a beautiful blond woman.

Bartling immediately got a sense of déjà vu. I've seen that woman before, he said to himself, and then the light glowed on in his brain. The woman on the screen was the same woman as in his garbage can photos.

He ran to his backpack, pulled out the pictures and looked at them again.

Yes, he said to himself, this is definitely the same girl.

Then he sat for a moment on his disheveled sofa and tried to decide what to do. First he thought about calling the police, then he hesitated for a moment, because, as he said later, "I have all these photographs with my fingerprints all over them." But finally he decided to call the Hermosa Beach Police Department, which was handling the missing persons case of one of its residents, a bathing suit model named Linda Sobek.

Unfortunately, Bartling's first communication with the Hermosa Beach police was less than fulfilling.

"I think I've got some information on the case of the missing woman, you know the one that's been on TV," he gushed, the second someone from the department answered his call.

"What is this information?" asked the officious woman at the other end of the line.

"On Saturday, when I was in the Angeles National Forest, I found some photos of her that had been dumped in a trash can, and I think there might be other stuff of hers in that trash can, too."

While Bartling could barely contain his excitement about his discovery, the voice at the other end didn't seem to think there was much to it at all.

"Let me get your name and telephone number, and I'll pass the information along to our detectives," she said.

Bartling gave her the requested information, then sat by the phone the rest of the night waiting for it to ring. It didn't. But as he sat, he watched TV and saw what a media circus Linda Sobek's disappearance had become. Her name and face were on every channel's newscast; teases featuring her visage graced scores of station breaks. Her case was the lead story again and again, and Bartling had information that he was sure could help—but nobody called him back.

That night he had trouble sleeping, afraid he would miss the phone call. But the call never came. Up early the next morning, still fatigued from lack of sleep, he decided to call again. This time he was more insistent.

"I've got to speak to a detective on this case," he demanded. Luckily Lieutenant Mark Wright of Hermosa Beach PD had just rolled in at that early hour, and he took Bartling's call. He turned out to be much more interested in Bartling's story than the receptionist the night before.

Bartling told the detective that he had found pictures of Linda Sobek and he thought that some of her other personal effects might be in the garbage still sitting in a huge dumpster behind Elk Grove Ranger Station.

"You've gotta get someone up there and make sure nobody takes that stuff away," Bartling told him.

Wright agreed. Asking Bartling to meet him on the way up into the mountains, he rounded up one of his sergeants, got into a cruiser and sped out to Elk Grove Ranger Station, more than an hour away from Hermosa Beach.

Up at the ranger station, Bartling quickly pointed out the dumpster where he had deposited all the garbage bags on Saturday morning, and the policemen looked at each other and sighed. There they were in their sport coats and slacks with hundreds of bags of garbage to sort through, not an appealing task, but handing Bartling their coats, they dove right in.

For twenty minutes or so they waded through the slop, trying to dodge the most heinous of the discarded waste, struggling to keep their neckties from collecting random bits of goo, and eventually they found what they were looking for. In one of the garbage bags they found Linda Sobek's DayPlanner, photographs of her and a couple of other items that piqued their interest.

One was a *Membership Roster and Media Guide*, published by the Motor Press Guild, a Southern California organization of auto journalists and photographers. That caught their eye, because they knew that Linda was a model who frequently worked in the auto industry. But the item that really got their attention was a borrower's agreement for a Lexus LX 450 sport utility vehicle, a vehicle that had been picked up from Lexus on Thursday, November 16, the day Linda Sobek disappeared. There was a name on the agreement. It attested that the vehicle had been borrowed by one Charles E. Rathbun, a photographer working for *AutoWeek* magazine.

Chapter 19

THERE'S A saying in Chicago: "Don't like the weather? Just wait a minute, it'll change." On Tuesday, November 21, 1995, the weather for Charlie Rathbun was about to change as radically as the shift from a sunny summer day to a destructive tornado.

His morning began pleasantly enough with the anticipation of some easy but lucrative work. He had a new photo shoot to do for *AutoWeek*. This time the vehicle was a Mitsubishi Montero, another sport utility vehicle but not quite as grand as the Lexus LX 450 he'd turned in the previous morning.

He'd already decided on how he wanted to shoot the Montero after talking with art director Marilee Bowles about her layout plans, and he knew it wouldn't involve a long drive, so he was expecting to have a fairly relaxed day. Generally he enjoyed his work. Going out in the field and finding great locations was fun for him, and enhancing his photographs on the computer was fun, too, if in a different way. Best of all, as a freelancer, he could keep his contact with jerks and creeps to a minimum.

After spending much of the morning puttering around the Canyon Drive house, he took a quick run over to his new place on Cheramoya. It was almost ready for move-in, and he couldn't help but be proud of himself for becoming successful enough to buy it. From his early childhood he had felt a sense of not belonging, and the new house was a

131

sign that he did belong, that he did have roots and that he did have a future.

In the afternoon Charlie gathered up his friend and sometime photo assistant Jack Petersen, and the two drove down to the Palos Verdes peninsula to finish the work on the Mitsubishi. P.V., as the locals call it, is a huge promontory that rises above the South Bay city of Redondo Beach at the foot of Santa Monica Bay. Filled with luxury homes, riding stables and breathtaking ocean views, it is an enclave of the rich perched less than thirty miles from downtown Los Angeles. Photographically it offers thousands of different aspects, some so rural one might think the setting was Iowa, others so exotic one might believe the backdrop was a South Seas island.

That afternoon, as the autumn sun began to vanish into the ocean haze, Charlie gazed into his viewfinder at the orange light lending a glow to the vehicle's dark flanks, and he liked what he saw. At automotive photography he was now an acknowledged expert. In his mind he had proven that for all to see, most especially Jim Haefner, Bob D'Olivo and the idiots at Petersen Publishing who had booted him out the door.

With his camera's shutter connected to a remote release, he exposed frame after frame, carefully setting the f-stop after each to make certain he would get the correct exposure. As with comedy, the art in photography is in the editing—what you leave in and what you leave out—and Charlie wanted to be sure he had enough choices when the film came back from the lab.

Finally it got too dark to shoot any more, and Charlie and Jack packed up their gear and stowed it carefully in the rear cargo area of the Montero. Driving downhill out of Palos Verdes, they began the long slog across the Los Angeles basin that would eventually take them to Hollywood.

Back in more familiar territory, Charlie dropped Petersen off, then drove over to his rented bungalow on Canyon Drive. Camera gear in hand, he strode up the steps and walked across the broad, old-time porch.

Charlie's sunny day was about to be ripped apart by a tornado.

When Charlie walked in the door, his roommate, Bill Longo, couldn't wait to tell him the news. But from Longo it came out less like news and more like a punchline.

"Hey, Charlie, did you hear about the missing model on Angeles Crest?" he asked, his eyes dancing in anticipation of the upcoming joke.

Charlie looked at him stupidly, waiting for the other shoe to drop.

"What I want to know is, where did you bury the body?" Longo continued, breaking into hilarious laughter.

To Longo's surprise, his roommate of five years didn't seem to get the joke.

"Come on, Charlie," he said, now beating a dead horse, "where'd you hide the body?"

Rathbun could only stare at him. Then, after a long pause, he choked out, "I don't really remember," and he walked out of the room.

Charlie's tongue-tied reaction was far different from his rejoinder to a similar question he had received the day before from another of his fun-loving buddies. At eight o'clock that Monday morning, as Charlie was sitting at his kitchen table with his friend Hoyt Vandenberg of *Sport Truck* magazine, he took a phone call from Dan Sanchez, a regular client. Sanchez had seen some of the *Hard Copy* television reports on the Sobek disappearance and in a slightly hysterical voice asked Rathbun, "Hey, have you heard about Linda Sobek?" And Charlie replied, totally deadpan, "Yes, I killed Linda Sobek, and I buried her body."

Maybe Lisa Kudrow was wrong about her former photographer's comic timing.

Minutes after Longo had tried his stillborn joke on his

roommate, Charlie Rathbun was glued to his television set, watching the ten o'clock news. In fact, he was so interested in the subject that he slipped a videotape into his VCR to record another channel, just so he wouldn't miss anything. Then, still rapt, he watched the eleven o'clock news as well.

He didn't like what he saw and liked less what he heard. Over the course of that ninety minutes the two very frightening words that Bill Longo had uttered in his abortive attempt to get a laugh were repeated over and over and over again during the newscasts.

"Angeles Crest."

When Longo had first spoken those words, Charlie knew the police had discovered some of Linda Sobek's effects up on the mountain. He knew because he had put them there.

Chapter 20

CHARLIE RATHBUN was shaken. Bill Longo couldn't help noticing how troubled his roommate seemed, although it was obvious he was trying to remain stoic. In all the years Longo had known him, he'd never seen his friend so upset, so scared. Charlie had watched the news reports on the Sobek case like a man possessed, and now, at 11:30 P.M. on Tuesday, November 21, Longo was certain his friend had something to tell him.

"Bill," Rathbun asked plaintively, "if you knew something about this case, would you go to the police?"

"I suppose I would," Longo shot back. "I guess it depends on what I knew."

"That's just it."

"What's just it?"

"Well, what if you knew something important? Something the police would really want to know?"

"Again it depends on what I knew, but I probably would."

"You know how the police twist things sometimes," Charlie said. "They hear what they want to hear."

"Shit, Charlie, what the hell do you know about all this?

Rathbun looked desperately at him, not certain what he should say, not certain if he should say anything. He turned away from his roommate for a moment, trying to get things straight in the turmoil of his mind, and then slowly, hesitatingly, he turned back.

"Bill," he said, the words coming with difficulty, "Bill, I was the last person with Linda Sobek."

Longo looked at him blankly, trying to compute all the ramifications of that simple sentence.

After a moment he asked, "Charlie, how do you know you were the last person with Linda Sobek?"

Charlie looked at him, pain contorting his face, and replied, "I know. I just know."

"Oh, shit, Charlie," Longo said, and though he wanted to ask his roommate a million questions that would help him understand what was going on and what was going through his close friend's head, he decided not to venture down that road any farther.

Twenty minutes later, Charlie was at the desk in his room, feverishly scribbling out notes to himself, notes he described later as "what I knew about Linda Sobek." During the evening's news reports on the Sobek case, he had seen a composite sketch of a man police wanted to question. Now, as he wrote out what he later described as scenarios regarding her disappearance, he described two men who he felt resembled the composite.

Both men were photographers, at least after a fashion, and both had known Linda Sobek. With that and the image of the composite fresh in his mind, Rathbun hand-wrote a scenario about her disappearance, suggesting one of the two men might be involved.

"[He] was a dead ringer for the composite," Charlie said later of one of the men. "He saw Linda at the SEMA show and promised her two to three hundred dollars to pose for him. [The other man] recommended her for a book. He was a scam artist who was in the country illegally. These were people who matched the composite sketch in this case."

But as Charlie worked on his scenarios for the remainder of the night and on into the next morning, he was laboring under a delusion. The composite shown on television had not been a composite from the Sobek case. There were no composites in the Sobek case, because the authorities had no idea with whom she'd last been. The composite he had seen and to which he was now trying to tie two of his professional rivals was from the Pandelios case, now more than two years old.

Despite all Charlie's efforts to direct the blame to someone else, his work had the ring of desperation about it. As the photographer had already admitted to Bill Longo, he was the last person to see Linda Sobek. He was only too well aware that the photographers at whom he was pointing the finger had had nothing to do with Linda's disappearance at all.

But the task Charlie had set for himself that night wasn't over. In the wee hours of the morning of Wednesday, November 22, 1995, the thirty-second anniversary of the assassination of one of Rathbun's heroes, John F. Kennedy, Charlie wrote two other scenarios as well. These short essays, composed at his computer keyboard, have been described as suicide notes, and Charlie has adopted that description of them as well, but others have disputed it from the day they were discovered.

"I accidentally killed Linda Sobek on a shoot," one printout began. "I've never hurt so much as a bird before." According to the note, he had been "hamming it up" on a photo shoot when he struck Sobek with the sport utility vehicle. "I'm sorry I let you all down," it concluded.

The second printout had a slightly different version of events. "I think she suffocated or choked to death," it said. "I did not intentionally choke her." In it Rathbun wrote that two lives were effectively over, just when his life was looking so good.

As daybreak brought soft light into Charlie's bedroom that Wednesday morning, life was not looking good at all for the balding photographer. Any second he feared that the police could be at his door, ready to arrest him and haul him off to jail, but at the same time, he was still uncertain what pieces of Linda's personal property had been recovered by the police in their search on Angeles Crest. Reviewing the videotapes he'd made of the newscasts, he had seen reports that items had been pulled from a dumpster at Elk Grove Ranger Station, but he continued to harbor hope that the authorities might not be able to connect him to Linda.

Okay, he thought, they had found her DayPlanner, but that didn't mean they knew he had hidden it there.

It was a rational hope, but fear continued to climb the back of his neck.

When he had cleaned out the Lexus before returning it to Joella Lamm, he had been unable to find the borrower's agreement, an eight-and-half-by-eleven-inch piece of paper that he often stashed in the glove compartment or simply tossed on the floor of the vehicle. The sheet had his name and driver's license number on it.

What if the authorities found that? he asked himself.

The answer was chilling.

Charlie knew he needed good advice, and he knew he needed it quickly. Realizing that the work day had already begun in Detroit, where it was three hours later, he picked up the phone and dialed Marilee Bowles at *AutoWeek*. A sweet-faced brunette with big, caring eyes, Bowles had some interests and experiences in common with Charlie, including a stint at Petersen Publishing Company, where she had once served as art director at *Sports Car Graphic* magazine. Over the previous year or so the two had become phone friends, and now Charlie was desperate for someone to talk to, someone he'd feel comfortable with.

Though Charlie wanted to talk with her about the Sobek incident, he had difficulty speaking directly. Instead he waltzed around it.

"Marilee, this is Charlie."

"Hi, Charlie," she replied in her soft voice. "You're up early today."

"Yeah, I had some trouble sleeping."

"Really?"

"Yeah, Marilee," he said, stumbling. "There's some stuff going on in the news that's been bothering me."

"What, Charlie?" Marilee asked, concerned by his tone.

"Well, have you heard about Linda Sobek? The model?"

"I don't think so."

"Well, she's a model out here, and she disappeared."

"Yes?"

"And I know something about it," he said. "Can I ask you something?"

"Sure, what is it, Charlie?" she replied, now frightened by what he might say to her.

"If you knew something, something that was important to the police, would you tell them?" he asked.

"Of course I would," she replied without hesitation.

"Yeah, I know you would, Marilee," he said. "I know you would. Let me ask you this. If you did something you shouldn't have done, something you're not proud of, do you think it's better to confess it?"

"Yes, I do."

"You're a good Catholic, aren't you, Marilee?"

"Yes, I am."

"And you believe in confession?"

"Yes, I do. Charlie, are you in trouble of some kind?"

"I might be," he said.

"What kind of trouble?"

"I can't tell you, Marilee. Thanks for talking to me."

He hung up the phone, leaving her sitting and worried at the other end. Charlie looked around his bedroom, stared at the winking screen-saver on his computer, saw the yellow light of the late-autumn sun trickling in through the window, and he shook his head. He had no idea what to do, but he knew he had to do something.

What Longo and Bowles did not know was that Charlie

had withheld from them the most important part of his story. Not only had he been the last person to see her but he also knew where she was—and that she wasn't coming back.

Chapter 21

THERE ARE those who say the most terrifying part of an aircraft crash is not the moment of death but the seconds or perhaps even minutes when the victims know they are going to die before the final, fatal impact. In that short span of time the terror that grips the victims must be excruciating. Early on Wednesday morning, November 22, 1995, Charles Edgar Rathbun, photographer, resident of Hollywood, California, was gripped by just that kind of terror. Each phone that rang, each car that approached, each footfall on the sidewalk outside his house engendered fear, because each of them could mean that the police were on his trail. Most difficult for him was the fact that he didn't know what the police knew. He didn't know if the police could in some way connect him to Linda Sobek on the day of her death. And the not knowing was killing him.

Finally he had to do something, even if it might have been the wrong thing. At just about 7 A.M. he placed a telephone call. To the Hermosa Beach Police Department.

"Hello, this is Officer Rickey," a no-nonsense voice at the other end of the line answered. "How can I help you?"

"Hi, this is Charles Rathbun."

"Yes?"

Charlie was relieved that the name had not brought immediate recognition. Obviously there wasn't an all-points bulletin out on him.

"I'd like to make an appointment to make a statement about the Sobek case," Rathbun continued tentatively.

"Yeah? Why?" the officer asked, wary of yet another crank call, a phenomenon that dogs virtually every high-profile investigation.

"Because I have some information that will be helpful to you," Charlie meandered on.

"Like what?"

Charlie searched his mind for a safe answer.

"I know where her DayPlanner is," he offered.

"That's nice, but so what?"

By that time, Rickey knew, Linda's DayPlanner had already been recovered.

"Well, I might have some other information, too," Charlie said.

"Okay, what is it?"

"Before I talk with you, I'd like to get in touch with my attorney, Jim Nichols."

"What did you say your name was?" the officer asked, his suspicions aroused.

"Charles Rathbun."

"How do you spell that?

"R-A-T-H-B-U-N. Charles Rathbun."

"You know, that sounds familiar. I think we found your name and number along with Linda Sobek's effects."

Charlie's heart leaped. They knew his name, but did they suspect him?

"Mr. Rathbun, what's your telephone number?" the officer continued.

Charlie gave it to him in a low, mumbling voice.

"Mr. Rathbun, I'm going to have another one of our officers call you back in a few minutes. Are you going to be home for a while?"

"Yes," Charlie said, "I think so."

"Okay, Mr. Rathbun. Thank you." And the phone clicked dead.

Charlie had hoped that the information he gleaned from the call would ease his mind, but instead of relieving his tension, the phone call to the Hermosa Beach Police Department intensified it. He paced around his room like an animal confined in a cage that was too small. He tried to make coffee, but he was too fidgety to wait for it to brew. He called up an image on his computer screen and tried to work on it, but his impatience wouldn't let him. The fear of the unknown, much more than the fear of the known, was eating him up inside.

Thinking that it might be good to get out for a while, he drove over to the photo lab, where he dropped off the exposed film from the Mitsubishi Montero shoot. Then he went to a Federal Express office, one of his constant haunts, and sent the edited Lexus LX 450 photography off to Marilee Bowles at *AutoWeek*.

But though he tried to maintain a normal schedule of mundane activities, the specter of his involvement in Linda Sobek's disappearance was hanging all around him. He couldn't escape it, and the terror inside him was becoming impossible to ignore.

He needed someone to talk to, someone who could understand and help. He again thought of his friend Jim Nichols, a man who was not only a good listener but also a trial attorney. Flashing through his address book, he found Nichols's work number and dialed it from a pay phone near the Federal Express office, but the secretary who answered told him, "Mr. Nichols is in court."

"Would you please tell Mr. Nichols that Charlie Rathbun called?" he asked her. "And tell him that I need to speak with him."

Hanging up quickly, he immediately dialed Shannon Meyer, and he didn't need his address book to remember her number. Up to just a few months ago, he had been dialing it at least two or three times a week for more than a year.

Shannon was sitting at her desk in her artistically furnished Burbank equestrian-district home when the call came in, and just hearing Charlie's voice was a shock to her.

"We hadn't seen each other for at least two or three months after the mountain biking incident where I found out he was jealous of my husband," Meyer remembered. "So I was surprised that he called, and then he sounded so serious.

"He said, 'Have you heard about the missing model? Well, I know what happened.' And then he started telling me this story.

"He had been doing a photo shoot with a blond model, nice looking, and he was showing her how to do doughnuts [industry slang for driving in a tight circle] when he hit her with the car and killed her.

" 'I left her there,' he said."

In addition to her job as an animation cell painter, Meyer was also a Reserve Deputy Sheriff for Los Angeles County, but she had never heard anything like this.

"I said to him, 'Charlie, is this a practical joke?' And he said, 'I'm not kidding. I'd like to send you something that will help explain this.' "

When Rathbun mentioned that he was thinking of going to the authorities, Meyer said, "I wouldn't go down there without an attorney."

Meyer immediately recommended that Charlie try to reach her neighbor and good friend Jim Nichols, and when Rathbun said he had already attempted that with no success, she insisted that he keep trying.

"I told him, 'If you can't get ahold of him, I'll get ahold of him,' " Meyer recalled. "I was trying to calm him down, telling him everything will be fine, and he said, 'I don't think it will be fine. I'll be gone for a long time.' "

Before Rathbun hung up, he asked Meyer to feed his cat while he was away.

That was the kicker, and Shannon wasted no time in calling Jim Nichols's office.

"I left a message saying, 'Charlie's in trouble, serious trouble,' " she remembers. " 'Please call him at his house.' "

Within a few minutes Charlie was back at home, contemplating what had become an almost impossible situation. He couldn't help wondering: when the other shoe dropped, would it have spikes in it?

Suddenly uncomfortable in his own house, he tried to decide what the best course of action was. Should I cut and run? he asked himself. Should I get in the car and head to the airport as quickly as I can get there? Should I take all my cash out of the bank and buy a plane ticket for South America?

He wandered from room to room. For some reason it all seemed unfamiliar to him, as if he'd been deposited in someone else's home. Instead of moving in a linear progression, time seemed to be standing still or worse, swirling in an unfathomable muddle, going forward and back, then forward again.

His head spinning with contradictory thoughts, he impulsively picked up the telephone and called Hermosa Beach Police Department again. Officer Raul Saldana, Hermosa Beach PD, by then a veteran of the Sobek investigation, took the call.

"Rathbun?"

"Yes."

"This is Saldana of the Hermosa Beach Police Department."

"Oh, Detective [Saldana's correct title is "Officer"], I've been expecting you to call and thought I'd call you."

"You called us earlier?"

"Yes. I think I have some information that might be helpful."

"Where do you live, Mr. Rathbun?"

"1937 Canyon Drive in Hollywood."

"I see. Are you married?"

"No, but I have a girlfriend."

"And what's her name?"

"Glenda Elam. E-L-A-M."

"And where does she live?"

Charlie provided her address in Hollywood.

"You called in about the Sobek case?"

"Yes, like I said, I have some information."

"Did you see Linda Sobek last Thursday? On November 16?"

"Yes, I did," Charlie replied. "I met her at the Denny's restaurant at Crenshaw and the 405."

"About what time was that?"

"Oh, I don't know. About eleven o'clock or so. Give or take."

"And what was the meeting about?"

"Well, I thought I might have some work for her. She modeled for me one time, and I thought I might have something coming up that she would be good for."

"And what happened at the meeting?"

"Oh, she was waiting for me when I pulled up, and she had her portfolio with her—you know, pictures of her in various poses. She wanted me to look at it."

"Yeah?"

"And so I looked at it for a few minutes."

"That was it?"

"Pretty much," Charlie said, getting calmer as the story grew. "I told her I would call her if I had something, and then I got back in the car and I drove off."

"And did she drive away, too?"

"I'm not sure. I don't remember her driving away. Maybe she stayed and got something to eat."

"What kind of car do you drive, Mr. Rathbun?"

"I own an Isuzu Trooper, but that day I was driving a Lexus LX 450. It's a big sport utility they're about to come out with, kinda like a Toyota Land Cruiser. I had just picked it up at Lexus."

"And you say you just talked to her . . ."

"Yeah, for about five or ten minutes maybe."

"And then you drove off?"

"Then I drove off."

"And you didn't see her after that?"

"No."

"Tell me, Mr. Rathbun, why has it taken you so long to come forward with this information? This woman has been missing for several days, and reports have been all over TV, radio and the newspapers."

"I don't know. I guess I've been very busy, and so I haven't been watching much TV. But last night I saw some reports, and I thought I should give you a call."

"Well, Mr. Rathbun," Saldana said, "I think you need to come in here to talk with us a little more."

"Come down to Hermosa Beach? To the police department?" Charlie asked, trying to disguise the trepidation he felt about that prospect.

"Yes, you need to come down as soon as you can."

"All right," Charlie said. "But that's really all I know."

"When do you think you can get here?"

"I don't know," Charlie stammered. "I've got some things to do this morning, and it'll take me almost an hour to get down there."

"Well, what do you think? About twelve, twelve-thirty? Can you get down here about then?"

"I can try," Charlie replied.

"Okay, Mr. Rathbun, we'll see you around noon or so."

The two men hung up simultaneously.

The phone call had done nothing to ease Rathbun's jangled nerves. Now he was convinced he needed a lawyer, but when he tried Nichols's office again a few minutes after hanging up with Saldana, he got the same answer he had before: "Mr. Nichols is in court."

Now more desperate than ever, Charlie pulled a bottle of Scotch out of a cupboard, unscrewed the top and started to drink. Then he went downstairs and got an antique .45-caliber automatic pistol out of its locked plastic case, knocking over his mountain bike in the process, and returned to his room. He lay down on the futon, the bottle in one hand and the gun in the other, and tried to decide what to do next.

If the phone call to the Hermosa Beach Police Department left Charlie more nervous than ever, it left Saldana, who had been working on the missing person case almost since the beginning, strangely calm. He wanted to hear how Rathbun would explain the fact that his Lexus borrower's agreement and Motor Press Guild book had ended up in the same trash can in the Angeles National Forest as Linda Sobek's DayPlanner and portfolio. Since that trash can was some fifty miles of driving distance from where the photographer said he had left the model, at the Denny's off Crenshaw at the 405, it was an unusual coincidence. But Saldana was also experienced enough to realize that there were often logical explanations for things that sounded very illogical on their face. After all, Rathbun *had* accepted his invitation to come in to the station for a voluntary interview. At that moment Saldana had something else on his mind. He was about to go into a meeting that would change the complexion of the case.

Chapter 22

SINCE THE first report of the disappearance of Linda Sobek had come in on Friday, November 17, 1995, the Hermosa Beach Police Department had been working on the case night and day. Though there had been no direct evidence of foul play, the investigation led by Lieutenant Mark Wright had pointed to what probably didn't happen—voluntary disappearance or suicide—if not what probably did. Hermosa Beach PD suspected foul play, but the personnel conducting the inquiry knew they were a long way from solving the case.

Though the investigators had already done a yeoman's job in moving the investigation forward, the Hermosa Beach Police Department was a small agency, unused to kidnapping, murder or other violent felonies. On the rare occasions when such crimes did occur within its borders, they were usually open-and-shut affairs, not mysteries requiring tedious and expensive investigation. It is not unusual for small jurisdictions like Hermosa to request assistance from a larger agency when a case calls for more powerful techniques and more experienced investigators, and so it went in the Sobek disappearance. Fairly early on, Hermosa Beach PD asked for the help of the Los Angeles County Sheriff's Department, which sadly enough has had a great deal of experience investigating homicides.

At noon on Wednesday, November 22, soon after Officer Raul Saldana had suggested strongly to Charlie Rathbun that he come on down for an interview, the key investigators on the case from both Hermosa Beach PD and the Sheriff's Department met in the squad room of the Hermosa facility. Around the table were Wright and Saldana of Hermosa Beach PD and Deputy Mary Bice, Deputy Nash Reyes, Sergeant Mike Bumcrot and Sergeant Mike Robinson, all of the Los Angeles County Sheriff's Department. There was a little tension at the table as well, because Hermosa Beach PD was understandably proud of its achievements on the case up to that point and was a little bit miffed about the Sheriff's Department suggestion that it step back to a second-fiddle position. The Sheriff's Department personnel, especially experienced veterans Bumcrot and Robinson, were sensitive to the situation, having participated in several multiple-agency investigations over the years, but the mood was dicey.

Wright and Saldana proceeded to review the results of the investigation up to that point. Having completed the initial interviews with family and friends, the group was told, Hermosa Beach PD was currently looking at a former boyfriend of Sobek's as well as some associates of the model. The biggest news, of course, was the recovery of Sobek's DayPlanner and the Lexus borrower's agreement from a dumpster in the Angeles National Forest thanks to the persistence of community service worker Bill Bartling.

The group waited expectantly for the arrival of Charles Rathbun, which he had promised in his phone call with Saldana, but twelve and then twelve-thirty came and went without a sign of him. The meeting was still in progress when the group got word that a search of Angeles Crest garbage cans, triggered by the DayPlanner discovery, had turned up Sobek's leopard-print curler bag and a few other bits and pieces. Bice and Reyes departed immediately for the Angeles National Forest to document the discovery.

Minutes later the remaining members of the group received a message that Sobek's white Nissan 240SX sports coupe had been discovered in the parking lot of the Denny's at Crenshaw and the 405. Wright and Bumcrot left the meeting to secure the scene and do further investigation, while Robinson teamed with a Hermosa Beach officer to conduct an interview with a man named Morgan Carey, who had been pulled off a plane at Los Angeles International Airport and taken to the Lennox Sheriff's Station. Carey, reportedly the brother of singer Mariah Carey, was rumored to have pursued Sobek romantically, but the interview netted no information that connected him to her disappearance.

Later that afternoon officials from the Lexus public relations department phoned the Hermosa Beach Police Department to tell them that the Lexus LX 450 prototype Rathbun had returned on Monday morning was now back in their possession after a loan to another automotive magazine. An officer went to secure that vehicle, and soon thereafter both the Lexus and Linda's Nissan were towed to Carson Street Sheriff's Station, where they were impounded for further investigation. Crime lab technicians immediately went to work on both vehicles, looking for fingerprints, blood and other trace evidence. The vehicles were also photographed from every angle, although it's doubtful that Charlie Rathbun would have approved of the technique.

As three o'clock came and went, with the veteran automotive photographer still a no-show for his scheduled interview at the Hermosa Beach Police Department, the task force sent a surveillance team to keep an eye on his Canyon Drive residence.

That team was barely in place when all hell broke loose in Hollywood.

Chapter 23

UNTIL YOU'RE under tremendous pressure, pressure that could involve life or death, you never know how you'll respond to it. Some cower and cry. Others rise to greater heights than they ever would have imagined, transcending fear in the face of forbidding odds.

As morning turned into afternoon on Wednesday, November 22, 1995, Charlie Rathbun found himself under tremendous pressure, and he responded with a paradoxical combination of sheer panic and taut self-control. Though he tried to maintain a normal schedule of routine activities, his involvement in Linda Sobek's disappearance plagued his thinking. He couldn't escape it, and the terror inside him was becoming impossible to ignore.

He got up from his futon, where he had been keeping drunken company with a bottle of Scotch and a handgun, and stumbled the few steps to his desk. There he made a phone call to Pete Ternes at the Oldsmobile public relations department in Michigan about the press kit project. Then he banged out a computer fax message to Shannon Meyer, double-clicked on Send and then went back to his bottle and his futon. Again he was contemplating suicide, and he expected the message he had just faxed to Shannon would arrive at her home after his death. At least, that's what he claimed later.

At three that afternoon Meyer was still trying to decide what to make of Rathbun's excited midmorning telephone call when Charlie's fax came rustling in. It resembled nothing so much as a transcript of a speech by a drunken man. It was filled with misspellings, some of the words were slurred, and one of the most poignant sentences in it was "I love you and I've always loved you." The fax made the already troubled Shannon even more troubled.

"I immediately thought it was a suicide note," Shannon said. "It was obvious he was at the end of his rope."

At the same moment that Shannon Meyer was receiving the suicide fax from Charlie, Jim Nichols was on his way home from the Van Nuys courthouse, where he was defending a medical malpractice suit.

"Shannon is a neighbor, and we're riding friends," Nichols said. "There's nothing lusty and dusty there, nothing like that. But late that afternoon I called her to see when we could go riding, something we do all the time. She immediately told me that Charlie thought he might be facing serious legal charges."

Nichols's first assumption was that Charlie had been involved in some sort of drunk driving incident, but he, like Meyer, was so aware of Charlie's off-beat sense of humor that he was uncertain whether the whole thing might be some oddball joke.

He asked Shannon her opinion, and she said, "He sent me a very weird fax this afternoon, and Charlie's told me some other stuff on the telephone, but some of the things are so bizarre, I'm just not sure."

After punching the End button on the call with Shannon, Nichols telephoned his office, and his secretary told him, "Charlie Rathbun called you earlier today, and he wants you to call him."

At the wheel of his car, nearing his Burbank home, Nichols thought to himself, "The guy may actually not be joking."

Just to make certain, Nichols called Rathbun's Hollywood home, but all he got was the recorded message of an answering machine. He didn't know what to make of that, and in the back of his mind he feared that his friend Charlie might already be lying in a pool of his own blood.

When Nichols reached the equestrian district, he immediately drove to Meyer's house and ran up the walk to her doorway. She answered his insistent knock quickly and shoved the fax that Charlie had sent her less than an hour before in front of his face. Nichols read it swiftly and was appalled by what it said.

"It seemed like he was building up nerve to do himself in," Nichols said. "Words were slurred, misspelled. It was clear that here was a guy who was totally despondent. Here was a guy who was ready to kill himself."

The pair tried calling Rathbun again, but again all they got was an answering machine. Then they sent him a fax, but there was no response from Canyon Drive. Feeling there was no time to lose if they were going to prevent their friend from committing suicide, Meyer and Nichols immediately hopped into his car and took off for Hollywood.

In less than a half a hour they had traversed the Cahuenga Pass and found themselves in front of Charlie Rathbun's antique bungalow, but the place was so quiet they couldn't tell if the photographer was there. In fact they weren't even certain he *lived* there.

As Shannon recalled, "There was a car in the driveway but it was not his personal car. It was a black sport utility. We knew he had bought a house, and we said to each other, 'Maybe he's moved.'"

They didn't notice that the black sport utility carried special Distributor license plates, a dead giveaway for a manufacturer's press fleet vehicle. The sport utility they saw was the Mitsubishi Montero that Charlie had been photographing over the past several days.

Desperate to make contact with their friend, the pair continued to place calls to Rathbun's telephone number, but answering machine pickups were all they got in response. As they sat in Nichols's car, trying to decide what to do next, Meyer spotted a man in a car a few doors down. Putting two and two together, she thought the Sheriff's Department might be watching the Rathbun house.

Intrepidly she walked over to the car and asked the nondescript man inside, "Are you with the Sheriff's Department?"

"No, I work at the market down the road," he replied unconvincingly.

Not knowing what to make of the entire situation, Shannon returned to Nichols's car, and the pair decided to make one more call to the Rathbun residence. Again the call was picked up by the answering machine, but figuring that Charlie might be monitoring it, they pleaded with him to talk to them.

"Charlie, we're going to call an ambulance if you're not out of that house in five minutes!" Shannon shouted into the phone.

Nichols was close enough to law enforcement to know that unstable suspects might do anything, and his friend Charlie Rathbun was giving every indication of being unstable. That knowledge created a fear gnawing in the back of his mind.

"I thought because he had a crush or a love interest in Shannon that if he was going to kill himself, he might also kill her," Nichols recalled. He pleaded with his companion to stay in the background if and when Charlie came out.

Two minutes elapsed, then three, then four. Meyer and Nichols were looking at each other, searching in vain for the tack to try next, when Rathbun popped out of the front door of his house. He was carrying a .45-caliber automatic.

Afraid that Charlie would flip out if he got near Shannon, the mild-mannered Nichols decided to take the lead role. He worked his way up onto the porch, where his friend was lurching about waving the gun but not pointing it in any particular direction. What he saw when he got close to Charlie scared him all the more.

"He was totally intoxicated, bombed," Nichols recalled later. "He looked like a guy who was sleeping on a park bench."

After all the good times the trio had shared at events involving The Spirit of the West Riders, Nichols was saddened that it had come to this. Charlie was so unsteady on his feet that he was staggering, and though most of the time the gun was pointed down, he continued to swing it carelessly. If that wasn't enough for the bespectacled lawyer, Shannon had followed him onto the porch.

"Put the gun down, Charlie," Nichols said, and Shannon picked up the chorus. "Put the gun down, Charlie. Put it down."

Though the two were trying to remain outwardly calm, inside they were experiencing the adrenaline rush of fear.

"I was concerned that he would shoot himself right there in front of me," Nichols said. "I was in panic that he would put that gun to his head and blow his brains out."

Despite the fear, Meyer and Nichols continued their efforts to get the gun from his hand.

"Put the gun down, Charlie. Put it down."

Suddenly Rathbun weaved toward them. A round exploded from the gun, hit the concrete porch and ricocheted into Shannon Meyer's arm.

Involuntarily she screeched, "I'm hit!"

Nichols whirled around to see if she was all right, and when he turned back toward Charlie, the photographer's expression was absolutely unchanged.

"I don't recall any reaction," Nichols said later, "and that's with a gun in his hand that's still smoking."

Meanwhile Meyer was screaming, not so much because of the pain but because she was upset at her initial reaction to being shot, which included a curse or two.

"I was so mad, I was screaming like a girl," she remembered. "I was shouting, 'Call 911! Call 911!' "

With one shot fired and Charlie still holding the automatic, Nichols decided drastic action was necessary.

"I knew I had to get the gun from his hand," Nichols

said. "I thought I would have to tackle him, but he was so unsteady on his feet, I wasn't sure what would happen if I lunged at him."

At the same time Shannon Meyer showed the value of her Sheriff's Department training and her own presence of mind by calmly walking back to Nichols's car and dialing 911 herself. At first glance her wound didn't seem too serious, but she was bleeding profusely, and she feared that without help she might bleed to death. After reporting that she'd been shot, Meyer clicked off the phone and watched the two men on the porch, very afraid for Nichols's life.

"Charlie, put the gun down," Nichols repeated, but he couldn't tell if Rathbun was even hearing him. Desperate to end the standoff, Nichols contemplated trying to tackle the much larger and much younger man, but then, to his great relief, Rathbun simply put the gun down on the porch. Warily Nichols swooped in, scooped it up and pulled the clip out of it. He tucked the heavy .45 into the waistband of his pants right at the small of his back.

With that, "Charlie turned around and went right back in the house, like a rat with a piece of cheese," remembered Nichols.

The lawyer followed him through the entranceway, and the sight that greeted him sent new chills down his back. The house was filled with guns. Rathbun, an antique firearms collector, had apparently been toying with several of his weapons while ingesting a great deal of whiskey.

Nichols persuaded Charlie to sit down on the couch, and he put his arm around his friend, who was drunk, soiled and smelling like a warm night on Skid Row. He said to him, "You sit right here, Charlie. I have to talk to Shannon. She was shot."

"Oh, my God!" Charlie cried out. "She was shot?"

The hulking photographer began weeping as Nichols ducked out the open door to check on Shannon, who was hurrying up the walk.

"Are you okay?" Nichols called out.

"I'll be fine," Meyer told him. "The police are on the way."

"Okay," Nichols said, somewhat reassured, and he turned to reenter the house.

"Jim, don't go back," Meyer called to him.

"I have to," he said, turning toward her for a second. Then he disappeared into the house.

He found Charlie in the living room, where he'd left him, but the photographer had risen from the couch and was staggering around again. Fearing that Rathbun might grab one of the guns scattered about, Nichols wrestled him back onto the sofa and sat down on the edge of one of the cushions, trying to maintain control of the situation. If anything, Charlie was more despondent than before. By the time Meyer entered the room, he was crying openly, and when Nichols tried to reassure him, he shouted, "I don't care. My life is over."

In the distance sirens were wailing, and moments later, a convoy of Los Angeles Police Department squad cars began piling into the street in front of the Rathbun home. Pulling their shotguns out, half a dozen officers got together to organize their next move.

Meyer sensed more potential danger and ran to the living room phone to call 911 again. She wanted to make certain that the police outside knew that Jim Nichols was not a threat.

"My only concern was for Jim," Shannon said later. "I was afraid Jim would be shot."

Before she even had time to hang up the phone, the police stormed into the living room, shotguns leveled.

"Onto the floor! Onto the floor!" the helmeted cops shouted, and soon Rathbun, Nichols and Meyer were all spread-eagled in the felony position.

"He's got a gun!" one of the cops suddenly shouted, and five men simultaneously dove for the .45 that was still tucked into the waistband of Nichols's pants. Instantaneously it was confiscated, but its presence marked Nichols as a suspicious character.

"Looking back on it, I think about how they could've shot me and nobody could have said a thing," Nichols recalled. "They would have got off scot-free, and I don't fault them for that. I had forgotten I had the gun on me."

Taking no chances, the police handcuffed both Rathbun and Nichols and led them off to separate squad cars, while Meyer flashed her Reserve Deputy badge and identified herself to police. Several officers examined her still bleeding wound, and then paramedics were called and told to meet their victim at Los Angeles PD's Hollywood Station, less than half a mile east on Franklin.

Rathbun and Nichols were transported to Hollywood Station in separate patrol cars. After medical aid, Shannon Meyer was soon to follow.

By five o'clock on that pleasantly cool Thanksgiving Eve, a suspect in the Sobek disappearance was in custody. Millions of Angelenos getting home early for the holiday saw the live reports from the scene attesting to that minutes after the arrest was made. But there remained an unanswered question that hung in the air. Where was Linda Sobek?

Chapter 24

To Sergeant Mike Robinson, a thirty-four-year veteran of the Los Angeles County Sheriff's Department, the phone call was good news at a bad time. It reported that Rathbun, now officially a suspect in the disappearance of bathing suit model Linda Sobek, had been apprehended at his home in Hollywood. A shot had been fired, the report continued, but no one had been seriously hurt.

A substantial, gray-haired man who looks younger than his fifty-five years, Robinson smiled at his luck. He couldn't have been more pleased that a suspect was in custody, but the trek from Hermosa Beach Police Department, where he had been manning the task force command post, to the Los Angeles Police Department's Hollywood Station was not very appealing to him. And it was less appealing when he remembered that it was the day before Thanksgiving. When most others were headed home, he knew damn well he'd be fighting bumper-to-bumper traffic all the way north.

Of course, looking back over his twelve years in the Sheriff's Department Homicide Division, Robinson had worked more than his share of nights, weekends and holidays. Among the high-profile cases he and his partner, Sergeant Mike Bumcrot, had worked were the notorious Compton police officer murders of 1993 and even further back, the Night Stalker investigation. Prior to that, during his fourteen years in Special Investigations, he had done battle against prison gangs, organized crime and even some unlawful members of Los Angeles's occult scene.

Yeah, he thought, as he pointed his car toward Hollywood, I guess I can stand a little traffic.

Soft-spoken but with a glint of hardness in his eyes, Robinson still liked his job, even after more than three decades.

"Oh, it's got its frustrations," he once said, "but every case has got its own personality, and every case is a learning experience that takes you in a different direction."

Though Robinson was contemplating retirement, the Sobek disappearance presented a variety of interesting challenges, and he wanted nothing more than to finish his career by putting the Sobek case in the Solved file. He would get that chance as the lead investigator, heading up the joint Los Angeles County Sheriff's Department and Hermosa Beach PD task force.

When he was dragged out of the back of the LAPD squad car behind Hollywood Station at the corner of Western and Franklin, Jim Nichols felt like a fish that had just flopped out of the fishbowl. For one thing, he was about as unused to sitting handcuffed in the back of a police car as he was to wearing spike heels and a spandex dress. Even more disconcerting was the fact that though he was a strong supporter of law enforcement and a believer in the death penalty, he knew his friend Charlie Rathbun was in a great deal of legal difficulty. He had an old-fashioned sense of justice, but he also wanted to make certain that his friend's rights as a citizen weren't thrown to the four winds. Nichols was a little miffed at the police for separating him from Charlie on the ride to the station, and he was afraid his friend might say something he would regret later, especially in his drunken state.

The fact was that Rathbun was already blabbering uncontrollably.

"I tried to save her, but I couldn't," he told officers in a plaintive voice as he was led into Hollywood Station.

"It was just too much for me," he wailed. "I never saw anyone die before."

Immediately upon getting out of the police car, Nichols announced that he was Rathbun's lawyer.

"I don't want him questioned," the attorney said grimly to anyone who would listen.

That statement, like the gun that had been found on his person, did not endear him to the police. Still in handcuffs, he was told to take a seat on a plastic bench in a corridor in the station, while Rathbun was hauled off to an interrogation room. Afraid that he would be "stuck in a cell with a lot of toothless, tattooed guys," the mild-mannered attorney demanded to know why he'd been arrested in the first place.

An LAPD officer who had been at the scene at Canyon Drive told him, "We're sorting it all out. We took a .45 off of you, so we had probable cause."

At the same time Rathbun was panicking not just about his arrest but also about the condition of his friend Shannon. When he caught sight of her being wheeled down the hallway of the Hollywood Station on a gurney, officers prevented him from running to her, but before she vanished out the door, he mouthed to her the words, "I love you."

Rathbun was hauled off to an interrogation room, pending the arrival of the team from the Sheriff's Department and Hermosa Beach PD. Nichols was taken to a holding cell, which to his great relief didn't contain any toothless men.

When the interrogation team did arrive, mild confusion reigned, at least for the first few minutes. The confusion was understandable. The task force had only recently been assembled, the Sheriff's Department had only taken the lead on the case a few hours before, and here they were in a facility operated by a third agency, Los Angeles Police Department. With a suspect about ready to admit his involvement, each agency wanted to make certain it got the credit it felt it deserved, and there were arguments over who should question Rathbun.

Things quickly were sorted out, and teams were assigned to question several of those involved in the late-afternoon events at 1937 Canyon Drive. Deputies Mary Bice and Nash Reyes, along with HBPD Officer Raul Saldana, began the initial interrogation of Rathbun. Sheriff's Sergeants Mike Robinson and Mike Bumcrot interviewed Rathbun's roommate, Bill Longo, and eventually Jim Nichols.

After cooling his heels for what seemed like hours in his cell, Nichols was more than a bit out of sorts. The cops had treated him like a criminal, taken his valuables, including his watch, and thrown him in a cell. That was enough to piss him off, but he was also convinced that his friend Charlie, drunk as he was, could not be doing himself any favors.

"As I sat there, I said to myself, 'He's spilling his guts; he's confessing to everything,' " Nichols recalled. "I assumed that he was spilling like a Rainbird [a kind of sprinkler]."

At the same time Nichols had only the vaguest idea of what Charlie might actually have done. All his information about the crime or crimes that Rathbun might have committed had come from his discussions with Shannon Meyer about Charlie's phone call and fax, plus what little he had overheard Charlie tell police before they were separated. In both phone call and fax to Meyer, Rathbun had mentioned hitting Sobek with a vehicle, so Nichols assumed that vehicular manslaughter was the charge being contemplated.

While Nichols fretted in his cell, Rathbun was being questioned by Bice, Reyes and Saldana, though questioning is a charitable description. Questioning implies an ordered structure that this interview lacked. Charlie, still much the worse for the Scotch he had imbibed, vomit covering his clothing, launched into a rambling, tearful, stream-of-consciousness monologue about what he claimed had happened to Linda Sobek.

The story he told stuck fairly closely to the one he had already related to Shannon on the telephone and to what he had written on his computer during the previous night and on into the morning. In fits and starts, he told the assembled investigators that he hadn't left Linda in the parking lot of the Denny's restaurant as he had indicated to Saldana earlier that day. Instead he had taken her to El Mirage dry lake to do a photo shoot on the Lexus LX 450.

"She's a friend of mine, she really is," Charlie stammered. "I care about Linda. She's a nice lady. She's, she's a good person. I don't care what she looks like. The model part doesn't matter."

While on the dry lake, he rambled, the two had attempted to do an action shot with Linda driving the vehicle, but she wasn't doing the maneuver properly, so he got into the sport utility in an effort to show her how. In the process of doing doughnuts, he said, he had lost control of the vehicle and run into her, knocking her to the ground. He ran to check her, but after trying to revive her, he determined she was dead.

"Oh, yeah, oh, yeah, I screwed up," he moaned. "Fuck! I hurt Linda. I hurt my parents. I hurt all my friends. I hurt her friends. Just by fucking not paying attention, just trying to get a little more dust off the tires, little more action out of the car."

"You were just trying to do your job," Saldana commented.

"My job isn't killing people. What fucking good is a picture if you killed somebody to get it? Oh, man, if they would give me the electric chair it would be mercy."

Panicked and not knowing what to do, Rathbun told Bice and Saldana, after he realized the model was dead, he decided to bury her.

"Where did you bury her, Charlie?" the investigators asked. "Where did you bury her?"

"In the desert," Rathbun replied absently.

The detectives were fascinated by Charlie's stumbling tale, so fascinated, in fact, that they ignored several of Rathbun's requests to speak to his attorney. They were desperate to find Linda, perhaps harboring the faintest hope that she might still be alive—at the very least wanting to put an end to her family's and friends' tragic vigil.

Though done in their zeal to find the missing woman, continuing the questioning after Charlie's request to speak to his attorney caused problems for the investigators later. They had violated his so-called Miranda rights, and their inattention to his requests would ultimately throw the case into turmoil.

As Charlie was completing his first round of interrogation, Nichols was finishing up his statement to Robinson and Bumcrot. During his interview he had complained several times about not being allowed access to his client, and at its conclusion he asked again if he could see Charlie.

The detectives told him that they would see what they could do and sent him back into the corridor where he had originally been held. He was unsure if he was free to go, and he was still worried about what his friend might be telling the police.

Nichols was pacing the hallway when Saldana emerged from the interrogation room where he had been questioning Charlie. The HBPD officer had a big smile on his face, and on Nichols's beckoning, he walked over.

"Whew! An interrogation like that is exhausting," Saldana said.

"You should try being held in a cell," Nichols shot back.

"Yeah, I'm sorry about that," Saldana replied. "We knew you probably didn't have anything to do with it, but we had to make sure."

"And now you're sure?"

"Yeah."

"Who were you interviewing?"

"Rathbun."

"Well, I'm his lawyer, and I don't want him questioned."

"Oh, it doesn't matter," Saldana said. "He's already confessed to the killing."

That news hit Nichols right between the eyes. Everything that he had been envisioning was seemingly coming true, with tragic results for his client.

"It was very disturbing to me," Nichols recalls. "Not on my watch, I said to myself. I didn't want this to happen while I was representing him."

With the cat at least partially out of the bag, investigators decided there would be no harm in letting the attorney speak to his client. They also hoped that Nichols might be able to persuade Rathbun to lead them to Linda Sobek.

Nichols was escorted into the interrogation room, and there at the table was Charlie Rathbun.

"He looked like crap," Nichols remembered. "His eyes were red, and there was vomit on his shirt. I was getting a sinking feeling in my gut that I was on a runaway train."

Nichols asked his client to go over what he had told the police, and he got the same story that Charlie had laid out for Bice, Saldana and Reyes. Charlie told him he had been trying to do a photo shoot with Sobek on the dry lake, and while showing her how to do doughnuts, he had lost control of the Lexus and struck her. When he determined she was dead, he panicked and buried her.

Nichols accepted the story at face value. He didn't realize that his entire conversation with Rathbun, a supposedly confidential attorney-client meeting, had been inadvertently tape-recorded by the police.

With the knowledge that their suspect not only had admitted to killing Sobek but also had admitted burying her, the members of the task force were as excited as ants at a picnic. They felt they were on the verge of solving the highest-profile case in Southern California since the Nicole Simpson murder. All they needed to wrap it up was to find the body.

But finding Linda Sobek, they were soon to find out, wasn't going to be as easy as they thought.

Chapter 25

WITH THE solution to the disappearance of the missing model seeming so near at hand, the investigators from the Sheriff's Department and Hermosa Beach PD were in a frenzy. Two issues were on their minds. First and most obvious was finding Linda Sobek. The second and lesser issue was which agency—Sheriff's Department, Hermosa Beach Police Department or Los Angeles Police Department—would get credit for solving the case.

As the investigators wrangled about the latter, they grew more and more eager to do the former. They had only the most marginal hope of discovering Sobek still alive. After all, Rathbun had told them that he had buried her on Thursday, November 16, six days earlier. Even if she had been buried while still breathing, and Rathbun said she hadn't been, it was a great leap of faith to believe that she might still be breathing nearly a week later. But the investigators were also sensitive to the ordeal Sobek's family and friends had been going through. The sooner they could find her—alive or dead—the sooner they could begin to give that large group some peace.

After hearing that expert trackers looking for Sobek's body would soon be at work in the Angeles National Forest, Rathbun told Bice, Saldana and Reyes that he would cooperate with them in locating the body of Linda Sobek. When Nichols was brought into the picture, he saw no

Linda Sobek as a five-year-old in 1973.

Courtesy of Elaine and Bob Sobek

The Sobek family in 1978 (*clockwise from top*): Steve, Linda, Elaine and Bob. Linda was very close to her family, particularly her mother.

Courtesy of Elaine and Bob Sobek

Linda worked out twice a day at Gold's Gym in Redondo Beach, California.

Courtesy of Elaine and Bob Sobek

Linda as a Raiderette.
Courtesy of Elaine and Bob Sobek

Charles Edgar Rathbun.

The Denny's restaurant at Crenshaw and 182nd Street, where Linda met Charlie on the final day of her life. Linda's Nissan 240SX sports coupe was found in this parking lot nearly a week after her disappearance.

Courtesy of the author

Sheriff's Department Sergeant Mike Robinson, chief investigator of the Linda Sobek disappearance and murder.

Courtesy of the author

The Dumpster in the Angeles National Forest in which police detectives found evidence linking Charlie to the crime. Police, alerted by community service worker Bill Bartling, arrived on the scene just minutes before the Dumpster was emptied.

Courtesy of the L.A. County Sheriff's Department

The crime scene in the Angeles National Forest where Linda's body was found.

Courtesy of the L.A. County Sheriff's Department

Crime lab experts examined every portion of the Lexus LX 450 prototype Charlie had been assigned to photograph.

Courtesy of the L.A. County Sheriff's Department

Charlie claimed this dent on the inside of the Lexus LX 450's door occurred during a scuffle with Linda. Sergeant Mike Robinson and criminalist Heidi Robbins proved otherwise.

Sheriff's investigators did "doughnuts" in the Lexus LX 450 near El Mirage to test Charlie's story.

Chief prosecutor Stephen Kay, a veteran of the Los Angeles County District Attorney's Office. He had won convictions against several Manson family members and serial killers Rory Norris and Lawrence Bittaker, among others, before taking on Charlie Rathbun.

Courtesy of the author

Assistant District Attorney Mary-Jean Bowman handled many crucial elements of the prosecution's case, including the cross-examination of the defendant.

Linda Sobek, the quintessential California bathing suit model.

Courtesy of Elaine and Bob Sobek

reason why he should withhold his cooperation, because he believed Charlie's word that the incident was essentially an auto accident. The civil attorney wanted Charlie to get credit for leading investigators to the body rather than waiting for it to be discovered by one of the search teams, since he fully expected an examination of the body would substantiate his client's story. Deep down he had another reason as well to urge his client to cooperate: he was the father of daughters and felt nothing could be more frightening than not knowing where your children are.

Sensing Bice and Saldana were about to put Rathbun in a police car and begin the search, Nichols invited himself along.

"We'll help you find her," he said to the officers, "but I don't want any questions. And I'm going with you."

So the quartet loaded themselves into a police car— Bice driving, Rathbun in the front seat so that he could point out where he had driven one week earlier and Nichols and Saldana in the backseat. By then it was nearly ten o'clock on the night before Thanksgiving, traffic was light, and the drive quickly assumed a strange, dreamlike quality.

"Suddenly we were racing into the night," Nichols remembered. "Without even asking, they seemed to know what direction to go in, and I thought to myself, They're going to find Linda tonight."

In the squad car Nichols was fearful that Bice was continuing to question his client, but he found it impossible to monitor the conversation up front since the voluble Saldana was keeping up a running commentary in the rear. He couldn't help wondering if the Hermosa Beach policeman really wanted to talk with him or if he was just gabbing to keep him from overhearing the conversation in the front seat.

The drive took the uncomfortable foursome up the Hollywood Freeway to Interstate 5, and then onto Highway 14, the Antelope Valley Freeway. Ironically, the route was familiar to Bice, since it was often part of her commute to work from her home in the high desert.

Just as Charlie and Linda had done a week earlier, the foursome exited on Pearblossom Highway and then they made their way onto the dry lake. What awaited them was the eerie aspect of El Mirage, its mottled clay illuminated weakly by a partial moon.

After they had driven across the tabletop flatness for a minute or two, Rathbun directed Bice to stop the car, and all four of the reluctant travelers got out, craning their necks around the area, made small by its immensity. Charlie walked a few steps ahead of the group and peered down at the clay surface.

"Yes, I think this is it," Charlie said, kneeling down on the edge of a dustbowl. "This is where it happened."

He was staring into what looked like a buffalo wallow, an indentation in the otherwise dead-level topography that was almost fifty feet across. There the clay was churned up into a soft powder as if by tires going over it and over it again.

"Is this where you buried her?" Saldana asked.

"No, no, not here," Charlie said, his voice subdued as he again surveyed the scene.

"Do you know where you buried her?" Bice asked.

"I think I can find it," Rathbun replied.

After an involuntary moment of silence in the place, the four got back into the police cruiser. In seconds they were under way again.

Bice and Saldana had originally decided to go to El Mirage so that Rathbun could retrace his steps from the supposed photo location to lead them to Linda Sobek. But after the motley band left the dry lake, Charlie seemed to grow ever more confused or reluctant to lead his captors to the gravesite of the missing model.

At first Bice and Saldana were affable, polite and cajoling. They tried to give Rathbun the impression that they were all in on it together, and once Linda was discovered, the entire nightmare would be over. They tried to maintain a positive air, and at times the drive took on the aspect of an outing. Saldana and Nichols traded stories about guns and horses, while Charlie tried to figure out where they were and where he had been on the fateful day when Linda Sobek died. But as the clock ticked onward, with Rathbun asking them to take first a right turn, then a left turn, then a right turn again, all to no result, their patience began to wear thin.

At Rathbun's suggestion they motored out of the high desert flatlands southward into the Angeles National Forest, and then they began hopping from road to road. Nichols thought Charlie seemed genuinely confused. Bice and Saldana began to feel that their prisoner was trying to con them, and that feeling grew as three o'clock turned into four o'clock in the morning. By that point Bice and Saldana were well into the twentieth hour of their workday, and their tempers were getting short. In contrast, Charlie, running on almost no sleep in the past day and a half, was actually becoming livelier.

"He was getting more and more sober," Nichols recalled. "And it was getting so he could verbalize very accurately."

From his position in the front seat Rathbun would describe a particular route to take with remarkable precision, but somewhere along the way, after minutes or even a half-hour had passed, he would suddenly say, "No, this doesn't look like the right road after all." Then the investigators would pull out the map and the process would start all over again.

By the time dawn of Thanksgiving Day showed at the horizon, the affable mood in the car had been replaced by animosity and mistrust. Not only was the temperature chillier, the atmosphere was chillier as well.

Sensing the mood change, Nichols decided to lay out a difficult question.

"Have you ever Mirandized Charlie Rathbun?" he asked Saldana.

"No, we never did," the Hermosa Beach officer replied.

"Well, you know that makes all the statements he made to you inadmissible in court, don't you?"

"Oh, that's no problem," Saldana replied. "We just want to find the body."

But by 5:30 A.M., after putting hundreds of miles into the search, they still had not discovered the body of Linda Sobek, and the two investigators were getting tired of chasing wild geese. They decided to bag the mission, taking Nichols to his car and turning their prime suspect over to the Hermosa Beach Police Department for transport to the Hermosa Beach jail.

While Charlie Rathbun was directing the fruitless search in the desert and in the Angeles National Forest, Robinson, Bumcrot and several members of the Hermosa Beach police searched Rathbun's residence on Canyon Drive and his new home on Cheramoya, a few blocks west. After a warrant had been obtained, the search began about midnight and was directed by HBPD, due to some confusion over which agency would be taking the lead in the case now that Rathbun had been detained.

Among the key pieces of evidence seized were what the police called the sorry letters and Rathbun described variously as scenarios and suicide notes. Found in Charlie's bedroom, the three pieces of evidence, one handwritten and two composed on his Macintosh computer, contained slightly different versions of the same story that Rathbun had told to the police at Hollywood Station, namely, that he had accidentally collided with Linda while at the wheel of the Lexus sport utility vehicle.

At first glance they seemed to corroborate what Charlie had said to investigators during the Hollywood police station interview. But there were also bits and pieces that seemed unusual, especially the handwritten note in which Rathbun seemed to be pointing the finger at the two photographers who, he thought, matched the composite sketch he had seen on television. The vast amount of verbiage also surprised the investigators. After all, how many people *rewrite* their suicide note?

Though Charlie had convinced his lawyer that the death of Linda Sobek was an accident, veteran detective Robinson was unmoved.

"My own feeling was, he wasn't acting like an accident," Robinson recalled. "From what I was getting at that point was that he had panicked and then he buries her, and he's throwing her property away. He's doing things that—I don't know—it just didn't feel right to me, like an accident."

From the moment that Charlie said he buried the body of Linda Sobek, he was going to have difficulty getting many people to believe her death occurred accidentally. Certainly many of us have been involved in auto accidents, some of them fatal, but when a fatal accident occurs, it's not the first impulse of most people to bury the victims.

Of course, as millions in the Los Angeles area awoke that Thanksgiving morning, only one person was certain Linda Sobek had been buried, because her body had yet to be found.

Chapter 26

As THANKSGIVING Day began in the Sobek residence in Lakewood, Elaine Sobek was trying to figure out what she had to be thankful for. Of course, she was grateful for her husband, her son, her daughter-in-law and two fine grandchildren, but as she sat in her lonely living room that morning, she wondered how Linda, her only daughter, her pet, could have been taken away from her so young.

Over the years the relationship between mother and daughter in the Sobek household had always been very tight, certainly tighter than in most families. People who knew both women saw the same soft exterior covering the same strong will. Day to day, both Linda and Elaine were pleasant, helpful and friendly, and quite ready to lend a helping hand to their neighbors, but if you got on their bad side, you could expect trouble. They weren't at all shy about giving adversaries a piece of their mind.

When Linda got into modeling and then began to seek out acting roles, some thought that Elaine lived vicariously through her daughter and managed her career. Those most unkind might have called her a stage mother. But there is no doubt that Elaine Sobek wanted the very best for her little girl. And there is no doubt that Elaine was more affected than anyone when her little girl disappeared.

Now, on Thanksgiving morning, after learning that a

suspect in the disappearance of her daughter was in custody, she began to attempt to reconcile herself to the fact that she would never see her daughter again. Suddenly a large part of her world had vanished.

About forty miles north of Lakewood, in the Angeles National Forest, Sheriff's Deputy Mary Bice was doing her best to try to end Elaine Sobek's pain. The investigator had been frustrated by what she interpreted as Rathbun's attempts to mislead and confuse his captors during the previous night's abortive search for Linda Sobek's body. After a brief rest she was back on the job, tracking down a report of a bloodstain found in Angeles Crest.

That morning a hiker in Red Box Canyon, one of the National Forest's many scenic backwoods areas, had come across some blood on the ground and reported the discovery to the authorities. The report drew attention because Sobek's DayPlanner, hair-curler bag and other effects had been found in the same general area, so Bice instructed Heidi Robbins, a Sheriff's Department serologist and criminalist, to investigate. But Robbins's analysis determined that the specimen was animal blood, and the lead was abandoned. Bice spent the remainder of the day organizing what would become a mammoth search for the body beginning the following morning, Friday, November 24. She ended her Thanksgiving Day no closer to finding the body of Linda Sobek than she had been twenty-four hours before, when Rathbun was arrested.

On Thanksgiving afternoon Jim Nichols engaged in a traditional holiday activity: he went visiting. The place he visited was hardly traditional, however, especially for a law-and-order advocate.

In the company of Phil Spangenberger, Charlie's closest friend, and Glenda Elam, Charlie's girlfriend, Nichols came calling to the Hermosa Beach jail, where the successful freelance automotive photographer was spending his first day in captivity, having been booked for murder that morning. Nichols quickly found that visiting a jail facility wasn't exactly like going over to granny's.

With a bright fall day glittering around them and the sparkling waters of the Pacific Ocean within view, the excursion to jail seemed horribly incongruous. As holiday revelers sought a little exercise to work off their turkey dinners on the Strand just a few blocks away, the trio of Rathbun's friends went through the tense process of trying to get Hermosa Beach authorities to grant a visit. HBPD was reluctant at best, especially since Sobek's body had yet to be recovered.

Despite their repeated pleas, Spangenberger and Elam weren't allowed to see Rathbun at all. Nichols, as his attorney of record, was granted less than fifteen minutes, and their discussion was guarded. He found his client looking drawn, gray and exhausted, and he wondered if Charlie might still feel suicidal.

"How are you doing?" Nichols asked.

"Oh, all right," Rathbun answered.

"Are they treating you okay?"

"Yeah, fine. No place I'd rather be."

"Charlie, this is serious," Nichols said. "It's important that you don't speak about this to anyone."

"You think so?"

"Yes, I think so, Charlie. Don't talk about what happened up there, not to the police, not to anyone. Do you understand?"

"But it was an accident."

"I know it was, Charlie, but you never know how they might interpret things you say."

"Yeah?"

"You might say some completely innocent thing, and they'll take it out of context and use it against you."

"Okay, I understand what you mean."

"Good."

"I'm sure they're going to ask me to help find the body."

"Yeah, I'm sure they are."

"Well, should I?"

"Look, Charlie, it was an accident, right? I don't see how helping them find her body will hurt your case. And I want you to get credit for it. I think that's a lot better than if they find it themselves."

"Yeah. That makes sense."

"But I don't think you should talk with anybody about this, and I absolutely don't want them putting you in a car to go look for the body until you've got proper counsel. You need a lawyer, Charlie, a criminal lawyer."

"Yeah, I know."

"Have you done anything about it?"

"I talked with my brother. He's a lawyer and he said he would ask around."

"Okay, that's good. I'd like to help you as much as I can, but I know you're going to need a criminal lawyer."

"Okay, okay."

"Is there anything I can get you?"

"Yeah, could you see about getting me my glasses? I haven't had them since yesterday."

"I'll see what I can do about that," Nichols answered. "Anything else?"

"I don't know," he said, his eyes getting a faraway look.

"All right. Hang in there. I'll tell the police that you're ready to cooperate in helping them find the body, but no questions. Okay?"

"Okay."

The faraway look was getting more pronounced, and Nichols left Charlie to his private thoughts, still worried that his client might not have taken his advice to heart.

"I was very concerned about Charlie continuing to talk," Nichols said. "If the police were going to get a conviction in his case, I wanted to make sure they'd get a righteous conviction. It bothered me that things weren't being handled the way I thought they should be."

Leaving the meeting with Charlie, Nichols was immediately confronted by Lieutenant Mark Wright and Officer

Raul Saldana, the two HBPD members most involved in the Sobek disappearance. Fearing that Nichols would persuade his client to refuse to help in the search for Linda's body, they were greatly relieved when he told them that Charlie would cooperate fully.

Then Nichols added, "I've instructed him to make no statements and to make no trips to search for the body without his lawyer present. He'll cooperate, but those are the ground rules. If you need to reach me, here is my home phone number."

He handed the policemen cream-colored business cards with his unlisted residence number scrawled on them.

"Thanks," Saldana replied. "I appreciate your professionalism. We want complete cooperation as well, and I can tell you that we'll ask for no statements without counsel present."

Nichols emerged into the late-afternoon sun and walked over to the car where Elam and Spangenberger were waiting. His worst fears had been quelled. Charlie didn't seem about to kill himself, and he wasn't spouting confessions about what he might have done to anyone who would listen. But Nichols also was certain that some sort of criminal charge would be leveled against his friend, and he knew he wasn't the attorney to defend him when that happened.

In the terms of his favorite subject, western history, Nichols felt he was fighting a holding action until cavalry reinforcements could be called in. And he had the Hermosa Beach investigators' word that Charlie wouldn't be questioned or pressed into a search for the body of Linda Sobek without proper counsel. That was good enough for him.

Chapter 27

"WHAT THE fuck?"
Jim Nichols had idly turned on the television in his tree-shaded home on the morning of Friday, November 24, 1995, when he saw something that caused his uncharacteristically vulgar ejaculation. What he saw was live coverage of his client, Charlie Rathbun, being led in handcuffs toward a waiting Sheriff's Department helicopter.

Across Southern California millions of viewers, many of them not working because of the Thanksgiving holiday, were watching the same pictures. The disappearance of model Linda Sobek had already become a national media event. Now it was about to become a live television event of unprecedented proportions.

Nichols, of course, was unconcerned about the number of people who were watching on television, but he was terribly concerned about what he was seeing. Not only was his client and friend about to clamber into a helicopter for what commentators were describing as a flight to search for Linda Sobek's body, but also there were reports that he had attempted suicide in the early hours of the morning. Mute testimony to that were the bandages apparent on Rathbun's wrists.

After Nichols's departure on Thanksgiving afternoon, Charlie had a sleepless night, filled with waking nightmares. He saw the dry lake, Linda Sobek, the inside of the Lexus LX 450, a bloodstain and the forest. They were not scenes he wanted to repeat in his head.

By the time morning came, however, he had become quietly composed. At breakfast time he was polite, answered his jailers' questions appropriately and seemed to have come to terms with where he was. Though Rathbun had threatened suicide less than forty-eight hours before, he appeared to be calm and rational. When he asked to clean up, one of the jailers gave him a bar of soap and a disposable razor.

Soon after the guard walked out of sight, Rathbun ripped the stainless steel blade partially out of its plastic covering and gouged it into both wrists. Blood began to spurt ominously from the cuts. Numb to the pain, Rathbun scooped up some of his blood and on the wall of his cell he finger-painted the words "I never meant to hurt anyone." Then he lay down on his bunk, perhaps never expecting to get up, maybe just waiting for someone to find him.

Minutes later there was chaos in the tiny jail. Noticing the bloodstained wall, a guard screamed for help. Several policemen responded immediately. Quick attempts were made to stop the bleeding, curses flew and a rapid decision was made to transport the injured prisoner to South Bay Memorial Hospital for emergency care. With HBPD so close to finding Linda Sobek's body and putting an end to the biggest case that had come its way in years, it didn't want to lose the key suspect to suicide, especially in its own facility. Rathbun was rushed to the hospital, where doctors were quickly able to stanch the flow of blood. With the cuts wiped clean, they put a series of stitches into the suspect's arms and covered the wounds with gauze and tape.

When the emergency had passed, Saldana, who had accompanied Rathbun to the hospital, talked to his prisoner.

"Charlie, we've gotta find Linda Sobek," he said.

"Yeah?"

"Yeah, we do, Charlie. Think of her family. Think of

her friends. We've gotta give them some peace, Charlie.''

"It was an accident. You know, I'm sorry, I'm very sorry about what happened, but it was an accident. I can't bring her back.''

"You can't bring her back, but you can help us find her. That'll look good for you, and it'll mean a lot to her family and friends.''

"It was an accident," Charlie repeated.

"I know, I know it was an accident. Let's prove it to everybody. Help us find her.''

Rathbun looked around the emergency room, considering what he should do. Several silent moments passed. Then he looked back at Saldana.

"Yeah," Charlie said.

"You'll help us find her?''

"Yeah, yeah, okay," he replied, the hesitation in his voice betraying a lack of commitment despite his words.

"All right, Charlie," Saldana said. "We'll get a helicopter that can take you right up to Angeles Crest. You can be up there in less than half an hour. Is that okay?''

"I want my lawyer with me.''

"You mean Nichols?''

"Yeah, yeah, Jim Nichols.''

"Okay, Charlie, I'll call him, but the helicopter's on the way. Is that all right?''

"Sure," Charlie said resignedly. "Sure.''

In his living room Nichols watched Rathbun climb into the giant Sikorsky helicopter, and he started to come unglued.

"My heart hit the floor," he remembered later. "I said to myself, What's with these police? They just do what they damn well want to do!''

As he continued to watch the live coverage, he learned that search teams had been working since nearly daybreak, trying to discover the body. Much of the live reporting originated from Mill Creek Ranger Station in the Angeles National Forest, the headquarters for the search, where reporters were waiting for the imminent arrival of the prime suspect.

Seeing a mammoth search under way, Nichols got even more upset.

"I told myself, 'They will rat-fuck him out of credit for finding the body,' " Nichols said, still rankled by the memory.

Impulsively he grabbed the phone and called the Sheriff's Department.

"Rathbun will cooperate in helping find the body," he told the detective on call, "but I don't want him questioned, not about how she died and not about how she was buried! Do you understand?"

"Yes, I understand," the detective at the other end of the line responded, "but you've got to understand we've got a missing girl here we've got to find. We're going to have to get back to you."

At Sheriff's Homicide a quick huddle of detectives ensued. Key members of the team then discussed the issue with Stephen Kay, the deputy district attorney whose office would be responsible for the prosecution of the case, and the plain-talking Kay had a simple recommendation.

"His lawyer has to be there," Kay told them. "Whatever you have to do to make it happen, make sure his lawyer is with him."

A Sheriff's Homicide detective called Nichols back immediately, telling him that a helicopter was being sent to Burbank airport that would take him to Mill Creek Ranger Station. They felt that their suspect was ready to tell them where he had buried Linda Sobek, and they didn't want to waste any precious time waiting for his lawyer to drive to Angeles Crest from his Burbank home.

By the time Sheriff's Department helicopters began shuddering their way from the South Bay and Burbank toward Mill Creek Ranger Station, the area was beginning to resemble a Vietnam-era airlift. Drawn by the search for the missing model, more than a half-dozen news helicopters had been circling over the breathtaking and difficult terrain since early morning, each attempting to get pictures of the discovery of Sobek's body.

Sheriff's Department Deputy Mary Bice, who had been leading the investigation into Linda's disappearance up to that point, and Sergeant Mike Robinson, who would soon take over from her, had arrived in the mountains together not long after daybreak. Within minutes they were directing their respective teams, which included the deputized civilians of the Sheriff's Reserve personnel, Forest Rangers and tracker dogs and their handlers. All of the Sobek family was on hand as well, plus scores of their friends who had volunteered to join in the search.

The search teams had a difficult job in front of them. The portion of the Angeles National Forest in which the search was being conducted is a rugged Alpine setting of steep rises and deep valleys, much of it covered with thick vegetation and topped by towering pines. Roads run along many of the ridges and down into the canyons, but between the roads lie hundreds of acres of unspoiled terrain that are forbidding to even the most practiced hiker. Finding a body buried somewhere in the region promised to be an excruciatingly difficult task.

Bice decided to center her team's initial search on Red Box Canyon, where the bloodstains had been discovered the day before. Robinson stationed his team in the Mill Creek area. Searchers proceeded to comb several square miles under the surprisingly warm late-November sun, but by noon hundreds of acres remained to be examined, no trace at all of Linda Sobek or any of her personal effects having been found. Privately some of the detectives began to wonder if her body was in the woods at all. They speculated on how convenient it would be for a perpetrator to suggest a search in one area when the body of the missing victim was in a different place miles away.

As the search droned on toward noon, with the sun reaching its zenith in the southern sky, a giant helicopter whirred its awkward way to Mill Creek Ranger Station carrying the man who could answer the tantalizing question: what happened to Linda Sobek? In it was successful Hollywood photographer Charlie Rathbun.

After the helicopter had touched down, its rotor blades still whirring, Rathbun was whisked off to the rustic wooden structure, his baggy white shirt flapping in the breeze, his eyes squinting to avoid the whirlwind of dust. With the press clamoring for a closer look, reporters shouting out questions, it resembled nothing so much as the landing of a presidential helicopter at Camp David with one notable exception: the President doesn't leave his Air Force helicopter wearing handcuffs.

While waiting for the arrival of Jim Nichols in the cramped office of a park ranger, Rathbun played with some paper clips. A HBPD officer kept an eye on him. Again Charlie became very voluble with the Hermosa Beach policeman, telling him, among other things, that he had "never seen anybody die before."

When the helicopter bearing Rathbun's attorney of record arrived a few minutes later, Nichols was ushered into the little office, and the attorney and his client were left alone to confer. Outside investigators could only hold their breath, hoping that Nichols wouldn't advise his client not to participate in the search.

"How are you doing, Charlie?" Nichols asked. "You okay?"

Involuntarily the lawyer's eyes focused on the bandages covering both of Charlie's wrists.

"Yeah, I think I'm okay," Rathbun replied wanly.

"You feeling all right?"

"I'm okay."

"Well, you know what we're here for."

"Yeah."

"They told me you volunteered to help them find the body."

"Yeah, I did."

"Well, I just want to make certain you get credit for

it. I don't want them finding the body and then claiming that you refused to cooperate.''

"Yeah, that makes sense.''

"Do you think you can find where you buried her?''

"I'm not sure, but I think so. The problem is it all looks so different in the daytime than it did at night.''

"Well, they expect to find the body this time, Charlie. They're not going to put up with any fucking around.''

"I know.''

"Their patience is running low.''

"I know.''

"I hope you haven't said anything to anybody about what happened.''

Rathbun did not answer immediately, and Nichols looked at him sharply.

"I might have said a few things,'' Rathbun allowed.

Nichols slapped his hand to his forehead and ran it back through his dark-brown hair.

"Damn it, Charlie. Didn't I tell you not to talk about this? Not to anyone!''

"Yeah, I know you did, but . . .''

"Charlie, listen to me. If we go out there into that helicopter, I don't want you saying anything to anybody. It can't help you, and it darn well might hurt you.''

"Yeah, okay.''

"And you agree with me?''

"Yeah, I agree.''

"So as long as you're sure this is what you want to do, let's go do it.''

"Okay.''

"I want you to find her and give her poor family some peace.''

"Okay, Jim, okay.''

Nichols knocked on the door, signaling that his conference was over.

"We'll cooperate,'' he said to the waiting detectives, who let out a big sigh of relief. "We'll cooperate, but no questions.''

The lawyer and his client were quickly led to the gigantic Sheriff's Department helicopter and shoved aboard. Lieutenant Wright of Hermosa Beach Police Department clambered into the mammoth fuselage with them, and at the signal from the ground, the clumsy machine lurched skyward, rising from the ground at what seemed like a maddeningly reluctant pace.

What followed was one of the most bizarre afternoons in the history of American criminal investigation. As the Sheriff's Department helicopter lumbered through the sky, its occupants trying to grasp where they were and where they were going, it was tailed by an armada of television news helicopters, each vying for the ''money shot''—the first glimpse of Linda Sobek's burial site.

At home millions of viewers watched the scenes with rapt attention. Nothing like this had ever been televised before. The only rough parallel to it was the famous low-speed chase of O.J. Simpson, but unlike the search for the missing model, that episode had taken on comic-opera aspects. In contrast, the search for Linda Sobek was tense and unrelenting.

In the bulbous helicopter, Rathbun, Nichols and Wright paid little attention to the smaller newscopters, which followed them like a school of pilot fish. They were too intent on trying to find the proverbial needle in a haystack—the body of a five-foot, three-inch woman in a forest that covered more than a hundred square miles. It quickly became clear that it would be no easy task.

As the minutes dragged into more than an hour in the air, with no sign that the search was closing in on the burial site, Sergeant Mike Robinson had to wonder why the decision had been made to search from the air in the first place. It had been his understanding that the helicopter had been sent to transport Rathbun from the South Bay to Angeles Crest. Once the suspect had arrived in the Angeles National Forest, the Sheriff's Department veteran fully expected him to be transferred to a waiting Sheriff's car, so that the search could be conducted from the same point of view Rathbun had when he disposed of the body in the first place. In fact, around one o'clock that sunny afternoon, Robinson and Mary Bice looped their way from Mill Creek Ranger Station to the valley floor north of the mountains, awaiting the arrival of Charlie Rathbun for just that purpose.

But in the air over the majestic pines of the forest, the search had taken on a life of its own. Inside the shuddering helicopter the noise was too great to allow Nichols and Rathbun to talk, so they wrote notes to each other on a tiny three-by-five-inch notepad, their pen fluttering nervously across the little pages. Rathbun directed the helicopter pilot this way and that, but he was having difficulty seeing clearly because he had lost his glasses in the fracas at his home two nights earlier, and they had not been returned to him. With Rathbun scrunching his eyes, trying to bring the scenery into focus, the air armada followed the big chopper down one dirt road and then up another. One hour grew into two, and then stretched toward three.

By that point several of the news helicopters had departed for refueling and hurried back, because on that Friday afternoon, as the drama unfolded on live television, there was no other place to be. Across Southern California, millions of television viewers watched the tantalizing guessing game. Would the suspect reveal where he had hidden the body? Would the authorities find the body before dark? Would the body prove that the death had been an auto accident?

On the ground Robinson looked at his watch and shook his head gravely. He knew that sunset comes early in the mountains, especially in late November.

"I was starting to panic, because we were running out of daylight," Robinson later recalled. "We had hundreds of people up there, and I could see this going into a second day, and it would be harder on a second day. Charlie might change his mind overnight."

Up in the helicopter Jim Nichols was beginning to have his doubts as well.

"I asked myself, Is this a replay of driving around the mountains like we did two nights before?" he remembered. "There were a lot of policemen in those mountains, and they were very eager to find the body. I just wanted to make sure Charlie got credit for it."

By three-thirty that afternoon the sun had begun to dip behind the peaks on the horizon, and the light was beginning to fade. Instinctively Nichols thought, It's now or never.

"Charlie, we've got to find her!" he wrote. "Concentrate."

Rathbun looked off to the west. A man who made his living by capturing light, he saw the daylight beginning to turn yellow, and he knew it would soon be orange, then red and then gone.

Writing on the pad, he gave the pilot some new directions.

The giant bird flew off, the news helicopters swarming behind it. Then, at Charlie's instruction, the chopper began to slow down and maneuver closer to the ground. It was over a road now—Santa Clara Divide Road.

"Close," Charlie wrote.

The helicopter pilot looked for a place to set down in the rough terrain, then expertly placed the big machine in the tight confines of the narrow, silt-filled canyon. Before its passengers alighted, however, Charlie wrote something else on the pad.

"Not here."

By now darkness was definitely closing around them. The cameras in the news helicopters above had their irises opened wide, the cameramen trying to gather as much light as possible as the sun plunged oceanward behind them, but it was becoming more and more difficult to deliver viewable pictures. Sheriff's Department detectives rubbed their heads in anger and exhaustion, resigned to restarting the massive search the following day.

But aboard the helicopter Rathbun, suddenly much more animated, wrote out new instructions. After receiving them, the pilot took off, maneuvered several hundred yards deeper into the canyon, and touched down again.

"I think that's the place," Charlie said, pointing to a concrete abutment surrounding a culvert pipe a few hundred feet away.

Investigators rushed to the spot. The sight that greeted them was heartbreaking. It was a makeshift grave, all right. It gave the impression of having been hastily dug and even more hastily filled in. Atop it were several large rocks that seemed to have been deliberately placed. And, most heartbreaking, up through the sandy soil stuck a woman's kneecap.

After a little over a week, Linda Sobek had finally been discovered. Not safe and sound, as her parents and her scores of friends hoped and prayed, but dead and buried in a shallow grave. Her body lay only a few steps from a lightly traveled road, and according to Nichols it was the only road Bice, Saldana, Nichols and Rathbun *hadn't* taken during the night-long search that began the evening Rathbun was arrested.

Chapter 28

EVEN AS he led investigators to the buried body of Linda Sobek, Charlie Rathbun continued to maintain that her death was an accident, the tragic result of losing control of the Lexus sport utility vehicle during a photo shoot. But as dusk turned to darkness on the night of Friday, November 24, the detectives from Sheriff's Homicide and Hermosa Beach PD just weren't buying it.

Sergeant Mike Robinson's gut had told him it wasn't an accident forty-eight hours before, and though he was experienced enough not to let his gut do his policework for him, there were things about Rathbun's story that just didn't seem quite right. Like other investigators on the case, he was willing to wait to see if the forensic examination of Linda Sobek's body supported Rathbun's version of the incident. But had he been a betting man, he would have bet against it. A homicide—that's what the Sobek investigation looked like to him.

There were others who felt the same way.

During the course of that busy day-after-Thanksgiving afternoon, the team that would eventually prosecute Charles Edgar Rathbun was getting itself organized. Several times that day, as television watchers noshed on turkey sandwiches and were sucked into the drama of the airborne search for Linda Sobek, veteran Deputy District Attorney Stephen Kay, the chief counsel in the District Attorney's Office's Torrance branch, called the home of

* * *

The following day, Saturday, November 25, 1995, the body of Linda Sobek was exhumed from its shallow grave. The meticulous process was conducted by Sheriff's Department and Medical Examiner's Office personnel with the help of a forensic archeologist. Laboring under a blue canopy placed overhead to block the view of the ever present news helicopters, the specialists were extremely careful to preserve anything that might later become evidence.

They found Linda clad in the same white unitard bodysuit she had been wearing when Charlie Rathbun had picked her up at the Denny's off Crenshaw little over a week before. There was blood on her face that at first glance seemed have come from an injury to one of her ears, but otherwise her body bore no obvious signs of having been struck by an automobile. In fact, it showed no obvious trauma at all, save one. The skin at her ankles was abraded in a circular pattern around her legs. These ligature marks, as the forensic examiners called them, suggested that something had been tied around her ankles before she died.

After the cursory on-site examination of the body, it was loaded into a waiting van for transport to the downtown Los Angeles office of the County Medical Examiner. There it would be scrutinized by experienced pathologist Dr. James T. Ribe, but the official release of his findings was weeks away.

More immediate was the task of positive identification of the body. Photographs of the dead woman were taken to the Lakewood home of Robert and Elaine Sobek, and there friends of the missing girl assured police that the body they had found was indeed the former Raiderette. Neither of her parents viewed the photos, having been warned by friends not to look.

As headlines heralded the unearthing of Linda Sobek's body on Sunday, November 26, 1995, Charles Edgar

Rathbun was shopping for a criminal lawyer. Facing arraignment on a charge of first degree murder the following day, he needed someone to represent him—and fast. Jim Nichols had offered to stand in for a criminal attorney at the arraignment, but both he and Charlie knew that the serious charge now being leveled against him demanded the services of a specialist in criminal cases.

About midmorning that Sunday, Mark Werksman, an attorney best known for his defense of entertainer Rick James in a much-reported assault trial, got a telephone call at his Manhattan Beach home. At the other end of the line was his father, a prominent Chicago attorney who had retired to Newport Beach, California. The elder Werksman told the younger that Robert Rathbun, yet another attorney, based in suburban Washington, D.C., was urgently seeking criminal representation for his younger brother. Would Mark be interested in talking with him?

The energetic young lawyer was very interested. Putting on a nice shirt and slacks, the California equivalent of a sport coat and dress pants, he drove to the Los Angeles County Jail in downtown LA to have a meeting with Charles Rathbun, who was being held in the medical ward under suicide watch.

The first meeting between attorney and client was guarded because it was conducted by means of telephone handsets and through a pane of glass, something that Rathbun would become used to over the next several months. Werksman, concerned that jail authorities would be listening in, cautioned his potential client against making any admissions. After a cursory review of the facts, they turned to the nitty-gritty business aspect. Werksman, a sole practioner, was concerned about practical matters such as hiring a forensic pathologist, an auto accident reconstructionist and additional experts and investigators.

''I anticipated that this was a case that would turn my schedule and perhaps my life inside out,'' Werksman recalled. ''I didn't know at the time if it would be a death penalty case; I didn't know at the time if this would be one of ten murders he'd be charged with.''

Werksman did some quick mental calculations about what he estimated the case would involve in terms of his time, plus additional investigators and experts. He wasn't just toting up his ultimate payday; he was trying to decide if the Rathbun family had the financial resources to do what needed to be done.

''You get a sense of how much time you're going to put into a case, how much your hourly rate ought to be, you think about how many hundreds of hours you're going to spend, what other commitments you're going to have to miss,'' he said, ''and then, on the other hand, you look at the benefits, the publicity windfall of being on the news every night, and you weigh that in.''

Charlie was very concerned about the cost of his defense, because he was afraid it meant the financial ruination of his family. At the same time he knew his very life could be at stake.

Werksman, cool, calm and relaxed, obviously wanted the case. He knew there would be no plea bargain in this one, and he was eager to face the challenge of a murder trial against one of the best prosecutors in the business. Before their hour was up Rathbun and Werksman had made a deal—Werksman would be defense counsel.

So by the time the weekend had come to a close, the battle lines had been drawn. The prosecution would go into court with a two-person team that would include one of the most experienced and successful prosecutors on the West Coast and a young but promising associate. The defense would counter with a smart, articulate former federal prosecutor who had been a defense attorney for six years, and in those six years he had never tried a murder case.

Chapter 29

ON THE morning of Monday, November 27, 1995—
the morning of Charles Edgar Rathbun's arraignment for the first degree murder of Linda Sobek—Sheriff's
Department investigators were feeling very fortunate indeed. What's more, the source of their good fortune was
very unexpected—none other than the suspect himself,
Charles Edgar Rathbun.

A decision Charlie had made more than a week before
was coming back to haunt him, namely, the site he had
selected for Linda Sobek's burial place. According to Dr.
James Ribe, the pathologist who examined Sobek's body,
Rathbun couldn't have chosen a better spot. Because of
the combination of climate, time of year and location, the
body that emerged from the shallow grave in the Angeles
National Forest was remarkably well preserved. In fact, it
resembled what investigators describe as a fresh kill rather
than a body that had moldered in the grave for more than
a week.

Because of this, the body began to yield a variety of
clues, clues that quickly convinced the investigators on
the case that the death of Linda Sobek had been no auto
accident. The ligature marks on her ankles were the first
suggestion of that, but before Ribe's autopsy was concluded, there would be several others.

Though Ribe cautioned detectives that he couldn't be
firm in his findings at that early date, he told them he

suspected the cause of death was asphyxiation by manual and compression strangulation. In more familiar terms, a hand around her neck had closed off her windpipe, causing her to suffocate. Not typical of an auto accident, that much was sure.

The previous Saturday night, soon after Linda Sobek's body had been transferred to the cold storage of the coroner's office, Sheriff's Department investigators, led by Sergeant John Yarbrough, conducted a second search of Rathbun's residence on Canyon Drive and seized additional evidence. Among the items confiscated were Charlie's computer, his camera, a wide variety of photographs and negatives and a cloth carrying-bag bearing the logo MacUser, filled with a variety of items including stripping tape and a tequila bottle. Those, plus the autopsy findings, would begin to point to a scenario far different from the story Charlie had told police when he was arrested.

When Sergeants Mike Robinson and Mike Bumcrot were put in charge of the Sheriff's Department task force on the case that Monday morning, they inherited more than three hundred clues from Hermosa Beach Police Department. Over the next two months an additional two hundred clues would come in. The task force immediately tapped into the Federal Bureau of Investigation's VICAP program, which provided them with information on similar crimes from around the nation. Within days, as publicity on the case increased across the country, scores of people provided the Sheriff's Department with information and background on Charles Rathbun. And the information some of them provided was intriguing, if not downright shocking. When it came to women, Charlie Rathbun obviously had a past.

One of the women in his past was Pam Downs (not her real name), a Colorado-based writer well known in rock-climbing circles. In July, 1995, she had met Charlie Rathbun on a photo shoot organized by Dan Sanchez of McMullen and Yee Publishing.

Flying into Ontario Airport from her home, the attractive, five-foot four-inch Downs was met at the airport by Sanchez, who she knew casually, and Rathbun, who she didn't know at all. Sanchez explained briefly that Rathbun had been enlisted as the photographer for the project. The threesome left by car for Joshua Tree National Park, a rock-climbing mecca in the California desert east of Los Angeles.

Though not a model per se, Downs had been pictured in some previous articles on rock climbing, and Sanchez wanted to use her attractive visage to enhance the photography in the upcoming magazine layout that would result from the trip. Rathbun turned out to be not only taken with that idea but also taken with Downs personally. During the shoot he encouraged his amateur model with compliments that would have made many men blush, and by midafternoon he had persuaded her to climb for the camera in shorts and a brief top.

"You're so attractive," Charlie told her. "I didn't expect this from a rock climber."

When the shoot was over, Sanchez and Rathbun took Downs out to dinner, and Charlie continued to lay on the charm. Compliments about her rolled off his tongue, but although she maintained a polite facade, she expressed no interest in him beyond a professional level. To Downs, one notable thing about Rathbun was that he didn't drink any alcohol that evening, because in her limited experience, photographers always seemed to enjoy a celebratory post-shoot drink. Something else she found both notable and amazing was his suggestion that she join her two male companions for a night in the desert.

"You know," Charlie said, "we're thinking of doing a dawn shoot. Why don't you spend the night with us out there? We'll do the shoot, and then we'll get you to the airport."

"No way," Downs said, trying to laugh the proposition off as if it had been a joke. "There's no way I'm going to spend the night out there in the desert with you guys."

Downs flew back to Colorado, never expecting to see or hear from Charlie Rathbun again. Instead she became the subject of a barrage of calls from the Hollywood-based photographer.

"I'd really like to work with you," he said. "I think you're terrific."

Downs tried to deflect his attentions, saying she was a writer, not a model, but Rathbun was insistent.

"I'll fly you into LA; I'll meet you in Colorado," he told her. "You just name it."

Though Downs declined to meet Rathbun anywhere, the calls kept coming. At first they were just an annoyance, but then they became much more, especially when Downs began to travel around the country only to be confronted by another telephone call from Charlie Rathbun.

When she was in California, she was in the habit of working out of an office in Redlands, and one afternoon as she sat at her computer, the phone rang and it was Charlie. An involuntary shudder ran through her body.

A couple of weeks later she was in Oregon visiting her parents. The phone rang and again it was Rathbun.

"How does he know where I am?" she asked herself, very troubled.

While attempting to remain polite and professional, she tried to give him the impression that she wasn't interested in a romantic relationship, but the impression didn't take. Soon thereafter Rathbun was informed that he'd be doing a photo shoot in Telluride, Colorado, and he immediately called Downs to try to arrange a meeting.

"I'll meet you any place you want," he said.

"I don't think so," she replied.

"Oh, you're probably like all these other women," he said, the hurt apparent in his voice, "you probably just don't care about me."

At that point Downs thought the calls might stop, but they continued until November 15, 1995, the day before Charlie picked up Linda Sobek for their tragic trip to El Mirage. That Wednesday Downs, who was in California on business, agreed to have dinner with Charlie the next evening. She was reluctant to do it, but she figured that it was smart to keep the professional relationship open, and she thought she might be able to get across to Rathbun that she was interested in nothing more.

But later that day Charlie called her back.

"You know, I think maybe we better not do dinner tomorrow night," he said. "I've got an early shoot the next day, and it's in Santa Barbara."

"Oh, all right," she replied, somewhat relieved.

"Hey, I've got an idea," he continued. "Do you want to go with me?"

Downs politely declined the invitation.

She wouldn't hear from Rathbun again until the following Monday morning.

"Gee, I'm really sorry we didn't get together," he told her. "I wanted to call you back so you didn't think I blew you off. You know, maybe we can get together one of these days."

By then Linda Sobek was dead and lying in a pebbly grave in the Angeles National Forest.

Chapter 30

IF PAM DOWNS's experience had been an isolated incident, the police would have been tempted to ignore it, despite the fact that the woman who testified to it was credible and certainly not seeking publicity. But as the Sheriff's Department task force kept moving forward, they were contacted by other women who had experienced similar occurrences.

One was Jessie Hutton (not her real name), a bartender at the Hyatt on Sunset, a woman who photo-assisted and sometimes modeled for Charlie. She had met him some months before the incident occured, and she had spent some time with him on a photo shoot near Palm Springs prior to his employment at Petersen Publishing Company.

When Charlie got a job at Petersen, he realized that she lived right across the street from the Petersen office building at 8490 Sunset Boulevard. Ready to rekindle an old acquaintanceship, he contacted her, and they got together occasionally. Because of her close proximity to Petersen, he also often asked her to come to the photo studio to act as a stand-in while he set the lights for a shoot. Sometimes this would be done late at night so that the setting would be ready when the model arrived for the photography session the following day.

Because she was there simply to help Charlie arrange the correct lighting, Hutton usually wore casual clothes to the sessions. She'd stand in place. Charlie would swing some lights into position, take a few Polaroids as a check and that would be that. But on the night in question, in preparation for a *Hot Rod* or *Car Craft* shoot, Charlie asked Hutton to put on a tight black dress before meeting him in the basement studio.

Once in the studio Charlie directed Hutton to stand in front of the obligatory car and began directing her as if it were a real photo session instead of a lighting test. He'd never done that before, and because she had some modeling aspirations, she got into the spirit of it and began to pose. After a few minutes of playful posing, Charlie offered her some Scotch. By then it was past one in the morning, and Hutton figured there was little harm in a short one, so she had the drink and resumed posing.

After a few more minutes Charlie said, "Hey, why don't you come over here and look at these Polaroids?"

She walked over to Charlie and took the photos from his hand, and while she was looking at them, he came up behind her and kissed her on the neck.

"What are you doing?" she demanded, swinging around violently. Enraged, she bit him on the cheek so hard that blood began flowing down his face.

He grabbed her, they struggled for a few moments and he fell on top of her. Before she could drag herself to her feet, Rathbun's hands were up her dress, trying to pull her panties off.

"What do you think you're doing?" she screamed.

"I thought I was going to fuck," Charlie shot back, annoyed by her resistance.

"No, Charlie, no, you don't want to do this!" she screamed.

He continued to grab for her panties as she flailed her legs wildly.

"No, Charlie, please! We can't! I just had surgery!"

"What?" he shouted.

"I just had surgery! Female surgery!"

His ardor cooled a bit. She managed to get free of his grasp and ran out of the photo studio.

Rathbun's version of the incident was significantly different. According to his account, Hutton had been playing with him, showing him—in his words—her tits and saying, "I'm not sure if I can model; do you think they're big enough?" Charlie says that after the teasing, he was running his hand up her thigh when she went wild and bit him on the cheek. He admits falling on the floor with her, but denies trying to rip off her underwear.

Hutton went to the West Hollywood Sheriff's Station to make out a sexual assault complaint against Rathbun, but when Charlie was questioned about the incident, he told police that he and Hutton had had a prior relationship. The complaint went to the District Attorney's office, but it was never filed because of the difficulty in proving a he said/she said case with no witnesses to the satisfaction of a jury.

One of Rathbun's former roommates in the house on Canyon Drive also had a bizarre story to tell Sheriff's Department investigators.

Polly Kirk (not her real name) was just nineteen years old when a woman who was then living in the house invited her to move in. Kirk had done some modeling for the woman in Phoenix, and she jumped at the chance to come to Hollywood, where she hoped to find additional modeling work.

Kirk took a room in the house, proceeded to look for a job and had begun to settle into her new environment when the woman who had invited her decided to move out abruptly. This left Kirk, naïve and completely sexually inexperienced, alone in the house with Charles Rathbun, but since he had always been such a gentleman, she didn't think anything about it.

Several weeks had passed without incident when Polly sat down on the floor of the living room one night, sighing with fatigue.

"You look tired," Charlie said.

"I am tired," she answered.

He moved to the couch behind her and started rubbing her back.

"Ooh, that feels good," she moaned.

"I'm glad."

He rubbed her back for several more minutes, and she continued to coo in pleasure, but then his hands began to roam. She straightened up immediately.

"Now, Charlie," she said. "Please don't do that. Let's just stay roommates, okay?"

"All right," he said, trying to hide the hurt. "All right. No problem."

And he got up and walked into his room.

Several weeks later, when nothing more had been said about the episode and Charlie's behavior had been exemplary, he announced, "I'm going to Palm Springs for a photo shoot this weekend. You're going to have the house to yourself."

"Okay, Charlie. Have a good time," she said, seeing him out the door.

That night, alone for the first time in the big 1920-era home, she stayed up late watching television. Trying to keep from scaring herself, she had locked up the place meticulously, making sure every bolt was thrown, every security bar in place, before she went to bed.

At about two in the morning she awoke in her bed in the loft of the house with a large man on top of her. He was wearing a hooded sweatshirt that made it hard for her to see his face, particularly in the darkness of the confined room, which terrified her.

"Do what I tell you and I won't hurt you," the black-hooded man commanded.

"Okay, okay," she replied nervously.

"Hold your hands behind your back!"

When she did so, her attacker wound tape tightly around her wrists. After subduing her, he tried to enter her vaginally, but because she was a virgin, he was unable to, so he proceeded to sodomize her. Then he turned her over, sat on her chest and forced her to orally gratify him until he ejaculated.

Finished with her, the hooded man vanished as quickly as he had entered. The police were called, and Polly spent the rest of the night in a nearby hospital. When the house was checked for missing items, the only thing that had been stolen was the rent money Polly had paid to Charlie before his departure.

It didn't surprise her, because from the moment the man was on top of her, she was sure it was her roommate. She was sure because the man bore the odor of Charlie Rathbun.

"He's got a distinct smell," she told investigators. "He smells like this house, like mildew and must."

When she had heard the man's voice, it only confirmed her suspicion. After spending some time recuperating at her parents' home in Arizona, she returned to the house to move her stuff out. Seeing her there, her roommate tried to commiserate with her.

"God, I heard about what happened," Charlie told her. "I'm so sorry."

Despite feeling certain that Rathbun was her attacker, Kirk refused to press charges. The semen of her attacker was never processed or filed, so there is no way to determine if her suspicion was correct.

Rathbun claims an alibi for the night when Polly Kirk was raped. He said that on the night in question he left home for a photo shoot and spent the night in Banning, which he said is east of Palm Springs. (Actually Banning is about twenty miles west of the famed winter resort.) Kirk claimed she was raped between 2 and 3 A.M. He asserted he was in Banning at the time and that a security camera in a local convenience store could prove he was there at 4 A.M., because, he said, "I went out to get some things."

Charlie additionally claimed the police, not Polly, first suggested that he might be the perpetrator, and added that when the police asked Kirk if they should question him, she said no. Charlie believes "she knows more than what she's saying about the incident," and he claims to suspect she knew her attacker.

Polly Kirk was not the only model to run afoul of Charlie Rathbun in the loft of the house on Canyon Drive, at least according to the testimony of others. Another model, Willa Sandaval (not her real name) told Sheriff's Department investigators that she was sleeping on the futon in the loft one night when she awoke to find Charlie on top of her, rubbing her back.

That was unnerving enough, but when she tried to move her arms and legs, she found she was in tied in four-point restraints, spread-eagled on the futon. According to her statement to police, the restraints were attached to eyebolts in the floor.

Sergeant Mike Robinson personally investigated her story, examining the floor of the Canyon Drive house for bolt holes and finding no evidence of them. But, he said, he didn't raise the carpet, and he theorizes that the restraints could have been attached to a piece of plywood under the futon.

Like Kirk, Sandaval said she could identify Charlie by his smell.

"If you put me in a room with ten guys and he's one of them," she told Sheriff's Department investigators, "I can pick him out by his smell."

Yet another woman, Cheryl Ortmann (not her real name) told police she had been advertising for modeling jobs in the *Recycler*, a local ad paper, when she got a call from Charles Rathbun. After speaking with him on the phone, she invited him to her house to talk about possible modeling assignments.

When he arrived at her door, he was wearing a sport coat and Levis, looked professional, acted professional, and she asked if he wanted to come inside. As the owner of a huge, well-trained Doberman pinscher, she felt safe despite the fact that she was the only one at home.

The two talked for a few minutes about possible gigs, and then Charlie asked Ortmann if she'd mind taking her dog into another room, because, he said, it was beginning to bother him. Since the Doberman often had an intimidating effect on people, she agreed and escorted the dog into the kitchen.

When she returned, the pair talked for a few more minutes, then Rathbun said, "You know, what I'd really like to do is see you in a tight dress with a choker chain around your neck."

With that, he jumped up off the sofa and wrapped his hands around Ortmann's windpipe. Sensing its mistress to be in danger, the dog started barking wildly in the next room, and Ortmann was able to gasp, "He can get out of there!"

Hearing that, Rathbun backed off.

Ortmann never reported the incident, fearful that it might injure her chances of succeeding in the modeling business.

Rathbun has offered explanations for both the Sandaval and Ortmann incidents. He claimed he had an ongoing relationship with Sandaval that went sour, although they remained off-and-on sexual partners. He said he believed her sexual assault story was designed to mollify her new boyfriend. As to Ortmann, he claimed he wasn't even in California at the time she said the incident happened and added that in those days he wore his hair much longer and sported a full beard.

The most damning story told to Sheriff's Department investigators about Charlie Rathbun dated all the way back to a rainy night in June, 1979. That night, Charlie, then 21, noticed his car had a flat tire and asked one of his coworkers, an attractive young married woman named Erica Ellis (not her real name) for a lift home. It was getting late. The Kroger's grocery store in which they worked was about to close, but she said okay. They walked out into the parking lot and got into her car. At first there was very little conversation, but as they drove along, Charlie finally spoke up.

"I really appreciate the ride," he said. "If it weren't for you, I don't know what I would've done."

"Oh, no problem."

"You know I live alone, so I don't know who I could've called to pick me up."

"Don't worry about it. It's just a few minutes out of my way."

"It's awfully nice of you. I hope there's something I can do for you sometime."

"Maybe," she said smiling.

"Did you know I'm into photography?" Charlie asked her, returning the smile.

"No, I didn't, but that's funny."

"What's funny?"

"Oh, my brother's about to get married, and they've been looking for a photographer."

"No kidding? I'd be glad to show you some of my work. I mean, if you've got a minute."

They pulled up in front of his dingy apartment building, and she looked at her watch. It was a little after midnight.

"It'll only take a minute," he coaxed.

"Well, okay," she said.

Inside his tiny apartment, the shy, retiring young man she had been with in the car changed his demeanor dramatically. After showing her some of his more prosaic work, he pulled out what she described as pornographic photos. As she looked at them in embarrassment, he came up behind her, started groping her and forced her to the floor. He proceeded to rip off all her clothing and raped her, saying, "If you'll let me do what I want, I'll let you go."

After the attack Ellis ran from Rathbun to a nearby apartment with her pants pulled on inside out. There the police were summoned, and she gave a statement in which she said Rathbun admitted he was "sick" and wanted to be punished.

Charlie Rathbun's version of the night's events, as recounted during the subsequent investigation and trial, was far different. He said he was friendly with Ellis, who was married and often complained to him that her husband was getting seriously into drugs. That night Ellis, who had borne a child by her husband and another child as a teen-ager, went up to his apartment and voluntarily had sex with the aspiring photographer. Unfortunately, he said, he had ejaculated in her when he wasn't supposed to, and because he had a bachelor's apartment, there was nothing for her to douche with. This angered her, and when she noticed it was getting late, she cried rape to explain her lateness to her husband.

"I had to laugh at her," he said. "She was in such a hurry to leave, she put her pants on inside out."

Rathbun also claims that after he was accused in the Linda Sobek case, Ellis told an interviewer that during the 1979 incident he penetrated her anally and a knife or knives was involved. Since neither aspect was in her testimony at trial, he suggested her credibility was zero. The Los Angeles County Sheriff's investigator who was sent to Ohio to interview her, however, found her very credible.

"She remembered the incident just like it was yesterday," Robinson said. "When she started to talk about it, she broke down crying."

During the trial Ellis pulled from a paper bag a pair of jeans that were ripped from one side of the crotch to the other, the jeans she said she was wearing the night of the alleged rape. But during the proceedings it was revealed that the police had never made a notation about her clothing being ripped, nor did they put any of her clothing into evidence. When the verdict came down from Ohio Judge Paul P. Martin in February, 1980, it was Not Guilty.

*   *   *

Though the vast majority of Rathbun's alleged harassments and assaults targeted women, an undercurrent of bisexual pursuit also circulated about the photographer. Not only had he once reportedly hit on a rumored bisexual, who was a Petersen veteran, but he also allegedly attacked a male member of the photo staff in a way the staff member interpreted as sexual.

"I was painting a reflector," that staffer remembered, "and I was wearing a spun-paper smock. I'm painting away, and he [Charlie] got behind me and rushed me. He grabbed the smock and ripped it from my tail to my neck. I was embarrassed. I was attacked by him, and I didn't do anything about it. I had a real rush of emotion."

The attack wasn't violent, the photo department staff member said. "It was weirdly playful."

At Petersen Publishing, Charlie's uncurbed desire to talk about sex and the way he conducted himself made him the center of uproar. He seemed to go out of his way to be argumentative, to pick fights and to get involved in controversy. At the same time he also seemed to go out of his way to win over new acquaintances and to help out his friends. It became clear to Sheriff's Department profiler Sergeant John Yarbrough that Charlie liked attention, and once he got attention, he liked to keep it. That's why he would rain flowers and phone calls on new lady friends and inveterately pick up dinner tabs and lunches for male buddies.

Women courted by him often complained that his attentions were obsessive. Unlike most men, who learn over the years to get it when women are uninterested in them, Charlie never seemed to possess that sixth sense. He would pursue long after the pursuee had had enough.

One technique that proved effective for Charlie in his pursuit of feminine charms was a combination of photography and alcohol. The idea of getting a few drinks into a woman to "loosen her up" certainly didn't originate with Charlie Rathbun. When he mixed the inhibition-depressant that is alcohol with the excitement of performing before a camera, he often found the combination resulted in sexual conquest.

As one of his fellow photographers had said, "A lot of women will fuck you for a photo shoot." Have camera, will travel.

In Charlie's case, he also found that alcohol and a camera sometimes resulted in a charge of sexual assault, as with Jessie Hutton. But unlike Hutton, the women on whom the combination had proven effective without violence were not likely to come forward to the police. Though they might have regretted their actions later, they got what they bargained for.

They say one definition of sexual harassment is an *unwanted* sexual advance. Obviously what is unwanted lies in the eyes of the beholder.

So as the murder case against Charles Edgar Rathbun wound toward its next landmark, the preliminary hearing, the Sheriff's Department task force had gathered a great deal of anecdotal evidence about their suspect. In contrast to the stories of sexual abuse, a few stalwart friends of Rathbun had come forward to tell police that he was an affable companion who seemed extremely generous and who possessed a sly sense of humor. They couldn't imagine that a guy like Charlie could ever be responsible for anything as heinous as murder. He seemed so mild, so quiet.

At the same time several women claimed Rathbun had sexually abused them, and those reports covered a period of more than fifteen years. Despite the allegations, however, the record showed that only one incident resulted in Rathbun's arrest, and that incident had ended in a Not Guilty verdict.

Investigators knew it would be an uphill fight to get any of the sexual abuse and date rape stories in front of the jury. Most judges, they knew, would immediately disallow them as unfairly prejudicial. But in their minds the allegations did demonstrate a pattern. The Sheriff's Department task force came to believe that the Sobek case wasn't an isolated accident. It was the culmination of an overall pattern of behavior.

Now, of course, they had to prove it.

Chapter 31

WHEN CHARLIE Rathbun was arrested as a suspect in the murder of Linda Sobek on Wednesday, November 22, 1995, speculation that he was a serial killer had already begun. Less than two weeks later, on November 30, Los Angeles County Sheriff Sherman Block fueled that speculation by announcing his opinion on the subject at a press conference.

In a blustering performance, the longtime sheriff postulated that Rathbun might not only be the killer of Linda Sobek but also might be connected to the deaths of Kimberley Pandelios and several other women whose murders remained mysteries. He singled out two Ohio cases: the unsolved murders of Stephanie Hummer, an eighteen-year-old Ohio State University student, and Stacy Fairchild, a seventeen-year-old retail worker. He also hinted that Rathbun might be a suspect in the 1990 sexual assault and murder of airline flight attendant Nancy Jean Ludwig at a Romulus, Michigan, motel and in the disappearance of Rose Marie Larner, an aspiring model who resided in Lansing, Michigan.

Though Rathbun was quickly cleared in the Ludwig case, news media speculation soon grew about Rathbun's possible involvement in other unsolved crimes. Included among them were the disappearances of Christine O'Brien and Paige Marie Rentkowski, both of Livingston County, Michigan, and the murder of Kym Morgan, a twenty-four-year-old photography student whose body was found in California's Los Padres National Forest, near Santa Barbara.

As defense attorney Mark Werksman said, "Police started to come out of the woodwork, trying to solve their unsolved crimes at Charlie's expense."

Though the serial killer speculation in the press was vexing enough for the defense team, Rathbun and Werksman had something else to worry about: the autopsy results. When a sketchy overview of the autopsy findings was released to the press in mid-December, 1995, there were a number of startling revelations. The most startling was that in the opinion of pathologist Dr. James Ribe, Linda Sobek had been sexually assaulted. Also stunning was the fact that Sobek had a 0.13 blood alcohol level, almost twice the level required to prove drunkenness in the state of California.

Earlier the coroner's office had announced that Sobek's injuries were inconsistent with an automobile accident. There were no abrasions, contusions or broken bones that seemed to have been caused by being struck by a careening vehicle. Now the medical examiner's office expanded upon that opinion, confirming that Sobek did not die as the result of auto accident injuries but by asphyxiation caused by neck and body compression.

According to the office's spokesperson, C. Scott Carrier, the asphyxiation was consistent with someone sitting on the victim's chest and strangling her and with a heavy person or object sitting or lying on the victim. The coroner's office would not give further details of the alleged sexual assault other than to say it occurred before Sobek's death and it appeared to be non-consensual.

Privy to the very detailed final report, detectives learned that the alleged sexual assault would have involved the insertion of some sort of foreign object into Sobek's anus. The report of an anal attack caused the task force to take a second look at an informant's tip regarding a Christmas card Rathbun had sent to a few select friends a year or two prior to the Sobek incident. The card's attached photo depicted a shapely female's bottom with a candy cane slipped in the crack of the butt cheeks. The greeting read, "Merry Christmas."

It was not clear how strongly Charlie gravitated toward anal sex. He would later explain that his first taste of anal sex came in Ireland. Traveling in the company of two Australian men, Charlie met a trio of saucy Irish girls who were looking for a good time. After the requisite drinks, talk and horseplay, the women seemed ready for more intimate conduct. But when the time came, Charlie discovered to his dismay that birth control was completely outlawed in solidly Catholic Ireland. With no condoms available to stave off an unwanted pregnancy, it looked as if the evening might come to a frustratingly rapid close when Charlie's companion suggested that Charlie "do her in the ass." According to Rathbun's later recollection, he neither particularly liked it nor particularly hated it. To him it was "just okay."

As a result of the sexual assault finding in the Sobek autopsy, on January 5, 1996, Rathbun was charged with sodomy with an unknown object in addition to the first degree murder charge he already faced. Via the discovery rules, which require the prosecution to provide the defense with virtually all the information about its case in chief, the defense quickly learned the details of the autopsy report and of the police work that came in its wake.

The new charge of sodomy had serious ramifications for the defense. It meant that Rathbun's case now qualified for the special circumstances section of the penal code. (In California, special circumstances is a term that applies to particularly heinous crimes, and it carries with it harsher punishments.) In Charlie's case the application of special circumstances meant that he might well face the death penalty when he stood trial.

*   *   *

With that trial still some months away, the news reports on the sodomy charge, the autopsy findings and the speculation over whether Rathbun was the next Ted Bundy had the defense reeling. But the resourceful Werksman had some arrows in his quiver as well.

The first shaft was launched on St. Valentine's Day, when he released a copy of his thirty-seven-page motion asking that all the evidence the police had gathered from the time Charles Rathbun had been arrested until after the search for Sobek's body had concluded be suppressed.

According to the motion, which was eventually filed on February 26, 1997, "From the moment the police began interrogating Charles E. Rathbun until after he led them to Linda Sobek's corpse, the entire course of the dealings between the police and the defendant was compromised by a blatant, sustained and systematic disregard for Mr. Rathbun's Fifth Amendment right not to incriminate himself."

In essence, Werksman's motion asserted that Deputy Mary Bice, Hermosa Beach PD Officer Raul Saldana and a variety of other law enforcement personnel had ignored Rathbun's right to avoid self-incrimination by continuing to ask him questions after he had requested legal counsel during the first interrogation, which took place soon after he was arrested at his home, and in subsequent interrogations. At no time did Bice or Saldana Mirandize Rathbun, that is, they failed to inform him: "You have the right to remain silent; anything you say can and will be used against you in a court of law; you have a right to an attorney; if you cannot afford an attorney one will be provided to you at no cost."

It was a startling omission, since nearly anyone who has watched detective shows on television can recite the Miranda rights litany almost by heart. School kids playing cops and robbers frequently spout it to one another. Yet on the night Rathbun was arrested, not one member of law enforcement thought to read the suspect his Fifth Amendment rights.

Equally inflammatory was the charge that Rathbun repeatedly asked for the advice of an attorney—at least a dozen times in the initial interview with Bice and Saldana—yet questioning continued and no counsel was provided. This, too, was an obvious violation of the Miranda code. According to the rules mandated by the federal courts, when a suspect being questioned requests counsel, all questioning must cease until the suspect is provided with an attorney.

Werksman's motion created a tidal wave of publicity.

"Miranda Rights Issue Imperils Key Sobek Evidence" ran the headline on the February 19, 1996, issue of the *Los Angeles Times*.

"I got calls from all over the country, saying, 'I'm sorry your case is going in the toilet,' " recalled Sergeant Mike Robinson of the Sheriff's Department task force.

The press speculated that the prosecution would defend the actions of the police officers on what is known as the public safety exception to the Miranda rules. The public safety doctrine holds that Miranda can be ignored when there is an urgent need for information that can aid in the protection or rescue of the victim of a crime. Legal experts suggested that the prosecution would argue that the police believed Linda Sobek might not be dead, and so could be excused for foregoing the niceties of Rathbun's constitutional rights in the interest of finding her still alive.

When the case came before Municipal Court Judge Benjamin Aranda on February 27 for the preliminary hearing, that is exactly what Deputy District Attorney Stephen Kay did argue, but there wasn't much steam in his argument. At the same time Werksman fought vociferously for all of Rathbun's statements and all the evidence that came as the result of his statements—including the evidence yielded by Linda Sobek's dead body—to be stricken from the case.

Aranda returned with what might be viewed as a compromise decision, but a compromise based firmly on the law. He noted that those questioning Rathbun offered no evidence that they had any reason to believe that Sobek was still alive during the interrogation. After all, the judge continued, she had been missing for more than a week. With those facts in mind, he ruled that the public safety exclusion to Miranda did not apply, and therefore he made inadmissible all the statements Rathbun had uttered during his various interrogations beginning at his arrest and continuing to the helicopter search for the missing model's body.

But in a decision that was to become absolutely crucial to the prosecution's case, Aranda further ruled that the helicopter search for Linda Sobek's body had been done within Miranda, since Jim Nichols, Rathbun's attorney of record at the time, had been allowed to meet privately with his client before the search and then accompanied him in the helicopter. The ruling meant that the body of Linda Sobek and the important evidence drawn from it could be presented at trial.

Some observers of the proceedings proclaimed a victory for the defense, because virtually all of Rathbun's statements to police over the course of the days immediately after his apprehension were thrown out of the case. But because Rathbun hadn't confessed to the crime for which he was charged—or for that matter any crime other than vehicular manslaughter—during those rambling hours of interrogation, the prosecution wasn't too upset about Judge Aranda's ruling. It was their contention that Rathbun's statements to the police in those early hours after his arrest weren't truthful anyway, but instead meant to cover his tracks.

In addition, the searches at Rathbun's Hollywood home had yielded the computer-written sorry letters that echoed essentially what Rathbun had said in the disallowed interrogations, namely, the death of Linda Sobek occurred in an auto accident and he was sorry it had happened. Since those sorry letters had been obtained in a legal search, the prosecution figured Werksman's motion had created a great deal of smoke but no fire.

Chapter 32

IF WERKSMAN'S salvo on the Miranda issue had more form than substance, the next volley he would fire off in defense of his client would have farther-reaching effects. In fact, the issue he raised would go on to become a pivotal factor in the trial. It all revolved around evidence that had come into his hands in a most unorthodox way.

On February 26 and 27, 1996, three months and a day from the date he had been arraigned on a count of first degree murder, Charles Edgar Rathbun stood before Judge Benjamin Aranda for the preliminary hearing on the case. In the courtroom that day, in addition to a crush of media and court-watchers, were Charlie's brother, Robert Rathbun, and his brother's girlfriend, Elizabeth "Betsy" Chapman.

Robert had been instrumental in finding legal counsel for his brother and wanted to see the proceedings for himself, despite the fact that the testimony he was likely to hear would be ugly. During the couple's few days in California, they stayed at Charlie's Hollywood home and commuted back and forth to the courtroom.

On Wednesday, February 28, 1996, the day after Charlie Rathbun was bound over for trial for the murder of Linda Sobek, his brother decided to visit him in the overcrowded high-rise that is the Los Angeles County Jail. Charlie was being held in isolation there in the same orange-barred cell that had housed Lyle Menendez.

Robert Rathbun was accompanied by Donna Tryfman, Werksman's legal assistant. Tryfman was in the habit of visiting Charlie at least once a week, and since Werksman had filed papers identifying Robert Rathbun as part of the defense team, she expected he would have no difficulty in getting a visit with his brother in the attorney's room, an advantageous place since conversations there are not monitored by jail authorities.

She was wrong. In the dingy, paper-strewn visitors area, Sheriff's Department guards informed Robert that they would not allow him to visit his brother in the attorney's room. With Robert cooling his heels in the waiting area, Tryfman made her visit alone, spent nearly an hour with Charlie and emerged with a piece of paper Charlie had given her to take to Robert. On the paper were a note and a hand-drawn map.

Robert appeared to know what the note was about and carefully pocketed it. He explained that he and Charlie had talked about it on the telephone previously, and Tryfman thought so little about it that she never mentioned it to her boss. A day or so later, both Robert Rathbun and Betsy Chapman packed up their suitcases and headed back to their home in Springfield, Virginia.

For Werksman the excitement triggered by Robert's visit began on the night of Sunday, March 14. That evening he received a frantic call from his client's brother.

"I have some evidence that I think might be very important!" Robert gushed.

"What is it? What is it?" Werksman asked.

"I have some photographs, some pictures of Linda Sobek that Charlie took."

"Photos Charlie took?"

"Yeah, I've got five rolls of film. Four rolls show her posing in clothes out on the dry lake, and the fifth roll—well, the fifth roll is hard to see because it's been damaged, but I think it shows her masturbating in the car."

"Masturbating?"

"Yeah, touching herself."

"My God, where did you get them?"

Robert Rathbun proceeded to tell the defense attorney that Charlie had spoken to him about several rolls of film had taken of Linda Sobek on the day she died. In that conversation Charlie had said that in his panic and remorse the morning after the model's death, he had taken the rolls of film and thrown them away in the Poppy Preserve, a protected wilderness area off Avenue I west of Lancaster, California. Looking back on the incident later, he had realized they might be valuable to his defense. In his jail cell Charlie had drawn a map of the area, which he passed to his brother through Donna Tryfman.

Robert explained to Werksman that on March 1, 1996, he, along with Betsy Chapman, drove to the place Charlie had indicated on the map, and the couple discovered five film canisters. They had no way to know if they were the same canisters Charlie had mentioned, but packing them carefully in their luggage, they returned home with the undeveloped film. More than a week later Robert developed the color film in his in-home darkroom.

"I can't see them too well because they're slides," Robert continued. "But it looks to me like Linda Sobek."

"Jesus, Robert."

"Do you think they're important?"

"Yes, I do. If these pictures actually show what you think they show, they could be very material to the defense. They could provide exculpatory evidence. This could show consent to have sex, and, you know, this is a special circumstances case."

"What should I do with them?" Rathbun asked.

"Why don't you do this? Why don't you package them up very carefully and send them to me via overnight mail? That way I can have a look at them, and we'll see what we've got."

The developed film arrived in Werksman's downtown Los Angeles office the following Tuesday morning. With Glenn LaPalme, a retired U.S. postal inspector who frequently served as an investigator for the defense attorney,

Werksman opened the package and eyeballed its contents. Excitement if not euphoria began to fill the room.

Four of the rolls depicted Linda Sobek posing under a hard blue desert sky. There was no doubt that the photos had been taken on El Mirage dry lake the day Sobek died. The other photos were harder to read but even more intriguing. Werksman and LaPalme, viewing them through a magnifying glass, could make out the image of a woman touching herself provocatively, but they were double exposures, and it was difficult to sort out detail. Since the woman's head was not shown in any of the photos, it was impossible to identify them positively as photos of Sobek.

"It looked like Linda Sobek naked, masturbating to me," Werksman recalled. "There was no face, but it looked liked she was in a Lexus."

He noticed that the logo on the steering wheel of the vehicle over which the images of the woman had been superimposed didn't seem like the Lexus logo, but he attributed that to the fact that it was a prototype vehicle.

After viewing the film, Werksman was convinced he was onto something. If he could prove that sex between Charlie Rathbun and Linda Sobek had taken place with her consent, he could negate the rape charge. That would knock out the special circumstances stipulation, which called for a mandatory sentence of life without parole if Charlie was convicted. A great deal was riding on the photos.

The defense attorney discussed the newfound evidence with several of his colleagues and also with his client. Charlie told him that he had taken all of the photos on the afternoon of Sobek's death. He said the double-exposed roll resulted from his excitement when he saw the beautiful model touching herself. In his rush to take some photographs, he inadvertently inserted a partially used roll that already contained shots of the Lexus LX 450's interior.

To Werksman it all sounded almost too good to be true, and he wanted to be extremely careful with the precious evidence. At first he contemplated having the photos enlarged into prints by an independent processor away from the prying eyes of the police.

"From a photographer friend of mine I got the name of a couple of labs where I thought I could get prints developed confidentially," he remembered. "I didn't want the media to get it. I didn't want the sheriffs to get it. And I knew the story was heavily publicized, and I knew that Rathbun was a local photographer, so I was afraid anywhere I went, any lab I went to, would recognize it because this was Rathbun."

The young lawyer was also afraid that an independent photo lab might somehow lose what he was beginning to consider the most important evidence in the defense case.

As he put it, "What if, with my luck, the lab loses them, or there's a fire, or they get destroyed or some minimum-wage knucklehead employee at the lab spills chemicals on them, and says, 'Mr. Werksman, I'm really sorry, the four rolls with Linda Sobek dressed came out fine, but you know that roll with the naked woman? We spilled some chemicals on it and it got ruined.' And then what am I going to say?"

Finally, after what he described as forty-eight hours of internal turmoil, he came to the conclusion that processing the photos in a commercial lab was foolhardy.

"I decided I wanted to do this through the court," Werksman recalled, "because I wanted to preserve the integrity of the evidence. I was concerned that the way they had been discovered and the length of time that had gone by made them suspect in terms of authenticity, and I thought the more I fuck around with them the worse it's going to be."

He called Judge Aranda to set an in chambers meeting with Deputy District Attorney Stephen Kay. At the meeting, which was also attended by Sheriff's Department Sergeants Mike Robinson and Mike Bumcrot, he told them he had in his possession exculpatory evidence regarding the rape charge against his client.

"What is it?" Kay asked.

"Photos of Linda Sobek on the day she died," Werksman answered. "Some of them depict her masturbating."

Kay, Robinson and Bumcrot could barely believe their ears.

"Where did they come from?" Kay asked pointedly.

Werksman explained the bizarre chain of possession as the detectives sat shaking their heads. When the defense attorney had finished his story, the five men decided that Robinson would take possession of the film and the Sheriff's Department photo lab would make two sets of prints from the slide positives, one set for the defense and one for the prosecution. Robinson would then return the film to the court. The evidence was sealed and subject to a gag order forbidding release of any information about it.

"I didn't want to exploit it for commercial purposes," Werksman said. "I wasn't going to tell *Hard Copy* about it, because I didn't want to offend the sensitivities of the family."

To say Kay and the Sheriff's Department detectives were skeptical about the evidence is putting it mildly.

As Robinson said, "I would've felt a whole lot better about it if they had called the authorities to document what they found right when they found it."

Though Robert Rathbun was an attorney and his girlfriend, Betsy Chapman, worked for a police agency in Virginia, they hadn't done that. What they had done was drop a hot potato right in the defense attorney's lap.

"I thought I had some very potent evidence," Werksman recalled. "And explosive."

Before the trial was over, the photos would become much more explosive than the defense attorney ever imagined.

Chapter 33

WITH CHARLIE Rathbun's trial scheduled to begin in September, 1996, the case continued to make news throughout the spring. In April the Los Angeles County District Attorney's Office announced that it would not seek the death penalty.

The decision surprised many people, including the Sobek family. During the weeks and months prior to the decision Rathbun had been portrayed in the media as the second coming of Ted Bundy or an upper-middle-class version of Richard Ramirez, the infamous Night Stalker. Now, however, the prosecution seemed to be backing away from that assessment by declining to seek the ultimate penalty.

Werksman was quoted as talking cocky in the April 19, 1996, edition of the *Los Angeles Times*.

His hopes undoubtedly buoyed by the photographic evidence provided by his client's brother, he told reporters, "They cannot prove the special circumstances [allegation of sexual assault] and they know it. They must have some doubts about whether the sex that they think happened occurred by force and without consent."

Deputy District Attorney Stephen Kay weighed in with another opinion. "If I had to guess," he told the *Times*, "I would say the two overriding factors were that Rathbun had no prior convictions and that he demonstrated remorse."

Of course, while he had no prior convictions, there was his 1980 trial for rape in Ohio and there were the various accusations of sexual assault. On the other hand, he had aided the police in the discovery of Linda Sobek's body, an effort which the prosecutors, giving the defendant the benefit of the doubt, construed as showing remorse. Jim Nichols's counsel to Charlie to help police locate the body certainly was a factor in keeping him from facing the death penalty, no matter what difficulties it might have presented to the defense later on.

Unspoken in the press were two other factors that led the District Attorney's Office to decline to seek death in the Sobek case. One, there was a perception that seeking the death penalty makes it more difficult to convict a defendant, and the Los Angeles County District Attorney's Office really needed a win in the election year of 1996. Two, Steve Kay had a strong desire to prosecute the case, and he knew full well he wouldn't get the chance if the state sought the death penalty.

Because of lengthy penalty phases during which the sentence is determined, death penalty cases usually take much longer to complete than those that don't involve the ultimate penalty. Because of that, in Los Angeles County they are routinely "sent downtown" to be prosecuted in the Criminal Courts Building, which has facilities for handling the crush of press. Kay was very aware that it would be impossible for him to prosecute a case downtown and run the Torrance branch of the DA's Office, so he was eager for the case to stay in his own backyard. He also liked his chances with the South Bay area jury pool, which in general is much more likely to convict than the downtown area group.

With all these issues swirling in the background, a District Attorney's Office panel made the final decision that the prosecution would not seek the death penalty against Charlie Rathbun. Instead the photographer faced a maximum sentence of life in prison without parole.

Approximately a month later, the eventual trial judge,

Donald F. Pitts, made three rulings that would have a material effect on the outcome.

Aggressively trying every angle he could think of to keep the pressure on the prosecution, Werksman filed for a change of venue, citing the inflammatory publicity surrounding the case. From his bench in Torrance Superior Court, Pitts summarily turned down that request.

"Despite all the publicity, I didn't really think we had much of a chance there," Werksman said later. "I mean they didn't even grant a change of venue for Manson, and that case generated far more publicity."

The refusal to change venue was a minor blow to the defense, but Pitts's second ruling struck at the prosecution's case. He refused to permit the prosecution to present testimony from four of the women who had alleged to Sheriff's Department investigators that Charlie Rathbun had raped and/or sexually assaulted them. Pitts disallowed the testimony on the grounds of its prejudicial nature.

Finally, the distinguished, gray-haired judge upheld Municipal Court Judge Benjamin Aranda's ruling that the findings derived from the body of Linda Sobek could remain in evidence at trial. Werksman had again sought to quash that evidence, citing the violation of Rathbun's Miranda rights when he was arrested. But like Aranda, Pitts ruled that Rathbun had benefit of counsel before and during the famed helicopter search that yielded the body.

With that, all that remained was to try the case. Before it concluded, the trial would become one of the most bizarre and titillating in California history.

Chapter 34

THE BUILDING that houses the South Bay District Superior Court is one of those modern buildings that isn't very modern any more. Fashioned of steel, concrete and stone, it replaces the grandeur and presence of the old-time courthouses with a sixties-style anonymity. It could house the office of your dentist or your chiropodist or your shrink but instead it houses Justice. At least, that's what we'd like to believe.

For much of the nineties the bland structure also housed the unassuming office of Stephen Kay, deputy district attorney. It was his home away from home, and he spent countless hours there, helping his staff fight the often-thankless war against crime. He knew it as he knew the penal code's murder statutes, and he felt as comfortable there as in his favorite easy chair.

As the trial of Charles Edgar Rathbun opened in a cramped and cluttered third-floor courtroom in the same dull-as-drainwater building where Kay kept his office, there was an excited buzz. The Sobeks—Elaine, her husband Robert and son Steve—and their supporters and well-wishers were out in force. Attractive women in their mid-twenties, friends of Linda mixed with the Sobek clan, hugging Elaine warmly and wishing Bob good luck. The gaggle of people had been waiting a long time to see justice done by their daughter, sister and friend, and they had an air of expectation about them that recalled a crowd getting ready for the big football game.

The courthouse Sheriff's Deputies made certain the Sobeks got front-row positions in the theater-style seats near the south wall of the courtroom. Across the room, near the north wall, the deputies placed the Rathbuns—Charlie's father, Horace, a wizened little man with a shock of reddish hair, his mother, Shirley, a woman who seemed to have more substance than her former husband, and their two daughters, Louise and Maryanne, both attractive and well dressed in an understated, upper-middle-class manner.

In contrast to the Sobeks, who seemed absolutely certain why they were there, the Rathbuns appeared more than a little lost, a bit dazed and somewhat embarrassed. No matter what their loved one may or may not have done, they were innocent of any wrongdoing toward the Sobek family, and there are no Miss Manners guidelines on how to act in a courtroom when one of your family is accused of murder in the first degree. They seemed to be trying to gauge the reaction to their presence, taking the temperature of the room to see how hated they might be by the others, even through no fault of their own.

You can say many things about Stephen Kay—in fact many people have said a great many things about him over the years and most of them have been good—but one thing you cannot say about him is that he's a man of few words. Far from it. He's as voluble as a proverbial Southern Senator, although his accent is California-bland.

Having given himself the task of opening the case for the prosecution, he made the most of it. After quickly warming up the ten-man, two-woman jury, he got right to the point of the prosecution's theory of what happened on Thursday, November 16, 1995.

"Charles Rathbun did not have a photo shoot of a Lexus LX 450 in mind when he drove out of the Denny's parking lot," Kay told them, his tenor voice growing higher with excitement. "What he had in mind was taking Linda Sobek to an isolated area, taking photos until he got excited, and then showing her what she deserved."

Kay's emotion grew as he told the jury that Rathbun had gotten sexually excited while Sobek posed for his camera. Then, the prosecutor asserted, the photographer had attacked her, ripped an earring from her lobe and tied her legs apart. With his victim struggling mightily against her bonds, Kay continued, Rathbun proceeded to sodomize her before strangling her and burying her to cover up his crime.

"Linda Sobek will come out of her grave, figuratively speaking, and into this courtroom and tell you what happened," Kay predicted. "She will tell you of the terror and the horror and the pain and degradation that she experienced."

Alluding to two of the prosecution's chief experts, Kay told the hushed courtroom that Deputy Coroner James Ribe and sexual assault expert Dr. Laura Slaughter would render opinions that would leave no doubt that Linda Sobek had been both sexually assaulted and strangled to death. The prosecutor also promised that their testimony would be accompanied by drawings and photos that would make clear Linda's various injuries.

Perhaps most interesting to outside observers was Kay's assertion that Rathbun had hated Linda Sobek. The prosecutor told the jury that the photographer's dislike for the bathing suit model began at a 1993 photo session and continued until the day he eventually murdered her. Backing up this theory, Kay promised to produce witnesses who would prove that Rathbun harbored a virulent hatred for the Hermosa Beach beauty.

Alluding to the MacUser carrying sack found in a Sheriff's Department search, Kay told the jurors that on the fatal day Rathbun had brought along "a little rape bag." Inside the piece of giveaway luggage investigators had discovered 3.1 grams of marijuana, an opened bottle of tequila, a length of rope and some road-striping tape that had a strand of Linda Sobek's hair on it.

By the time the lanky Kay yielded the floor, he had painted a picture of premeditated rape accompanied by what could have been premeditated murder. According to the storyline presented by the prosecutor, Rathbun had called Sobek that morning for one reason. He had a deep hatred for her that he wanted to pay off by raping and murdering her. The photographer had no need to employ her as a photo model, because he had already arranged to photograph the vehicle the following day, using his girlfriend as the driver. Instead Rathbun had conceived a plot to drive to the desolate El Mirage dry lake, overpower Linda Sobek, tie her up and rape her. Then, to make certain she didn't talk, he may have planned to kill her. It was a dramatic, inflammatory performance that left Elaine Sobek and many others in the courtroom in tears.

The opening statement by defense counsel Mark Werksman was considerably less evocative. Speaking in deliberately measured tones designed to match the gravity of the case, Rathbun's advocate chose to dwell on the alleged rape as the key issue in the case.

"When all the evidence is before you," he said, "you will see a complete picture emerge instead of a partial picture."

He called the jury's attention to Sobek's 0.13 percent blood alcohol level, noting it was higher than the state limit for illegal intoxication. Hinting broadly that in her inebriated state Sobek had found Rathbun appealing sexually, he asserted that the intercourse between the two had been consensual. Trying to walk a fine line between being explicit and offending the jury, he also told the jury that Sobek wore provocative clothing, posed in a sexually provocative way and eventually allowed herself to be photographed in the nude.

"There are two sides to the story," Werksman concluded.

Deliberately holding some things back, Werksman did not paint as vivid a picture as his opposite number had. Still, it was obvious from his opening statement that proving the sex between Rathbun and Sobek was voluntary would be the linchpin of the defense case. For Charlie Rathbun, his freedom was riding on the photos his brother had provided Werksman.

Chapter 35

AFTER THE explosiveness of Kay's opening arguments, the prosecution's case in chief versus Charles Edgar Rathbun moved forward at a much more prosaic pace. The first to testify was Elaine Sobek, a brown-haired fiftyish woman whose looks failed to hint at her daughter's lush beauty.

Elaine Sobek made no secret of her hatred for Charlie Rathbun. As she answered Kay's questions, she kept a laserlike stare on the man she was convinced had murdered her daughter. Finally, a little unnerved by her single-minded attention to the defendant, Kay moved her microphone so that she would be forced to face away from him.

Dramatic as her confrontation of Rathbun was, the real drama came when she was asked to identify photos that had been found in the Angeles National Forest trash bin. When Kay held up one of the photos of the vibrantly alive Linda, Elaine dropped her face into her hands and immediately began sobbing.

"Yeah, that's Linda," she said, "Oh, God. My poor baby."

She also testified to the last time she had spoken with her daughter—a short discussion about an upcoming family barbecue that occurred about ten-forty-five on the morning of November 16.

*　　*　　*

In an attempt to prove that Rathbun hated Sobek and thus had a reason to rape and murder her, the prosecution produced two former colleagues of Linda's, Cherie Michaels and Stella Henderson. Both were well-known members of the Los Angeles bathing suit modeling community, and both had worked with Rathbun over the years. In fact, prior to the trial, Charlie numbered them among his friends.

Under the prosecution's questioning, the attractive Michaels outlined her modeling and acting experience and then spoke about a 1994 photo shoot she had done in Malibu. Rathbun was the photographer for the session, and as the two of them drove to the photo location, they began discussing possible candidates for a swimsuit layout in *Sport Truck* magazine.

"What about Linda Sobek?" Michaels asked innocently.

According to the model, Rathbun reacted violently to the name. She said he clutched the wheel angrily and sputtered, "She's a little bitch, and she deserves whatever she's got coming to her." He added that he would never work with her again.

In cross-examination, Werksman asked if she had relayed Rathbun's comment to Sobek, and Michaels replied she hadn't since she didn't want to injure Linda's feelings. She also admitted that even after the negative remark about her friend, she had continued to work with Rathbun and even allowed him to house-sit at her home when she was out of town.

Another actress-model, Stella Henderson, had a similar tale to tell about the defendant. With Rathbun sitting stoically at the defense table next to the nattily dressed Werksman, she told the court that on a 1994 assignment for *All Chevy* magazine, she had engaged in a nearly identical conversation with Rathbun.

When the name Linda Sobek came up, Rathbun shot back, "Oh, I'll never work with her again. She's a bitch and difficult to work with."

Subtler but perhaps more chilling testimony came from Joella Lamm, the Lexus public relations employee who had lent Rathbun the Lexus LX 450 sport utility vehicle. Under prosecution questioning, she told the court that when the photographer returned the vehicle the Monday after Linda Sobek's death, he said, "I was thinking about you over the weekend." One thing no one disputed was that Charlie did a lot of thinking about women, and apparently the shock of Linda's death had had little effect on him in that regard.

According to Lamm, the photographer went on to say he had considered riding his bicycle on Saturday or Sunday and wanted to ask her to join him but didn't know how to get in touch with her. With that as the preamble, he asked her for her home telephone number, and she gave it to him.

Bill Bartling, the unemployed maintenance man who first discovered Linda Sobek's photos and DayPlanner in the Angeles National Forest, took the stand to tell his story. Another witness, magazine editor Dan Sanchez, testified that Rathbun told him, "You're going to see Linda Sobek's picture on a milk carton some day." And Sheriff's Department criminalist Kenneth Sewell was one of a number of witnesses who contributed bits of information that the prosecution hoped would lead the jurors to conclude Rathbun's behavior after Sobek's death was suspicious. Sewell testified that he had collected a number of items from a trash can at the Rathbun residence on Canyon Drive shortly after Charlie's aborted "suicide attempt" and subsequent arrest. The search, conducted approximately a week after Sobek went missing, netted a pair of white tennis shoes and two lengths of rope. None of the items was ever definitely connected to the crime.

More to the point was the testimony of two Lancaster women, both of whom claimed they saw Charlie Rathbun at a Kmart in the Antelope Valley community a little after dark on November 16, 1995. The first said Rathbun walked right by her and headed to a pay phone as she stood outside the store smoking a cigarette. Telephone company records showed that two suspicious calls had been made from the phone—one to the home of Glenda Elam, Charlie's girlfriend, and one to the residence at 1937 Canyon Drive.

The testimony of the second woman was even more damning. She told the court she had waited on Rathbun as he bought a pair of gloves, a shovel and two bottles of Snapple iced tea. One of the reasons she remembered the transaction, she said, was that Rathbun had asked for a price check on the shovel. A receipt found in one of the Angeles Crest trash bins had spurred detectives to question Kmart shoppers and employees.

Perhaps the most baffling part of the prosecution case was the succession of witnesses who proclaimed Rathbun hated blondes and thought of them as "throwaway people." One of them quoted Rathbun as saying, "Women in California are nothing but peroxide and silicone." A living contradiction to this prosecution theory was Glenda Elam, both blond and attractive and a frequent courtroom visitor.

Testimony about Rathbun's supposed hatred for Linda, his hatred for blondes in general and his inappropriate behavior after the model's death were simply preludes to the most shocking portion of the prosecution's case in chief. Dr. James Ribe, a Senior Deputy Medical Examiner and the coroner who had conducted the autopsy on Sobek, delivered graphic testimony about her injuries. He described in detail the hemorrhages in Sobek's anus, indicating that the penetration that caused them had most likely not been done with her consent.

He also described his theory on how Sobek had been asphyxiated. He noted her legs appeared to have been tied apart in such a way that she couldn't close them, although she struggled furiously to do so, leaving the ligature marks on her ankles. At some point during what he believed was a struggle with her attacker, that attacker ripped the earring out of her right ear, violently twisted her right arm and squeezed her neck with at least one of his hands. Sobek died in a facedown position, blood flowing from her ear.

"It was a painful death," he concluded.

Under cross-examination the medical examiner admitted that there were no external marks on Sobek's neck consistent with strangulation, but he pointed to several subdural hemorrhages in the musculature of the neck as the basis for his finding that someone had wrapped at least one hand around her neck. He acknowledged the existence of a third ligature mark running up Sobek's calf, but did not provide a theory of how it had occurred or what it might mean.

Through questioning, Werksman pointed out that Ribe's testimony at trial was significantly more specific than it had been at the preliminary hearing, when he concluded that the model had died from asphyxiation caused by strangulation, a chokehold or the use of some device. Ribe countered that his theory had evolved naturally over time.

The feisty defense attorney tried very hard to block the testimony of Dr. Laura Slaughter, a San Luis Obispo, California, expert on sexual assault. With the jury out of the courtroom, he argued before a sphinxlike Judge Pitts that her testimony should be disallowed, noting that she was trained as an internal medicine practitioner, not a pathologist.

"She hasn't conducted an autopsy since medical school," he railed. "This woman does not have experience of any persuasive amount to tell the jury what happened to Linda Sobek."

Defense counsel also pointed out that Slaughter had not attended the autopsy or examined Sobek's body at a later date. (The latter would have been impossible, since Sobek's body was cremated immediately after the original autopsy was completed. Today those ashes sit in the closet in Linda's childhood bedroom.) Instead of examining the body, Slaughter had viewed the postmortem photos before rendering an opinion.

Judge Pitts was unmoved by Werksman's argument, said he was impressed by Slaughter's credentials and permitted her to testify. The defense attorney predicted that Slaughter "would concoct a detailed scenario," and while the word "concoct" is prejudicial in its connotation, she certainly did present a vivid picture.

According to her testimony, Sobek's attacker used a blunt, rigid object to sodomize her. Under questioning by the prosecution, Slaughter floated the sensational theory that the blunt, rigid object had been the barrel of Charlie Rathbun's .45-caliber automatic. Gasps rose from the courtroom as those gathered pictured the innocent and beautiful Linda Sobek, struggling mightily against the ropes that bound her legs open, while the cold steel of a gun was inserted into her anus.

"The injuries wouldn't cause death," she said, "but they would be extremely painful. I think she was in terrible pain."

Slaughter's testimony hit home with the jury, but what jurors didn't know was that Slaughter had formulated her theory just the night before she testified, during a brainstorming session with the prosecution team, including Kay and his associate on the case, Mary-Jean Bowman.

"Now just what could he have used?" Slaughter had wondered out loud. And then she seemed to have a brainwave. "The gun!" she shouted. "That's it, the gun!"

It was the same weapon that had been seized in the commotion on the porch of the Rathbun residence, the same weapon that fired the shot injuring Charlie's friend Shannon Meyer. Despite the explosiveness of the theory, though, the prosecution never produced a witness or evidence to give credence to the suspicion that Rathbun had the gun with him at the dry lake.

By the time the prosecution case in chief concluded, it had presented the testimony of more than thirty witnesses and had painted a picture of a man who hated Linda Sobek so much that he was bent on paying her back by raping and perhaps even killing her. According to the scenario, Rathbun was a misogynist who hated blondes most of all. Before leaving home that morning, he had planned to rape Linda Sobek, bringing with him a "rape kit" of marijuana, tequila, tape and rope. Despite his claims, he had no need to use a model or even do a photo shoot that day, because he had already set up a photo session with the vehicle for twenty-four hours later.

After Sobek had been raped, strangled and buried, the prosecution contended, Rathbun had gone about his business as if nothing had happened—in fact, making tasteless wisecracks—until Bill Bartling's discovery in the Angeles National Forest garbage can connected the photographer's name to the crime. Then he began to panic. He tried to construct scenarios that would make the murder seem like an accident and thought about pointing the guilty finger at some of his photographic rivals. But those efforts unraveled; he was arrested and eventually led police to the body, which in turn yielded many more clues.

For the prosecution it was a good start, but Stephen Kay, Mary-Jean Bowman and Mike Robinson had a big surprise waiting for the defense. For them, the best was yet to come.

Chapter 36

DEFENSE ATTORNEY Werksman wasn't holding anything back. He knew he had to get the jury's attention quickly. So as one of his first witnesses, he brought Robert Rathbun to the stand to lay the groundwork for the introduction of the photographs Charlie's bother had provided. Those photographs, the feisty defense attorney believed, would negate the charge of sodomy with an unknown object and send the prosecution's case tumbling like a house of cards.

Shy and rambling, Robert Rathbun proved to be a reasonably effective witness as he described how he had followed a map provided by his brother to the Poppy Preserve off Avenue I. While there, he said, he and his girlfriend found five rolls of film, which they scooped up and took back with them to Virginia. The slightly built, boyish lawyer matter-of-factly described how he had developed the film and shipped it off to Werksman.

The prosecution's cross-examination pointed up the difficulties in finding items as small as film canisters in a place as big as the Poppy Preserve, especially after the canisters had conceivably been lying there for almost three months during California's harshest season of the year. But Robert Rathbun stood firm, and the prosecution didn't press the issue with much vigor.

Werksman then moved on to his expert pathologist, Dr. David M. Posey, a former Army surgeon and past member of the Los Angeles County Medical Examiner's Office. He was the second forensic pathologist the defense had contacted in regard to the case. The first, Dr. Michael Baden, an esteemed pathologist based in Albany, New York, had rendered an opinion very similar to Posey's, but Rathbun's defense counsel was afraid he might be carrying too much baggage into the courtroom with him. Werksman was worried about Baden's "florid New Yorker" presentation style and even more worried that the pathologist had recently appeared as an expert witness for the O.J. Simpson defense.

"I wasn't sure how that would fly with a white, male Torrance jury," Werksman recalled.

Instead the garrulous defense counsel had decided to enlist the services of a locally based forensic pathologist. Posey's credentials were somewhat less impressive than Baden's, but he had worked in Los Angeles and Riverside counties and possessed the speech patterns of a Californian.

Not surprisingly, on the witness stand Posey contradicted Ribe's theory of the cause of Linda Sobek's death. He said that asphyxiation resulted not from strangulation but from compression of the neck and chest against an inert surface.

"Like the door of a car?" Werksman asked.

"Yes, that is possible," the Palos Verdes-based Posey answered.

After a review of the autopsy results, Posey told the court that the absence of external injuries on her neck and chest convinced him that asphyxiation had occurred through some means other than a hand or hands closing Linda Sobek's windpipe.

"The findings for manual strangulation were just not there," he said.

He theorized that the fatal injuries to the model could have resulted from compression to her neck and chest as she lay in a prone position.

"Could this have happened in, say, the backseat of a vehicle?" Werksman asked.

"Yes, it could," Posey replied.

Posey's direct testimony sent the defense home happy that afternoon, but the following day the prosecution scored some points on cross-examination. Under the hawklike questioning of Stephen Kay, Posey admitted that Sobek's injuries, including trauma to her neck, right ear, right arm and anus, indicated the bathing suit model had been assaulted, a blow to the defense's position that sex between Sobek and Rathbun had been consensual.

"How do you explain the ligature marks, the injuries to the insides of her ankles?" Kay asked.

"I really have no explanation for that," Posey answered.

But the defense knew it desperately needed an explanation, and it had only one witness who might be able to provide one. That witness was Charles Edgar Rathbun. Charlie was eager to testify, and Werksman felt he had no choice but to put him on the stand.

Chapter 37

ON THE morning of Friday, October 18, 1996, Charlie Rathbun brimmed with eagerness. He flashed his customary smile to family and friends as he walked into the courtroom and took his place at the defense table with practiced confidence. Outfitted in a loose-fitting dark-blue suit, wire-frame glasses covering his owlish eyes and a close-cropped haircut accentuating the bald spot on the crown of his head, he looked like a veteran accountant ready to deliver a positive profit-and-loss statement. Instead he was prepared to testify to his version of the events of Thursday, November 16, 1995, the day Linda Sobek disappeared.

The aging little courtroom was filled to capacity on that crisp morning in expectation of Charlie's testimony. The Sheriff's Department had set up a lottery system to allocate the few seats that weren't assigned to the Sobek family, the Rathbun family or the press, and court watchers had lined up before 6 A.M. in an effort to land a place inside.

At the prosecution table Stephen Kay, Mary-Jean Bowman and the mustachioed Mike Robinson harbored a great deal of anticipation about just what Rathbun would say. How would he try to explain all the evidence that had been stacked up against him? they wondered. How could he have the gall to testify at all? Then they thought about the special surprise they had in store for the defendant and inwardly they smiled.

When Rathbun was called to the stand, he walked his gangling walk up to the witness chair and settled in, adjusting the microphone in front of him casually as his lawyer, a head shorter than his client and dressed to the nines, waited for Judge Pitts's signal to proceed. When that beckoning came and Werksman lobbed in the first question, he began to speak in a clear, low-decibel voice that often had an off-the-cuff air about it.

Charlie told the court how Marilee Bowles, the art director for *AutoWeek* magazine, had given him an assignment to shoot photographs of a Lexus LX 450, a new vehicle the company was about to introduce. On the spur of the moment he had decided to call Linda Sobek immediately after he had taken possession of the sport utility, and he dialed both her home phone and pager numbers, which he had received from her at the SEMA show a couple of weeks earlier. When he paged her, she called back almost immediately. They struck a deal for her services for the day at a rate of three hundred dollars, and she promised to meet him at the Denny's restaurant at Crenshaw and 182nd Street an hour later, around 11 A.M. While he waited for her, he said, he shot some photographs of the Lexus's interior in a nearby parking lot.

Linda arrived at the appointed time wearing a white workout suit and suede lambskin boots with her hair in rollers. In her arms were her curler bag, her DayPlanner and her portfolio, which she asked him to review. Leaving the parking lot, they immediately got onto the 405 freeway headed north toward the photo location.

Rathbun said his original plan for the photo shoot of the upscale vehicle had been horse country outside Santa Barbara, an area that he knew well from other photo assignments. But monitoring the weather on the radio as they continued up the 405, he determined that Santa Barbara, like the South Bay, was socked in with a low, thick overcast, so he switched destinations, deciding to go to El

Mirage dry lake, an area that promised better weather.

"Did you mention this to Linda?" Werksman asked.

"Yes, I did."

"And did she object?"

"No, she just wanted to make certain she was home in time. She said she had some kind of an appointment that night."

On the drive he and Linda chatted amiably, comparing notes on mutual acquaintances and the modeling and photography business as they continued northward on the 405, then Interstate 5 and finally the Antelope Valley Freeway.

"We're were on the same career paths," he said. "And we knew a lot of the same people."

At Acton they exited the freeway for a few minutes to purchase gas and some snacks. Rathbun said he believed Sobek made at least one telephone call while they were there, but he wasn't certain whom she called. The pair then resumed their journey to El Mirage without incident, arriving on the vast mud flats at about 1 P.M.

By going inland, they had driven from under the marine layer of overcast and were now basking in bright sunlight. As an experienced photographer, Rathbun knew that photos shot in the harsh sun would be full of hotspots and other unpleasant effects. He decided to wait until the sun slipped down toward the horizon, and he figured in late November that would occur about four o'clock.

Using an unfortunate turn of phrase, he noted, "We had some time to kill."

While lounging in the Lexus, Linda asked the photographer if he had anything to drink, and rummaging through his MacUser bag, something he used as a catchall on photo shoots, he found an open bottle of tequila, remains of an Oldsmobile session done a week or so before. He said he kiddingly bet her twenty dollars she wouldn't have a drink and, though reluctant at first, she had one and then several more drinks over the next half-hour or so.

"Did it bother you that she was drinking?" Werksman asked.

"No," Rathbun replied. "I knew I'd be using her for only fifteen minutes."

According to the defendant's testimony, the tequila seemed to unleash a playful spirit in Sobek, and sensing the positive mood, he offered to take some portfolio photographs for her, using the wardrobe she had brought.

"Did you see her as an attractive woman?" the defense attorney asked.

"Yes, I did," Rathbun replied. "In fact, I asked her, 'Could I shoot you nude sometime?' She said, 'All photographers are the same.' "

Rathbun recounted that the conversation continued in that same vein.

"I told her she had a great body," Rathbun went on. "I told her she should try to get in *Playboy Lingerie* as a lingerie model. She told me she had done some nudes that she intended to send to *Playboy*."

Deciding to shoot some photos that might end up in her portfolio, Rathbun suggested that Sobek change into one of the outfits she had brought with her. In the back of the sport utility she pulled off her workout suit and put on a beige outfit. At Rathbun's direction she posed for three rolls of photos on the moonscape of El Mirage. The photographer said he thought that his model was having fun with the session, giving him a sexy smile, generally glowing for the camera.

When he suggested she do a wardrobe change, he said, she returned to the Lexus, picked up the tequila bottle and had yet another drink.

"She told me I owed her another twenty dollars," the photographer testified in a calm voice. "Those were her words; they weren't mine."

From the defense table Werksman then picked up three photographs, which were introduced in evidence as defense exhibits W, X and Y.

"Do you know who the woman is in these photos?" Werksman asked.

"Yes, that's Linda Sobek."

"And when were they taken?"

"These are some of the photos I took while we were on the dry lake. Photos for her portfolio."

The photos depicted a smiling, sexy Linda Sobek posing provocatively against the stark backdrop of the dry lakebed. Several buttons on Sobek's outfits were undone, presumably for tantalizing effect, and in the pictures in which she was wearing the white lace dress, the jury and courtroom attendees were able to catch glimpses of her breasts and pubic hair.

"When you were taking these photographs, could you see private parts of her body?" Werksman queried.

"Yes, I could."

"And how far apart would you say you were?"

"Oh, about twenty-five feet."

By the time the photos depicting Linda in the second costume were completed, the model was very relaxed and playful, according to Rathbun. When she climbed into the backseat of the Lexus to rest for a few moments, Charlie said he caught a quick look at her crotch, and she didn't seem to mind. To Rathbun, that was an invitation.

"I started kissing the inside of her left thigh," he said. "I asked her if she wouldn't mind being touched, and she said, 'You mean like this,' and she started massaging her vagina."

With Sobek masturbating herself in the backseat of the Lexus, according to Rathbun's account, he reached for his camera, quickly loaded a roll of film and snapped off several frames using the camera's motor drive.

With just the touch of a swagger, the defense attorney immediately produced four more photographic enlargements, which were tagged defense exhibits Z, AA, BB and CC.

"Can you tell me what these are?" he asked.

"Yes, those are double-exposed pictures."

"And what is in those pictures?"

"It's Linda Sobek masturbating herself," Rathbun replied flatly. "I don't believe you'll see her face in any of the photos."

Werksman displayed the photos to the court for several moments, and the reaction on the Sobek side of the courtroom was one of abject shock.

Continuing with the testimony, Rathbun said that after putting down his camera, he rapidly became sexually excited, and he started to masturbate himself as well.

"So you touched yourself?" Weksman asked.

"Yes."

"Were you sexually aroused?"

"Yes, and I started touching Linda. I said to her, 'Do you want to take this all the way?' And she said it wouldn't be safe because we had no birth control."

Werksman then backtracked a little to make certain the story was clear for the jury.

"Now, let's go back to the photographs for a minute," he said. "Can you describe them exactly, please?"

"Yes," Rathbun agreed evenly. "They are double exposures of the interior of the Lexus superimposed over Linda Sobek touching herself. I got excited with what was going on, and when I loaded my camera, I guess I must have grabbed a partially shot roll of film that already had the interior shots on it."

"And so you shot the new pictures right over the old ones?"

"Yes. I shot about six to ten photos of Linda and then I got back to what Linda showed me she wanted."

"And did you ever think about your girlfriend, Glenda Elam, during this time?" Werksman asked.

"No, I didn't," Rathbun replied. "Hormones motivated me to do what I was doing."

"And then what happened?"

"She told me she couldn't risk getting pregnant again."

Almost before the words were out of the defendant's mouth, Kay was on his feet, screaming, "Objection!" The prosecutor was irate that Rathbun had managed to sneak in the fact that Sobek had had at least one aborted pregnancy, and Elaine Sobek glared at the defendant, pure hate in her eyes.

Judge Pitts called Kay, Bowman and Werksman together for a brief sidebar, as Charlie sat awkwardly in the witness chair. After Werksman had been properly scolded, Charlie's resumed his testimony in an even voice, as if he were discussing restaurants or types of film.

He told the court that when Sobek turned down the opportunity to have conventional sex with him, he stuck the tip of his index finger into her anus.

"She didn't stop me," he said, "so I thought it was an alternative to sex. I started masturbating her that way. I had no intention to harm her in any way."

But when his fingers went deeper, Rathbun continued, "She sat up quickly and told me to stop in no uncertain terms. She seemed more indignant than anything else."

According to the defendant's testimony, Sobek then relieved herself in some nearby shrubbery, washed off her hands with some glass cleaner and changed back into the workout suit she'd been wearing when they met that morning.

By then, Rathbun said, "It must've been a little after 3 P.M. I was a little bit apologetic. She was slurring her words, pretty drunk."

That, abruptly, was the end of the day's sexual encounter between Linda and Charlie, according to Rathbun's account. What followed was strained silence and then Linda's demand that Charlie hand over the film that showed her touching herself. Rathbun told her that was impossible, since the roll of film containing those shots was mixed in with other rolls of film, and he didn't know which one it was. The tense lull continued until the sun dipped low enough in the sky to begin the photo shoot.

By this time, even though Linda was "pretty drunk," Rathbun testified that he decided to go on with the photo shoot by asking her to drive the sport utility for action photographs. She agreed and drove for several minutes while Rathbun tried to line up a shot, but she couldn't get the hang of what he wanted.

"I tried to explain it to her," he said, "but she wasn't getting it, so then I decided to demonstrate for her the kind of driving I wanted her to do."

Climbing into the Lexus, he started to do doughnuts on the sun-hardened dirt and suddenly lost control of the vehicle, sending it barreling right toward Linda.

"I gave it gas at the ten o'clock position," he told the court, "and the rear end started sliding out. I cranked the wheel hard right to straighten out, and then I came skidding to a halt."

But during the few seconds when the sport utility was out of control, it had come very near the model, and she disappeared from Rathbun's sight.

"I could've hit her with the passenger-side fender," he said. "As I backed up, she fell to the ground about five feet from the car. I didn't see her impact the ground."

Rushing to her side, he said, he found her lying on her stomach, blood dripping down her hand. As he grabbed a pair of men's underpants from his bag to wipe the blood, Linda, angry about his careless driving, called him a shithead.

With Sobek screaming, "Oh, God, oh, God!" he helped her into the middle passenger seat of the Lexus and wiped out the inside of her mouth with a chamois. Recalling that he was worried about the vehicle's interior, he said he got towels and put them under her head.

"She didn't seem coherent," he said. "I knew right away the shoot was over, the day was done."

According to the defendant, he contemplated taking her into Palmdale to get medical attention, but he said that idea was interrupted by Sobek's outburst.

"As I got in back to climb into the driver's seat, she started swearing at me," he testified. "She said she had a video coming up, this was going to ruin it and she was going to sue me.

"I yelled 'Fuck you!' at her," the photographer continued coolly. "I said, 'At least the car isn't damaged.' Her reaction was to kick the door and say, 'Fuck you!' "

Werksman produced exhibits depicting the passenger-side door of the Lexus.

"And this is where she kicked?" Werksman asked.

"Yes, she kicked the door, and I grabbed her foot because I didn't want her to damage the car. Prototype parts are scarce."

Sobek's continued efforts to kick the door angered Rathbun, because, he said, he was responsible for the vehicle, so he began to wrestle with her and finally climbed on top of her.

"I sat right on her," he told the enthralled courtroom. "The minute I sat on top of her she started elbowing, and I held her upper body down."

At first, he said, Linda struggled against the weight, calling him an asshole in the process, but he continued pinning her down on the seat, pressing her head and her neck.

"She struggled for about thirty seconds; then she got very calm," he went on. "I thought she was playing opossum."

"Did you feel her body go limp?" Werksman asked.

"I couldn't tell when her body went limp," Rathbun replied tonelessly. "I don't recall her going limp."

According to Rathbun, he sat on top of her for a minute or less. Yet when he got up, Linda Sobek was unconscious. And, according to Rathbun, he panicked.

Chapter 38

PANIC CAN be a horrible thing. Driving away the calming voice of rationality, it can compel people to do exactly the wrong thing at exactly the wrong time. So it went with Charlie Rathbun in the fading light of that grisly Thursday afternoon. At least, that's the way he told it.

As his testimony continued under the guiding hand of Werksman, Rathbun explained to the courtroom that after Sobek suddenly ceased moving under his weight, he pulled her from the vehicle onto the ground and attempted to revive her.

"I tried to take her pulse," he said, "and I gave her mouth-to-mouth resuscitation."

His efforts were of no avail, he said, and, getting more panicky by the minute, he tried to lift her back into the vehicle.

"I grabbed ahold of her by her wrist," he said, "probably pulling her wrist out of its socket."

"Did she appear to be dead?" Werksman queried.

"I thought she was in trouble," Rathbun replied.

Having difficulty lifting her back into the sport utility, he says, he pulled an Ace bandage from his prep kit and tied it around her ankles, forming a truss that helped him hoist her back onto the seat from which he had just taken her. Once she was back on the seat, he had difficulty pulling the Ace bandage off her.

"Did you realize she was dead?" the defense attorney asked.

"Not yet."

Climbing into the driver's seat, Rathbun continued, he roared off toward Palmdale with Linda Sobek, rapidly expiring or perhaps already dead, lying motionless on the middle seat.

"I just wanted to turn it over and make it somebody else's problem," he told an amazed courtroom full of spectators, with the hint of a smile coming to his face.

"Did it occur to you that you could kill somebody by sitting on them?" Werksman asked.

"No. I checked to see if she was breathing," the defendant continued. "She wasn't. I looked in her eyes, and I saw that they were fixed and dilated."

For the first time during the trial Rathbun began to show some emotion. Sobbing, he took off his glasses and covered his eyes.

Pitts immediately granted Werksman's request for a five-minute recess.

Rathbun was able to compose himself in a very short time, and when his testimony resumed, he told the gathered spectators, "I thought of leaving her there and abandoning her."

Instead, he said, he put her on the ground. Then, thinking better of his plan to ditch her body as if it were a broken-down sofa, he picked up the dead weight of her body and put it back in the vehicle. He drove off, but about five miles farther down the road, he checked Linda one more time.

"I don't think I took her out of the car," he said matter-of-factly.

Still in what he described as a panicked state, he drove right through the city of Palmdale, got on the 14 freeway, then found himself on Avenue I in Lancaster. With the dead body of Linda Sobek under a car cover on the middle seat, he stopped at an Arco station to get something to drink.

"Did you go to a pay phone and call for help?" Werksman asked.

"No, I was just so thirsty. I had this incredible thirst,"
Rathbun replied.

After the quick stop at the Arco station, he drove to a
nearby Kmart discount store.

"Did you say, 'I have a dead woman in the car who
needs help?' " Werksman asked.

"No, I went inside the Kmart and grabbed two Snapple
iced teas," he said. "Then I bought a shovel and some
gloves. I went to the garden shop at Kmart, and a teenaged
boy waited on me."

"Did you tell him why you were buying the shovel?"
Werksman asked.

"No. I went outside, and I saw a woman smoking."

"Was it your intention to bury Linda Sobek?"

"I don't know what my intention was," Rathbun replied. "From there I drove home."

"Did you telephone anyone from Kmart?"

"Yes, I called Glenda Elam."

"And what did you say to her?"

"Well, I didn't know what to say to her. I mean, what
should I say? Hi, Glenda, I've just killed somebody—
how's your day?"

After the call to his girlfriend, he said, he dialed his
home to check his message machine. Still confused, dazed
and panicked, according to his own account, he drove
home with the rapidly cooling body of Linda Sobek still
lying on the leather seat. He went inside, called Glenda
again and flipped his computer on. But he couldn't think.

Restless, he climbed back into the Lexus and drove off
with the body on the middle seat and the newly purchased
shovel and work gloves in the cargo compartment.

"Why during all this time did you choose not to call
the authorities?" Werksman said, asking an obvious question.

"I had too many loose ends in my life," Rathbun answered.

"Did you think something bad would happen to you?"

"Yes."

After driving all the way to Avenue I and then south on Highway 14, he told the court, he headed into the Angeles National Forest, going up an isolated dirt road.

"I pulled over at one point and sat on a wall near a culvert pipe," he said. "I had only been there once before."

After again gazing into the face of the now very dead Linda Sobek, he claimed he again began to panic about what had happened, and that is when he decided to bury her. He pulled out his new shovel, dug a shallow hole, dropped in the lifeless body and started shoveling the sandy soil over it.

"I was worried about coyotes eating Linda," he said. "So I put rocks over her grave."

His voice was starting to break again as he continued, "I left as quickly as I could."

The tension in the courtroom had become horrendous. Jury, spectators, even the jaded members of the courtroom staff seemed ready for an end to the tale of horror. But as he told it, the night was not over for Charles Rathbun.

At 4:19 the morning of November 17, he was in the Lexus again, buying gasoline at an Arco station near his home. From there, he said, he drove to the Poppy Preserve east of Lancaster, where he took shots of the vehicle as dawn exploded over the desert. After that it was on to the Angeles Crest Highway.

"I was trying to figure out where I had been the night before," he said. "I thought I could clean her up and turn her in to the authorities."

Instead he dumped Linda's curler bag, her DayPlanner and with it, inadvertently, his Motor Press Guild membership book and the Lexus loan agreement in trash bins by the roadside. Then he headed home once more.

"I made my bed and I had to lie in it," Rathbun said. "I've got twenty-four hours to put my life in order."

"Why did you feel that way?" the nattily attired defense counsel asked.

"Because I didn't think I could explain what happened," he told the stone-faced jury. "I had no idea you could suffocate someone by sitting on them."

Rathbun went on to give a cursory description of the rest of his Friday and then the rest of his weekend. The things he did sounded quite mundane, especially compared to the twenty-four hours that had come before it.

On the courthouse steps following the day's testimony, Werksman and Kay gave separate reviews of Rathbun's performance.

"What he has described is very credible. It has a ring of truth," the defense attorney told the orderly crowd of press waiting for the afternoon sound-bite. "Rathbun broke down on the stand. That was real, that was genuine."

Werksman pointed to the photographs of Linda Sobek that had been introduced during his client's testimony and claimed they proved the sex between Rathbun and Sobek was consensual.

Then he added, "He was responsible for this. He shouldn't have been drinking, although it's not illegal to get drunk and have sex with a professional model. He was in a state of panic, and he regrets how he behaved. Now he has to live with the consequences."

When the stick-thin Kay stood before the microphones, he had a strangely positive glint in his eye.

"What you saw on the stand today was a very cold-blooded killer," he said. "And those tears were crocodile tears. Just wait until the prosecution's rebuttal case."

Asked if he thought Rathbun had seemed sorry for the death of the bathing suit model, Kay replied, "I believe Rathbun is sorry for himself. Did he show an ounce of remorse? No, no remorse."

Then the veteran prosecutor gave a hint about what was to come.

"We didn't know exactly what Rathbun would say," Kay told the gathered crowd and millions of others on live television. "But now that he has spoken, we are certain we can prove his guilt beyond a shadow of a doubt. By his testimony today Mr. Rathbun has sealed his fate."

Chapter 39

A WEEKEND came and went before Rathbun would take the stand again, and when he did, his testimony was anticlimatic compared to the fireworks he had tossed with his story of the previous Friday. Though its delivery had been low-key to the point of deadpan, the tale he told had struck a raw nerve within the Sobek camp.

Dressed in a charcoal suit slightly too big at the shoulders, Rathbun began by telling what had happened to the five rolls of film he had taken of Linda Sobek at El Mirage, including the now infamous "masturbation" pictures.

"I was on a hill at the Poppy Preserve, and I threw the film canisters away," he said. "It was pre-dawn, and they scattered on the hill."

"Why did you throw them away?" his defense attorney questioned.

"It was film I shot the previous day," Rathbun answered. "And anything that reminded me of the day before I wanted to get rid of."

Skipping right over the eventful weekend, Rathbun also testified about his meeting with Joella Lamm, which occurred when he returned the Lexus the Monday morning after Sobek's death. He talked about his Mitsubishi Montero photo shoot in Palos Verdes and acknowledged that he had started to follow the Sobek case sometime on Tuesday, November 21. That night, after his roommate

258

Bill Longo had facetiously asked him, "Where did you hide the body?" he said, he had begun to watch the television coverage of the case, going to the length of taping some of the reports on his VCR.

As Tuesday night turned into Wednesday morning, he said he could feel the pressure.

"Things were getting out of hand," he told the court. "Things were building to a head."

Not knowing quite what to do, he said, he retired to his room, where he wrote what he described as "just a bunch of scribbled notes of what I knew about Linda Sobek." Under his attorney's gentle questioning, he acknowledged that one of the notes described two fellow photographers.

"These guys looked like the composite I saw on TV," Rathbun said.

"Was the purpose of this note to mislead the police?" Werksman queried.

"No, not really," Rathbun replied lamely.

The photographer described in detail the wild events of Wednesday, November 23, 1995, the day he was arrested. He recalled the early-morning phone call to *AutoWeek*'s Marilee Bowles, to whom he hinted about his crime, and the two phone calls with the Hermosa Beach Police Department. During the second call, Rathbun admitted, he told Officer Raul Saldana he had simply met with Sobek at the Denny's restaurant, looked over her portfolio for a few minutes and sent her on her way.

"That was a lie, that was misleading, wasn't it?" Werksman asked.

"Very misleading," Rathbun agreed.

By the time he telephoned his friend Shannon Meyer, Rathbun claimed that it was becoming impossible for him to keep his secret much longer.

"Did you tell Shannon Meyer?" Werksman asked.

"Sort of," the photographer answered. "I told her I hit her with the car and killed her."

"Why didn't you tell her you suffocated her?"

"I couldn't."

Before he hung up with Meyer, Rathbun testified, he asked her to feed his cat, because, as he said, "I figured I'd be tied up for a while. I didn't want the cat to starve, and I had decided I was going to kill myself."

After a second call to Saldana, Rathbun said, he started to go ahead with the suicide plan. He opened a bottle of Scotch, downed about half of it, and passed out within forty-five minutes. When he came to, he went downstairs to pull his .45 automatic from its gun case, then started banging out a suicide note on his computer.

"It started out as a To Whom It May Concern letter," he said, "but then it became a letter to Glenda. I told her I had everything going for me and I screwed it up. I hit her with the car and killed her."

"Why didn't you admit you suffocated her?" Werksman asked.

"I couldn't own up to it," Rathbun said. "I couldn't admit it to anyone else and even myself."

After writing a second suicide note with minor changes in it, he said, he tried to send a delayed fax to Shannon Meyer. Then he loaded his gun, walked out to the futon and lay down. He said he must have fallen asleep, because "I woke to hear Jim Nichols and Shannon Meyer yelling for me not to commit suicide."

The accused photographer gave a cursory sketch of the events on his porch that led to his arrest, and then launched into by-play with counsel designed to demonstrate how cooperative he had been with the police.

"You told them that you had buried Linda Sobek's body?" asked Werksman.

"Yes, I believe so."

"Did you agree to help police find the body?"

"Yes."

"Could you have driven there on your own?"

"No."

Rathbun went on to describe his suicide attempt in Hermosa Beach jail and the helicopter search that culminated in the discovery of the body.

As the direct examination of the defendant wound down, Werksman went after the nitty-gritty.

"Had anything ever happened to cause ill will between you and Linda Sobek?" he asked.

"No," Rathbun shot back.

"Any reason to dislike her?"

"No."

He asked his client his explanation of the testimony from the two models, Cherie Michaels and Stella Henderson, who claimed he hated Sobek.

After clarifying the dates of the conversations with the two models, Rathbun said, "I didn't call her a fucking bitch. Linda needed work, and I had heard that Linda was a little bitchy, not a little bitch. Hard to work with. I had heard that she was just difficult. I didn't call her a bitch. And about that part 'she'll get what she deserves,' I meant that in economic terms. As a freelancer you always get what you deserve."

"Did you say you'd never work with Linda Sobek again?"

"No."

"Did you have any problem with Stella Henderson?"

"No."

"Did you have any discussion with her regarding Linda Sobek?"

"No."

"Did you intend to hurt Linda Sobek?"

"No."

"Did you intend to kill Linda Sobek?"

"No, definitely no. My only intention was to hold her down."

"Did you penetrate her with a gun?"

"No."

"Did you place any object inside her?"

"No." Then he added, biting his lip, "Just my fingers in her vagina."

"Did you cause tearing or ripping of her vagina?"

"No."

With that, the defense turned Charles Rathbun over to the prosecution for cross-examination. Although earlier in his testimony the defendant had testified that he had penetrated Linda Sobek anally, he now said that he had penetrated her vaginally. Oddly, however, that slip didn't cause comment in the post-testimony crush of press. Instead Kay, feeling better than ever about his chances, said jocularly about the man he suspected of being a serial killer, "The evidence is overwhelming in this case that he likes cats. We have never contended that he doesn't like cats." The prosecutor promised to get the case to the jury by the end of the week.

Chapter 40

W HEN MARY-JEAN Bowman prepared for her cross-examination of Charles Edgar Rathbun, she knew it would be the cross-examination of her life. A Niagara University graduate who once had the idealistic plan of becoming a public defender giving legal aid to the indigent, she had subsequently rediscovered her inner conservative and taken a job as Assistant District Attorney with the much maligned Los Angeles County District Attorney's Office.

Joining the case well before the model's body was discovered in the Angeles National Forest, she won the job of cross-examining the man she was certain had murdered Linda Sobek, because, as she delicately put it, "I tend to be a bit more brief" than her boss, Stephen Kay.

"We also thought it might be easier for me to trip him up," Bowman added.

It's likely that Kay, who enjoys irony more than most, couldn't resist the extra psychological twist of having his blond-haired female colleague cross-examine the man who allegedly hated blond women.

In the months before the trial began, Bowman had written five or six versions of what would become her cross-examination, an opus that eventually ran for more than twenty single-spaced pages. Her twin goals were to get into Rathbun's head, as she phrased it, and to call him on as many lies and contradictions as possible.

263

When she stood before the bland-faced defendant at 2 P.M. on Monday, October 21, 1996, she certainly hit the ground running. Bowman began the examination by asking Rathbun what clothing Sobek was wearing when he picked her up at Denny's on the day of her disappearance, and when he described the "white workout outfit and rough-out [suede] boots," she retorted, "That's the outfit you buried her in, isn't it?"

"Yes," Rathbun replied evenly.

"And you lied to Detective [Officer] Saldana about leaving her at Denny's, didn't you?"

"Yes," he agreed.

Bowman, her cherubic face made plump by pregnancy, quickly tried to establish that Rathbun had been going on with his life in a relatively stress-free fashion until he heard that the police had discovered Sobek's DayPlanner and the borrower's agreement for the Lexus LX 450. But the defendant claimed that in the week following Sobek's death he had no idea that the police had recovered those items.

When Bowman attempted to get Rathbun to acknowledge he hated Sobek, she inadvertently allowed him to make some headway with a reasonable explanation of why he hadn't used the blond model for a *Truckin'* magazine shoot after she had been recommended by one of her model-friends. He told the Assistant District Attorney that the editor of the magazine had requested a girl next door type, something the buxom, babish Sobek was not.

Jumping to the day of Sobek's death, Bowman asked, "When you got up there [to the dry lake] you said you had some time to kill?"

"It was a bad choice of words, but yes, we did have some extra time," he responded.

"According to earlier testimony, Linda had a 6 P.M. appointment?"

"I don't know about that. All I know is I was planning on getting her back by seven-thirty."

Bowman tried to embarrass the defendant by producing

Linda Sobek's DayPlanner and then asking him to find the place where he had written his name and telephone number when he had met with Sobek at the 1995 SEMA show. As he fumbled through the pages, he said, "I don't see any of the flyleaf pages I would have written it on." The assistant DA's question implied that Rathbun had ripped out the page that would have connected him to the model before discarding the DayPlanner in the Angeles National Forest, but it was a point that went undelivered.

Bowman did get her points across in an exchange about the photos of Sobek that Rathbun took on the dry lake. After a reasonably calm exchange about how many rolls were taken and what wardrobe the model wore, the assistant DA went on the attack.

"When she was changing clothes, you twisted her arm, threatened her with a gun and forced tequila down her throat, didn't you?" she asked, her soft voice rising in righteous rage.

"No," Rathbun answered.

"Then you used your gun to force her to keep drinking tequila, didn't you?"

"No."

"You didn't use that Ace bandage. You tied her up!"

"I never tied her legs up."

"You took advantage of her when she was changing clothes, and you penetrated her anus with the gun, didn't you?"

"No."

"So you mean to tell us that she just got into the Lexus and started masturbating?"

"No," Rathbun said, unfazed by her string of difficult questions, "I encouraged her, I must admit. I ran my hands on her thighs."

Bowman retrieved some photos from the prosecution table and held them at arm's length so that the defendant could get a look at them.

"Are these the photos you said you took of her while she was masturbating?" she asked.

Rathbun eyeballed them for a minute or so and replied, "I'm not sure [exhibit] BB1 is the interior of the Lexus."

"You testified before that it was the interior of the Lexus."

"I didn't take a good look at it."

"At 3 P.M., after the penetration of her anus, didn't you tie her up and take bondage shots?"

"I never had her tied up," Rathbun replied. "I've never taken any bondage shots."

"Don't you have an interest in explicit bondage photos?"

"No."

"What about the photo with the candy cane in the anus area?"

Werksman leaped up to object, but by then Rathbun had already answered, "That wasn't a bondage photo."

After eliciting a coherent if unemotional description of the near miss with the sport utility vehicle, Bowman queried Rathbun about the dent in the interior door panel of the Lexus, while holding yet another evidence photo.

"She made the dent with her bare foot," Rathbun said.

Bowman hammered the defendant to explain why he had never stopped at a hospital or even made a phone call after he determined his companion was in trouble, and he told her, "As far as I know, there is no hospital out there."

Under continued questioning, the photographer claimed he wiped the unconscious Linda Sobek off with Windex and used an Ace bandage around her ankles to keep her limbs from flapping as he lifted her into the vehicle. He said he removed the Ace bandage when he was on Avenue I some time before he buried her.

Responding to Bowman's questions about his buying spree in Kmart, Rathbun said, "Time got very distorted. At around five-thirty at Kmart I bought a shovel and gloves. It took me just moments to buy a shovel, and the gloves were right next to the shovel. I threw away both the shovel and gloves in Angeles Crest not long after I buried her.''

Homing in on his phone calls from the Kmart parking lot, Bowman got Rathbun to admit that he used change rather than his calling card.

''I figured it was a local call,'' he said.

''Where did you tell Glenda Elam you were?''

''I told her I was north of Santa Barbara,'' he replied. Actually he was about sixty miles from that charming coastal town.

After grilling Rathbun on how he had disposed of various pieces of potential evidence, including the Day-Planner, the leopard-print curler bag and his tennis shoes, Bowman dove into the sexual encounter between Rathbun and Sobek.

''Now these sexual activities, were they initiated by Linda Sobek?'' she asked coolly.

''Yes.''

''She was sexually interested in you?'' Bowman said, not trying to hide her incredulity.

''I guess spreading her legs and exposing herself led me to believe that.''

''And you say you masturbated her? For how long?''

''I'm not sure how long I masturbated her,'' Rathbun replied. ''Maybe one to two minutes. She was lubricating. She was keeping her legs apart, getting aroused.''

''Were you aroused?''

''Yes.''

''Did you have an erection?''

''Yes.''

''Did you want to have sex?''

''Yes.''

''Now, you testified that you started masturbating yourself, and then she masturbated you for a very short time, and then you inserted one and then two fingers into her anally?'' Bowman queried, disgust dripping from her voice.

''Yes.''

"Wasn't it your gun?" she shot back.

"No."

"Wasn't she restrained?"

"No."

"Why was there blood on this gun?" she asked, brandishing the weapon in front of the jury.

"Objection!" shouted Werksman.

"You know this gun tested positively for blood?" she continued.

"Objection! Objection, your honor!"

When order was restored, Bowman questioned the balding photographer about the various items in the MacUser bag, which included a table leg, marijuana, gloves, tape, a foam cupholder, a blue towel and a badge bearing the logo *AutoWeek*. Rathbun acknowledged the items with a so-what shrug, but Bowman wasn't through with him.

"Linda Sobek found you repugnant, didn't she?"

"No," Rathbun scoffed.

"You just had to show that little bitch, didn't you?"

Werksman objected again, but after the ruling Bowman resumed her onslaught.

"Did you have her legs restrained?"

"No."

"Did you anally penetrate her with her legs restrained?"

"No.

"Wasn't she in horrible pain?"

"No."

"You took her up to that lake bed for just one reason, didn't you?"

"Yes, as a photo model."

"As a photo model?" Bowman repeated sarcastically. "There are no pictures of Miss Sobek with the Lexus."

Bowman elicited the biggest reaction from the remarkably calm, nearly stonelike defendant when she questioned him about the so-called sorry notes.

Asked what he was intending to accomplish with the

notes, he replied, "I was telling them about myself. Two lives are effectively over. And life was looking so good. I can't face a manslaughter charge." He began to break up, biting his lower lip. "If I just had that thirty seconds to do over," he said.

The session ended for the day, but Bowman was not ready to let Rathbun off the hook. Wearing a houndstooth check dress as court resumed the following morning, she showed a series of photos that depicted injuries to Linda Sobek's right ear, her anus, her genitalia and her hand, asking the defendant how they had come to be there. Charlie answered each question blandly. He managed to remain even-tempered when Bowman slammed him with more questions about the Kmart telephone calls, places he had deposited Sobek's personal items and the allegation that he had called Sobek a little bitch.

Summing up, Bowman cited Rathbun's list of lies.

"You lied to Shannon Meyer, didn't you?"

"Yes."

"And to Officer Saldana?"

"Yes."

"And to Bill Longo?"

"Yes."

"And to Glenda Elam?"

"Yes."

"And to Deputy Bice?"

"Yes."

Bowman thrust a photo into the defendant's hand.

"This is [People's Exhibit] 110, one of the disputed photos that you contend is Linda Sobek masturbating," Bowman said crisply.

"Yes."

"Are you as sure these are Linda Sobek as you are sure you didn't murder Linda Sobek?" the assistant DA continued, her fury rising.

"Yes," Rathbun responded simply.

"Have you ever gone by any other name?"

"Objection!" Werksman shouted. He knew quite well from viewing the discovery materials the name that Bowman wanted to bring out in open court. It was a nickname several acquaintances told police Charlie used at cocktail parties: Grant Savage, the Dick of Death.

After a sidebar, Bowman's final words were, "No further questions."

Chapter 41

T HE DEFENSE redirect examination of Charlie Rathbun was a study in backtracking, bridge-building and general repair work to the defendant's injured credibility. Of course, that could describe the redirect examination of most accused killers. In its cross-examination the prosecution takes its best shots, and then the defense attorney tries to shore up its battered theory of events. Looking at the subjects covered in redirect, a jury can form a good picture of just where the defense thinks its opposition has scored.

As Werksman questioned his well-composed client for the second time, it became obvious that the defense wanted to defuse the prosecution theories that the gun had been used to penetrate Linda Sobek and that the so-called portfolio photos were taken under duress.

The energetic defense attorney quickly elicited from his client the fact that he had purchased the .45 automatic legally, although that hardly proved it had not been used to assault the dead model, and then he turned to the issue of the photographs of Linda on the dry lake. Rather than defusing the issue, however, under questioning, the photographer appeared to agree with the prosecution's contention that a visible hole in Linda's stocking and a price label on the bottom of her shoe were both unusual and unprofessional in photos meant for her portfolio. One conclusion that the jury might have drawn from his admission was that Sobek didn't pose for the photos of her own free will.

A thornier issue for the defense was the matter of the "masturbation" photos. On direct examination Rathbun had stated quite bluntly that the images of the naked woman touching herself were superimposed over images he had taken of the Lexus interior. On redirect Rathbun now identified the interior as that of an Oldsmobile Intrigue prototype he had shot a couple of weeks prior to the Lexus shoot. He explained that the stylized Oldsmobile rocketship-within-a-circle logo on the steering wheel resembled the Lexus L within a circle, and that had confused him. Following Werksman's lead, he went to some length to describe how a half-shot roll of Oldsmobile film had ended up with him on a Lexus shoot.

The defense attorney also questioned his client on why he hadn't told the authorities about the sexual encounter he had with Sobek when he was questioned after his arrest.

"There are a couple of reasons," Rathbun replied. "It was embarrassing for both parties, and it had nothing to do with the way she died."

As a disgusted Elaine Sobek bolted from the courtroom, Rathbun added, "It was my hope not to have to tell about sex with Linda Sobek. It was something that was not going to do anybody any good."

Asked about anal penetration, Rathbun held up his left index and middle fingers, and said, "I used these two fingers. I don't know their dimensions."

It was immediately determined that his index finger was three and a half inches long, his middle finger four inches long. Neither resembled the barrel of a .45 automatic.

The redirect concluded with Werksman drawing from his client the hardly startling information that he and Sobek had chatted about personal rather than business issues during their four and a half to five hours together.

Bowman required less than ten minutes for her recross-examination of the accused killer, essentially going over old ground.

Her parting question was, "She rejected your sexual advances, didn't she?"

"I'm sorry," the ever polite Rathbun answered. "That's just not true."

Warily the defense rested, fearful that the prosecution would spring something on them that had not appeared in discovery. Before the afternoon was over, Werksman would find out that his nagging suspicion had been correct.

The prosecution's rebuttal case started innocuously enough. Peter J. Ternes, Oldsmobile's assistant director of public relations, told the court that he had assigned Charlie Rathbun to photograph an Oldsmobile Intrigue prototype and had already received photographs of the vehicle from Rathbun. The dark-haired, gray-suited Ternes added that the photographer had mentioned to him that he would be shooting the Lexus LX 450 on the dry lake on November 16 and had said he would be happy to tell him how it had gone because Oldsmobile was planning a shoot at the same location eleven days later. Ternes's testimony negated Rathbun's claim that his decision to go to El Mirage came on the spur of the moment because of bad weather.

Following Ternes on the stand was John Shaw, a photographer for the Los Angeles County Sheriff's Department Crime Lab. Wearing a silk jacket and with his spectacles perched on the top of his head, Shaw described the laborious process of reproducing the coroner's photos of Linda Sobek's dead body and the double-exposed "masturbation" photos originally provided by Robert Rathbun. It became obvious that the prosecution intended to compare the photos of Linda Sobek's genitalia depicted in the coroner's photos with the genitalia of the woman Rathbun purported to be Linda Sobek in the photos his brother claimed to have found in the desert.

Feeling that his case was slipping into the abyss, Werksman labored mightily in cross-examination to impeach the credibility of the reproductions. He asked about deterioration, color change, increased contrast and distortion.

"So what you have is a copy of a copy of a negative of a positive?" Werksman asked.

"You have second and third generation photos," Shaw answered.

"Do you have distortion?"

"It could look quite close to the original," Shaw responded.

About the only positive for the defense was Shaw's admission that the film Robert Rathbun claimed to have discovered showed emulsion deterioration.

"There was evidence of being exposed to the elements," Shaw said. "Evidence I received indicated that it had been out in the desert, out in the heat and the rain. Some of the emulsion was torn off by water."

That testimony tended to support Robert Rathbun's story of the discovery of the film.

With the way paved for a closer examination of the "masturbation" photos, the prosecution called Sheriff's Department criminalist Heidi Robbins to the stand. Robbins, an attractive blonde dressed in a blue suit and sporting a ponytail, had participated in the Sobek investigation almost from the beginning. At the request of Deputy Mary Bice, she had checked out a suspicious bloodstain in the Angeles National Forest on Thanksgiving Day and had also participated in the search for Sobek's body on the day of the infamous helicopter marathon.

Prepared to hear about the comparison photographs, the court heard instead about one of Linda Sobek's stockings, which had been found in her leopard-print curler bag. Robbins said she had discovered a bloodstain on the foot of that black stocking, but the amount of blood was so small that it couldn't be typed.

With that weirdly inconclusive detour concluded, Robbins began her photo comparison with side-by-side looks at the interior of the Oldsmobile Intrigue prototype and the Lexus LX 450 prototype. Showing the pictures to the jurors, she pointed out that the vehicle in the double exposures was the Oldsmobile, not the Lexus.

That was mildly damaging to the defense, but it was nothing compared to what was coming. The prosecution was about to spring the trap it had been baiting since Kay and Robinson had first examined the film allegedly discovered by Charlie's brother months before. What the amazed jury was about to see were side-by-side comparisons of female genitalia.

Referring again to the prints, Robbins compared a photo of Sobek's genitals taken after death to two photos from the set of "masturbation" photos provided by Robert Rathbun after his trip to the Poppy Preserve.

With no small amount of glee Robbins reported, "[The woman in] AA1 and Z1 [the two "masturbation" photos] is not Linda Sobek."

The trap had been sprung, and the prosecution made certain the jury didn't miss their point. Displaying more photos side by side, the criminalist voiced her opinion that the pubic hair of the woman pictured in the "masturbation" photos was markedly different from that of Linda Sobek in the autopsy pictures.

"As you can see in the perineal area, there is a lot of pubic hair, dense and dark. There are several ingrown hairs and what looks like razor stubble," Robbins recounted to a thunderstruck courtroom. "On the other hand, Sobek's is sparse, fine, uninterrupted and has not been shaved."

Showing another comparison slide, she continued, "Here there is coarse, visible, dark pubic hair and what seems to be a rash, very distinct and different from Linda Sobek."

Even more graphic was the next slide, which showed, as Robbins described it, "the posterior view of a woman pulling her buttocks apart."

"You can see this landmark formation in this photo," Robbins said, "and again it is absent in Linda Sobek."

With Werksman sitting pensively at the defense table, the Sheriff's Department criminalist went on to describe several other photos, pointing out what she perceived as differences between the woman in the photo Robert Rathbun had provided the defense and the body of Linda Sobek.

Just when it looked as if the situation couldn't get any bleaker for the defense, Mary-Jean Bowman asked her blond-haired colleague, "On a scale of one to ten, how certain are you that the woman portrayed in these pictures is not Linda Sobek?"

"Ten! I'm certain," Robbins replied. "They are completely different women in those pictures."

When Werksman rose to do cross, it was as if he couldn't believe what his ears were telling him.

"You said that you are sure they are completely different people?" he asked, inadvertently allowing Robbins the opportunity to affirm it once again.

"They are completely different women," she replied.

After a little jousting with Robbins about the composition of the fabric under the masturbating woman, Werksman tried to draw a line of differentiation between the photos of a live female and that of a dead one.

"You're talking about the body of a woman who had been dead for ten days, who was way past rigor mortis," he rambled in search of a question. "You're talking here of a still photo after ten days of sloughing and decomposition."

At the conclusion of the day's testimony, the prosecution team and the Sobek family were exuberant. Kay and Bowman had strategically waited to challenge the purported photos of Linda Sobek masturbating until rebuttal. That way, they had been able to hold out their discovery material on the comparisons until the defense had rested its case in chief, a case that tied Rathbun's credibility to the "masturbation" photos.

After Werksman had turned the five disputed rolls of film over to the court in March, it hadn't taken long for the prosecution to smell a rat.

"After we had looked at the photos for ten minutes, we knew they were phony," said Kay, who favors the anachronistic speech of an Erle Stanley Gardner DA.

The deputy district attorney talked freely about a falsification of evidence case versus Robert Rathbun (something that, at this writing, hasn't been filed despite the repeated pleas of Linda's family). The Sobeks had been informed of the prosecution gambit, and they proved they could keep poker faces. When Rathbun introduced the disputed photographs in his testimony, they somehow were able to remain mum despite the outrageous things the defendant said about their loved one.

Werksman, obviously a bit rattled by the timing of the prosecution's revelations, vowed to fight back.

"This is the first time the prosecution has said that the defense has manufactured evidence," he said. "They chose to bring it up now to gain tactical advantage."

After the trial Werksman would say he was expecting the prosecution to challenge the photos but on different grounds from those actually put forward. He had thought his opponents would suggest the shots had been taken under duress or that Rathbun's hands, not Sobek's, were those pictured.

The following day the feisty defense attorney did battle back, but his persistent questioning failed to impeach Heidi Robbins's certainty. She stood her ground when he debated her ability to come to the conclusion she had reached, and her testimony drew a laugh from the gathered court-goers. When Werksman referred to a portion of anatomy on one of the photos as a buttock, she corrected him with a firm, "This is a vagina."

After failing to put a dent in Robbins's armor, the defense was one-two punched by the next prosecution witness, Dr. Marianne Gausche, a physician, surgeon and expert in emergency medical care who was employed by Harbor-UCLA Medical Center. Like Robbins, Gausche used comparison photos, and like Robbins, she came to the conclusion that the woman pictured in the double-exposed "masturbation" photos was not Linda Sobek.

"They are not the same person," the short-haired blond told the jam-packed courtroom.

Perhaps not surprisingly, her testimony was a bit more clinical than that of Robbins. She talked about pubic hair distribution and a lesion at the base of the labia that was present on the woman touching herself but not present on the body of Linda Sobek.

She theorized, "Miss Sobek might have shaved at the bikini line," not a big stretch of imagination considering she was a bathing suit model. Perhaps most telling was her discussion of the women's clitoral hood. She described Sobek's as having a "nice triangular pattern, while it is rectangular on the other person."

On cross, as he had with Robbins, Werksman tried to shake Gausche's testimony, but it was largely a no-go. He got her to acknowledge that most of her work was done on live human beings, not corpses, but a rundown of her credentials only served to make her seem a stronger witness.

Prompted by questions from the defense attorney, Gausche took the court on a tour of female genitalia. Werksman pointed to a portion of a photo that the doctor described as a lesion and asked her if she thought it looked like the head of a Phillips screw.

"No, I don't," Gausche replied.

The embattled defense attorney tried to get the emergency room physician to admit that there might be differences between the body of a living woman and that same body after death, but he made little if any progress.

By the time the cross-examination was over, the doctor

and lawyer seemed to be merely bantering with each other.

"To me they look different," Werksman said, referring casually to two vaginas.

"I spent hours with these photos," Gausche countered.

"That's just the point," he tried. "You mind's eye could see anything you want to see."

Gausche wasn't buying it.

"In my opinion," she said flatly, "they are not the same."

In light of the day's explosive testimony, the defense case was in a shambles. The jury could not have failed to see the inference of the testimony by Robbins and Gausche—the "masturbation" photos were fakes and Charlie's story of consensual sex with Linda Sobek was just as bogus. But the defense attorney, hoping that his fancy footwork in cross-examination might have muddied the issue, was still looking on the bright side.

A writer approached Werksman at the defense table after court was adjourned and asked him, "Do you have an expert to counter this testimony?"

"Do you really think I need one?" he answered.

Chapter 42

THE TESTIMONY from Robbins and Gausche had injured the defense case mortally, but before the prosecution rested, Sergeant Mike Robinson was on hand to deliver the coup de grâce. It was fitting, since Robinson had directed the task force that had gathered the ammunition the prosecution presented in court. Speaking in low tones, the imposing, gray-suited Robinson told the court about his examination of the right rear door of the Lexus LX 450.

When Rathbun was on the stand, he had testified that Linda Sobek had kicked the closed door of the sport utility when the pair struggled in the middle seat of the vehicle, and a result of that confrontation was a dent in the interior door panel. But after Robinson and Heidi Robbins had measured and photographed the inside of the Lexus, it was Robinson's opinion that what Rathbun had sworn to was impossible.

Using arrows to mark the upper and lower extremities of the dent, Robinson had shut the door of the vehicle and looked across the passenger seat from the opposite side. He found the bottom arrow to be well below the seat level and the top arrow only visible by an inch. In addition, an armrest on the seat blocked access to the door panel.

"If the door was closed, would it be possible for a human foot to kick and make a dent that size?" Kay asked.

"I don't see how this could be done," Robinson answered.

In the midst of Robinson's testimony, jurors filed past a bulletin board to look at the photos that the Sheriff's Department detective and criminalist had taken of their experiment.

Seeing another nail about to be driven into the coffin that the defense case was becoming, Werksman attacked Robinson for measuring a Lexus production vehicle, not the prototype that Rathbun had driven on the day of Sobek's death.

"Detective, oh, I mean Sergeant, you're a sergeant, right, not a detective?"

"Yes," Robinson replied balefully.

"A detective outranks a sergeant, doesn't he?"

"Yes."

"Sergeant, did you find the points of impact?"

"There appear to be possibly two points of impact."

"All right, and I see the armrest is curling toward the side of the car?"

"Yes."

"And you don't believe it could be done wearing shoes or not?"

"Yes."

"Barefoot?"

"No."

"There are three inches between the side of the seat and the door. Would it be possible if she were wearing heels?"

"I still don't think . . ."

"Objection!" Kay shouted. "The defendant testified that the victim was barefoot."

"I'm just asking hypothetically, Your Honor," Werksman said, appealing to the poker-faced judge.

"I'll allow it," he ruled.

"What if she were wearing a three-to-four-inch heel?" Werksman queried.

"I don't think I could make that dent with my fist," Robinson shot back.

"Detect—ah, Sergeant, did you seek to recreate the scenario by having somebody actually kick the door?"

"Lexus was real cooperative," the veteran investigator smiled, "but I didn't think they'd let me kick that door in."

As laughter erupted in the court, he continued, "Sobek could if she had a clear shot at it, but not in the configuration it was in, with the door shut."

That was all for Werksman, and when he passed the questioning over to the prosecution for redirect, Kay had just one question.

"Could this dent have occurred if you closed a door on a dead body?" he asked.

It was a question that would never be answered, since Werksman objected immediately and the objection was sustained.

The prosecution rested, and it was left to a scurrying Werksman to try to undo the violent rifts the prosecution had pulled open in Rathbun's story.

If you were ever to get a job as a casting director and be given the assignment to cast a private investigator, you should call Glen LaPalme, the defense's first rebuttal witness. Accompanying his gray hair is a vague down-at-the-heels scruffiness that says this guy has spent a lot of time in the street. Looks in this case are in no way deceiving. LaPalme has served sixteen years as a private investigator after eight as a U.S. postal inspector. He told the court that he possessed a doctorate from Claremont College, but his testimony this day didn't require an advanced degree.

As he told the court, on Saturday, August 24, 1996, he had accompanied the forensic pathologist Dr. David Posey to examine the Lexus LX 450, and he watched Dr. Posey reenact the scenario Rathbun had testified to at trial. Producing photos, he displayed a picture of the right rear door of the Lexus held in the open position. The two experts then positioned a Post-it note in the center of the dent.

"I'm positive I was able to see the Post-it note, looking across the seat," LaPalme said. "It appeared possible to me."

Kay asked LaPalme why he hadn't shut the right side door and then tried to take a picture of the Post-it note. LaPalme gave a waffling answer, and Kay let his testimony fly off into obscurity.

Next on the witness stand for the defense was Elizabeth "Betsy" Chapman, Robert Rathbun's girlfriend, the woman he said accompanied him on the excursion to find film rolls in the Poppy Preserve. A dark-haired woman in her forties, Chapman worked for the Fairfax, Virginia, County Police Department, giving Breathalyzer tests and taking blood samples.

Speaking in a slightly southern-tinged drawl, she said, "He [Robert] had a note with directions on it, written in pencil on white lined paper. There was a narrative section of eight or nine lines and drawings."

Switching between the drawings and a regular map, she said, she helped Robert negotiate his way to the Poppy Preserve west of Lancaster on Avenue I. Getting out of the car, they started looking around on a hillside that was easily visible from the road, and after a few minutes, Robert Rathbun called out that he had found a roll of film.

"I went over to look at it, and it was a blue and yellow undeveloped film roll," she said. "I found the next three rolls within five to ten feet of each other. We were walking around and looking, and I saw some bit of blue sticking out. It was a roll of film."

An anomaly the prosecution never mentioned, the film canisters that Robert Rathbun had overnight-mailed to his brother's defense attorney and were later introduced into evidence were the green and white of Fuji film, not yellow and blue, the colors Kodak favors.

According to Chapman, the film roll canisters were embedded in some sand and appeared to be badly crushed. She and boyfriend Robert put them in a zipper pouch, which she then deposited in her purse, and the couple returned to Charlie's house on Canyon Drive, where they were spending the week. When their stay in California was over, the couple returned to Virginia with the film canisters. On March 13, some twelve days after they had discovered the film, she said, Robert called her to say he was going to develop it.

"Did he sound excited?" Werksman asked.

"No, he didn't sound excited," she replied. "It was more informational."

Inside the walk-in closet that he had converted into a dark room, Robert Rathbun developed the film, Chapman continued, and she got a chance to view it before it was shipped off to the defense attorney in a piece of Tupperware.

The following day Robert Rathbun told much the same story as the defense went to all the lengths it could to attempt to shore up the authenticity of the photos, which were their magic bullet against the rape charges. Rathbun didn't have anything new to contribute.

Werksman asked him pointedly, "Would you manufacture or fabricate or alter evidence in order to assist your brother in this case?"

"No," the Virginia attorney replied. "I would not."

Court-goers expected Kay to attempt to savage the defendant's brother on cross-examination, but the prosecution apparently felt his testimony spoke for itself. And they were awaiting the imminent arrival of the defense's last-second forensic witness, Norman I. Perle.

Norman I. Perle was not an original member of the defense's witness list. When he appeared in court on the afternoon of October 25, 1997, it quickly became obvious that he was there for one reason and one reason only—to combat the prosecution's contention that the woman in the ''masturbation'' photos was not Linda Sobek.

To prove his contention that the woman in those photos was indeed the bathing suit model, he exhibited to the court a series of transparencies on an overhead projector. According to the salty-haired Perle, the overheads were derived from enlarged portions of the color prints of the autopsy photos and the doubled-exposed "masturbation" photos.

Early in his testimony he noted a thigh blemish that he said appeared in both sets of photos, and he showed several overheads to help demonstrate that contention.

"This is something that's physically on the person's body," he said. "I found that mark on both photos."

"And so given that, would you conclude the women are one and the same?" Werksman asked expectantly.

"Absolutely," Perle replied.

Using another series of transparencies, Perle showed markings on the labias and skin protrusions in the autopsy photos and the "masturbation" photos and testified that these, too, were the same.

Perle concluded, "I think the characteristics I'm identifying show they are the same person."

Asked by defense counsel about Heidi Robbins's prepuce-versus-prepuce comparison, Perle opined, "It would be like mixing apples and oranges. The lighting is different; the optics are different. The genitalia shape is affected by death."

Not surprisingly Werksman was hearing what he wanted to hear, and he quickly moved to seal the impression Perle was giving.

"Are you sure that the woman in each set of photographs is, in fact, the same woman?"

"Yes," the witness replied, "with the highest degree of certainty—9.9 on a scale of one to ten."

"9.9?" Werksman asked.

"You have to leave some margin for error."

"So you are confident at a scale of 9.9 the women are the same?"

"Yes."

Werksman passed his witness over to the prosecution for cross, and Mary-Jean Bowman was ready and waiting.

"What is your education, Mr. Perle?" she asked.

"Up to fifty-one units," Perle answered.

"Isn't it true you're several units short of an Associate of Arts degree?"

"I'm not sure that that's true," Perle replied. "I've taken other courses. I've worked with people outside of the field. I've taught and published articles."

"But you don't have a bachelor's degree?"

"No."

"Isn't it also true that you work out of your home?"

"I have a home office."

"With a high school diploma?"

"Like I say . . ."

"You have no training in sexual assault, do you, Mr. Perle?"

"No."

"No training in anatomy and physiology?"

"No."

"No training in medicine?"

"No."

"No training in vaginal or rectal exams?"

"No."

"In the area of photographic imaging, would you describe to us what a double exposure is?"

"Double exposure? Well, a double exposure is almost always done intentionally. And as to my credits, I am a member of the American College of Forensic Examiners."

"Mr. Perle, isn't it true that all it takes to become a member of that organization is sending in three hundred dollars and taking an ethics test?"

"No, that is not true."

"Well, then, Mr. Perle, what are the requirements?"

"You must pass a written test, write an ethics paper, give a compilation of your expert testimony, file references, pay fees. I had to provide references. I've been certified since May of 1996."

"Didn't you give false testimony—"

"Objection!" Werksman called, not at liking the way things were going for his forensic expert. "May we have a sidebar, Your Honor?"

As Werksman, Bowman and Kay conferred briefly with Judge Pitts, Perle remained in the witness chair, his hand on his chin, the most forlorn man in the world. When Bowman resumed her cross-examination, he got no respite.

"Didn't you falsely exaggerate your credits in Orange County Federal Court ten or fifteen years ago?" she asked.

"I wrote I had a resume with an AA degree," he said. "I did it anticipating that I would get the degree. I wasn't forced to delete anything."

"After you were sworn in as an honorary deputy sheriff in Madeira County, weren't those badges taken back?"

"No, that's not true at all."

After Bowman elicited from the witness that he was being paid one hundred seventy-five dollars an hour for his services, she asked him when he had been retained by the defense. That brought another objection and sidebar.

When questioning resumed, Bowman referred to one of the overheads Perle had shown during direct examination.

"In your earlier testimony you referred to a blemish on the thigh of the women?"

"Yes."

"Isn't that the women's *buttocks*, Mr. Perle?" Bowman said snidely, raising her voice to emphasize his mistake.

"Yes, yes, I believe you're right," he fumbled.

"So now we have a blemish on the thigh and the buttocks?" she mocked. "Is that your testimony, Mr. Perle?"

After embarrassing the defense expert as much as possible, Bowman withdrew the question and turned the witness back over to Werksman. The defense counsel tried to save face by having Perle repeat the presentation of some of his overheads, hoping against hope that some single juror might be able to make sense of the confusing and obscure presentation.

That completed, the defense rested its case; the prosecution did likewise, and all that remained were the jury instructions and the final arguments. The big question was: had the jurors heard the case in the same way the day-to-day courtroom observers had? Or was there at least one juror who identified with the successful Hollywood photographer Charlie Rathbun?

When Robinson returned to his home that night, having heard all the testimony and having viewed all the genitalia photos day upon day, he was in a bad mood, depressed and disgusted by it all.

"You know something," he told his wife, "in all of this I'm afraid of one thing: I'm afraid we've lost sight of Linda Sobek. That beautiful, lively, vibrant person has been reduced to pictures of her private parts."

For a woman who had refused to do nudes for so many years, it was an especially sad way to be remembered.

Chapter 43

BEFORE THE three lawyers in the case made their final statements, there was one piece of business to be transacted—the jury instructions. These instructions are a much overlooked piece of the jurisprudence system, but in the Rathbun trial, as in many others, they would prove to be very important. Though it might seem as if these instructions are done by rote, in the Rathbun case, each side had a strategy.

The prosecution wanted a murder in the first degree conviction, and the instructions gave it two ways to get there. The jury could simply find that Charles Edgar Rathbun had committed premeditated murder, that is, he planned to kill Linda Sobek and he did so. Or it could find that Rathbun killed Sobek in the commission of a felony, in this instance rape and forcible anal penetration with an unknown object, and the defendant would still receive a murder-one conviction even if the jury didn't find premeditation. As the California statute is written, the homicide need not have occurred while the felony was in progress for the felony-murder rule to apply. If there was a rape and if death occurred in some way as a result of that rape, the felony-murder rule would be invoked.

Also coming into play was the "special circumstances" section of the penal code. In this case "special circumstances" was added to the charge because the prosecution contended that the murder was committed "to facilitate the avoidance of detection.'' In other words, Rathbun could have killed Sobek in part to prevent her from filing a complaint against him about the sexual abuse.

The defense strategy on jury instructions was simpler but riskier. After consulting with his client, Werksman decided to forego a jury instruction on murder in the second degree, a very serious crime but one that does not carry a mandatory life-without-parole penalty as does murder one with special circumstances. In essence, he was hoping (gambling?) that some of the jurors would find enough doubt to hold firm against a murder-one conviction. That being the case, if the jurors chose to compromise, they could not choose the charge of second degree murder, which carries a very stiff penalty, but would be forced to choose voluntary manslaughter.

On Monday, October 28, the nine-man, three-woman jury was officially and formally reminded that Rathbun had been charged with one count of murder in the first degree and one count of unlawful anal penetration with an unknown object. Over the course of the case three male jurors had been excused—one for not revealing a prior conviction and the fact he had been a police informant, the second for discussing the case with other jurors and a third for a family emergency. One of the excused men was replaced by a female alternate, the other two by men, so the constitution of the jury remained nearly the same, mostly male.

That's just the way both defense and prosecution wanted it to be. When the jury had been empanelled more than a month earlier, Kay and Werksman each had made preemptive challenges against several female potential jury members. Kay's reasoning was that some females might not be able to relate to the beautiful model. Werksman felt that females might not relate to the middle-aged photographer. Once the predominantly male jury was in place, Kay said to Werksman jokingly, ''Well, Mark, one of us has to be wrong.''

Soon the world would see which one, but first would

come the final arguments of prosecution and defense.

Mary-Jean Bowman, in a black pinstripe suit tailored to accommodate her pregnancy, drew a very simple picture for the jury. Speaking in measured rather than passionate tones, she laid out an easily grasped premise.

"What happened to Linda Sobek?" she asked. "She was a beautiful, young, attractive model." Displaying the portfolio photos that had been recovered from the garbage can, now labeled People's Exhibits 1 to 4, she continued, "These are pictures of a young, beautiful, smiling, happy person."

Pointing at Rathbun, she went on, "Because she's beautiful, we don't have to wonder what happened. She was taken to a remote area, bound, anally raped, strangled and buried. There is really only one question you need to answer: Was she sexually assaulted? Was that anal penetration consensual? If it wasn't, he's guilty of first degree murder, because she was killed in the commission of a felony."

Having established the premise, Bowman then backed it up with a recounting of the evidence. First there were the anal injuries, crushing tissue against bone.

"No one would consent to that," Bowman asserted.

Then there were the ligature marks that showed Rathbun's gratification was accomplished against her will, as did the injuries to her ear, right wrist and left brow.

"Binding her legs apart," the blond assistant DA railed. "Is this something a normal person would consent to?"

After running over a laundry list of lies, falsehoods and prevarications the defendant had admitted to, she asked, "Why else would he lie to so many different people at so many different times? Why didn't he ever say anything about consensual sex with Linda Sobek? Because it wasn't consensual!"

Trying to make eye contact with individual jury members, the prosecutor asked the obvious question, "If you have an accident and kill somebody, do you take the body and bring it up in the mountains and bury it? No! You call 911!''

She then went through a ledger sheet of what she called big points.

One, in the doubled-exposed photos, the vehicle is not the Lexus. Two, in those same pictures, the woman is not Linda Sobek. Three, the dent in the door of the Lexus could not have been made the way Rathbun said it was. Four, the defendant's call to Glenda Elam on November 16 saying he was near Santa Barbara miles from where the crime was committed. Five, Linda Sobek's hair on the roll of tape in the MacUser bag. Six, blood on Linda Sobek's stocking. Seven, the ligatures that kept Linda Sobek's legs bound apart.

''We know all this,'' she said, ''but I don't know when; I don't know where. I don't know a lot of things, and we may never know them. But we know enough. We know he killed her to keep her quiet. He couldn't face shame, and she called him every name in the book.

''You don't have to believe he intentionally tried to kill. You know the answer. There can be only one verdict in this case. There are no compromises here that Charles Rathbun deserves. The verdict you must find is murder one.''

With the assistant district attorney holding a photo of Linda Sobek, court was adjourned for the day.

Werksman knew he had few cards left in his hand, so in his summation the following morning he pounded away at the key factor he felt had been absent from the prosecution's case: motive.

''The question is why?'' he asked. ''Why would Charles Rathbun rape and murder Linda Sobek?''

In an interesting turnabout, Werksman used the grisliness of the crimes as the reason his client couldn't have committed them.

''This is not a garden-variety rape,'' he told the rapt jury. ''This is not a garden-variety murder. They are saying this man became a savage animal, and yet they haven't proved it.''

Like Bowman, Werksman had a laundry list to run through, but his was a list of positives in his client's life.

"This man had a great job," Werksman continued. "He had just bought a home. He had a girlfriend. He had the esteem of friends. Why would he do such a thing?"

The defense attorney went through an exhaustive recounting of his case. He repeatedly referred to Sobek's 0.13 blood alcohol level and clung to the theory that the woman in the "masturbation" photos was Linda Sobek touching herself, not an impostor. He told the jury that Sobek's asphyxiation was much more likely to have been caused by compression of her head and neck than by strangulation, as the prosecution claimed. In fact, Werksman reminded them, that was the original finding of the coroner's office, before Dr. James Ribe changed his mind only weeks before the case went to trial.

He also vilified the prosecution for the introduction of the theory that Sobek had been sodomized by Rathbun's gun. Noting that Rathbun had thrown away a great deal of other evidence, he asked why he would keep a piece of evidence as important as the weapon used in the crime.

Werksman concluded his impassioned plea with a veiled appeal for mercy. He told the jury that Rathbun had admitted he had made mistakes and he had admitted he killed Linda Sobek, but if he was deserving of a conviction at all, it should be for involuntary manslaughter, not murder one.

"I'm not here telling you that you should give Charles Rathbun a medal for what happened," he said. "I'm telling you there was no rape. There was no murder."

The final word was left to veteran prosecutor Stephen Kay, who was more eager than he had ever been to win one for the much maligned Los Angeles County District Attorney's Office. Yet oddly enough, as he prepared to give one of the most important final arguments of his career, his loyalties were in some ways divided. The 1996 election was just a week away, and Kay had made no secret of the fact that he supported the challenger for the office of District Attorney, John Lynch, in his race with incumbent Gil Garcetti. With the race too close to call, he knew that a guilty verdict in the Rathbun case might be enough to keep Garcetti in office.

From the moment his summation began, there was no doubt that the distinguished prosecutor was not going to let politics stand in the way of his sense of justice. In a speech as emotional as his colleague Mary-Jean Bowman's had been clinical, Kay pulled out all the stops.

"He killed her," he said in an almost evangelical tone. "She didn't deserve to die. She was a decent human being. She didn't deserve to spend the last moments of her life on earth being tortured at the hands of the human monster, Charles Rathbun. From her grave Linda Sobek calls out for justice. Don't let her cries go unanswered."

As his delivery brought tears to the eyes of many in the courtroom, Kay again described the prosecution's theory of the crime. Rathbun took the beautiful model to an isolated place alone, thinking he could have his way with her sexually.

"I think he took her out there to see what he could get," the prosecutor told the attentive jury.

When she rebuffed his advances, Kay insisted, he became violent, trussing her in ropes and then sodomizing her savagely.

"Can you imagine the fear she must have had?" the prosecutor asked. "Can you imagine the pain? The helplessness?"

When Rathbun's frenzy was over and he realized how far he had gone, he had only one recourse, Kay insisted, he had to kill her to keep her from talking.

"The motive for the killing was to avoid detection," Kay asserted. "He didn't kill her just because he hated her. After what he did to her, how could he possibly let her live?"

Almost as heinous as the killing, the prosecutor continued, was the cold-blooded way Rathbun tried to conceal his crime. Claiming the photographer took his time about buying a shovel, as if he were contemplating buying a bottle of fine wine, Kay said Rathbun methodically buried the body and threw away evidence that might link him to Linda Sobek's death.

"Panicked?" the prosecutor scoffed. "This guy had ice water in his veins."

Kay pointed to the photographer's behavior over the next several days after burying Sobek and disposing of her possessions, asserting it was business as usual—until authorities discovered Sobek's personal effects along with his Motor Press Guild book and the Lexus borrower's agreement with his name on it.

The prosecutor pointed to the discovery of that evidence as crucial in making the case against Rathbun. Again referring to Sobek's beauty, he told jurors, "If those had been pictures of me, I'd still be buried up in Angeles Crest somewhere." But because Sobek's attractiveness grabbed Bartling's attention, her murderer could be brought to justice.

The final pieces of evidence pointing to Rathbun's guilt, Kay said, were the fabricated "masturbation" photos that purported to show Sobek in the nude. Those photos were the last desperate attempt to establish some sort of alibi in the face of mounting evidence, the prosecutor concluded.

"The Rathbun brothers tried to play us all for fools," he said.

Finally running out of steam after nearly four hours, Kay sent the case to the jury. As they had throughout the trial, the stunned Rathbun family remained mum, while the tearful Sobeks felt confident of a guilty verdict. But as Elaine Sobek noted about her daughter, "The only thing that can't happen: Linda can't come back."

Waiting for the jury to return—it has become the fodder of cliché nearly as frequently as the anachronistic scene of the father in the anteroom waiting nervously for his child to be born. In the Rathbun case the waiting took less than twenty-four hours, short by big-trial standards but excruciatingly long for the Sobek family.

It proved to be a troubled Halloween night for them after the case went to the jury on Thursday, October 31, 1996. Though convinced that Rathbun was guilty of the murder of their beloved daughter and sister, Elaine, Bob and Steve Sobek were frightened by the specter that some in the jury might be taken in by Rathbun's cool demeanor and glib answers.

But they were cheered when the jury announced it had reached a verdict the following morning. After just six hours of deliberation and one ballot in the jury room, the nine-man, three-woman panel found Charles Edgar Rathbun guilty of murder in the first degree with special circumstances and guilty of anal penetration with an unknown object.

Charlie Rathbun took the jury's pronouncement with baleful resignation, while his mother, whom police theorized was the root of his alleged hatred of blondes, gasped, "Oh, God!" At the same time Elaine Sobek greeted the verdict with a shout of "All right!" as if she were at a football game.

Though Rathbun had given an explanation for nearly every piece of prosecution evidence during his nearly four days on the witness stand, the jury just didn't accept his story. In fact, some members of the jury found his matter-of-fact answers just another reason to believe he committed the crimes.

"Once we started deliberating, we figured out how much he was lying," juror Doug Loos told the *Los Angeles Times*. "We just picked him apart. We didn't set out to do that."

Juror Greg Mars agreed, saying, "It just seemed he was lying on the stand about everything. He changed his story too many times."

As the prosecution exulted, Elaine Sobek shook the

hand of every juror, thanking them and saying, "God bless you guys."

Werksman took the jury's judgment stoically.

"There was the public perception that he was guilty from the very beginning," the subdued defense attorney told a large gathering of print and electronic media reporters. "Naturally I am disappointed with the verdict, but I have a lot of faith in the jury system. I accept the verdict."

On the steps of the mundane court building, Kay and Bowman could barely contain their joy at the conviction.

"I think we did the best we could have," Bowman said, speaking for a prosecution team that had finally won a high-profile case in Los Angeles County.

"No jury in the world would acquit Rathbun with the powerful evidence we had," Kay told the press. "Nothing can bring Linda back, but perhaps this verdict can bring some closure to her family."

He resisted any inclination he might have had to electioneer for his candidate for District Attorney, John Lynch. He was later criticized for that by some of his more partisan colleagues, especially when Lynch went down to a razor-thin defeat to Garcetti the following Tuesday.

The sentencing hearing that followed a month and a half later had the feel of a family reunion, at least on the prosecution side. The key members of the prosecution team—Kay, Bowman and Robinson—hugged various members of the Sobek family. Kay looked as ebullient as a father about to walk his daughter down the aisle in marriage, and the longtime prosecutor had some helpful hints for the Sobek family about the remarks they had prepared to give. "Just remember, no swear words," he advised.

The mood was considerably less buoyant across the courtroom. Werksman and Rathbun sat quietly side by side at the defense table, thinking private thoughts. The dapper defense attorney had arrived early so that he could provide his client with one of his final services in his behalf—a freshly cleaned suit packed in a cardboard box, provided so the photographer wouldn't have to appear in jail clothing. As news photographers took shot after shot, Charlie sat in the freshly dry-cleaned garments, calmly waiting for what he knew was inevitable.

When court was called into session, Werksman was the first to speak.

"There is nothing I or my client can say, nothing I can say that will make up for the injury and pain the Sobek family has suffered," he said. "Apologies are terribly inadequate."

Yet still there was no apology from Charles Rathbun. He refused to speak at the hearing, and as Werksman continued, it became obvious he didn't want to express remorse even through his attorney.

"My client maintains this death was a tragic accident," Werksman continued. "He says he never meant to harm Linda Sobek; he never meant to kill Linda Sobek."

The defense attorney's remarks only served to inflame the already bitter Sobek family.

Robert Sobek, the first to speak, responded with some text he had written as a letter to Rathbun, a letter intended for the photographer's prison file.

"Until the tragedy of my daughter's death I have never really known what it's like to despise someone like I despise this person," he said. "God will punish you, Charlie. I hope they put you away for a long time."

His son, Steve, presented a homespun story of his own daughter's fears in the wake of her aunt's death and spoke of the loss simply.

"We're never gonna see none of Linda's kids or anything," he told the court movingly.

Then his mother, Elaine, addressed the court, fire in her eyes.

"I still wonder how many people he has done this to," she said, her resolve obvious. "Why can't he answer our questions? Why won't he look at us?"

Then she turned directly to look at Rathbun, who was sitting at the defense table, writing out answers to some questions a writer had sent to him through his attorney.

"How can you sit there like that every day?" she sputtered. "Doesn't this bother you? Why can't you tell us where you took her?"

Kay's presentation to the court was remarkably graphic.

"This was a vicious and brutal sexual assault and murder," he told the stoic Judge Pitts. "Linda Sobek was repeatedly sexually assaulted while her legs were bound. This kind of attack defies comprehension. There were repeated full-force blows in her anus. The injuries to her hymen must have made her feel as if she were ripping apart."

With the dignity of a James Earl Jones, Pitts gave Rathbun a stinging reprimand.

"Mr. Rathbun, I don't know if you recognize the pain and suffering you have caused," he spoke to the rocksteady defendant. "Linda Sobek experienced a death of unspeakable horror."

After running down the findings of the original probation report, findings that noted the defendant had no prior record but dwelled on the enormity of the crime, Pitts continued, "The defendant gave the victim no consideration. He deserves no consideration himself."

For the rape of Linda Sobek Rathbun received eight years in prison. For the murder he received the mandatory sentence of life in prison without the possibility of parole.

As Charlie had anticipated when he made provision for his cat to be cared for some months before, he was going away for a long, long time.

Chapter 44

BY THE time Charlie was arrested, I had been following the disappearance of Linda Sobek for several days, largely because, given the media attention, it was impossible not to. The fact that Linda was from Hermosa Beach and I live in neighboring Manhattan Beach made her story all the more immediate.

On the day Charlie was taken into custody, I viewed the television coverage that originated live outside his Canyon Drive home, and over the course of the next several days, I watched transfixed as the Sheriff's Department search-and-rescue teams combed the Angeles National Forest looking for the missing model's body. Seeing a former coworker handcuffed in police custody gave me an unsettling sensation, and I wanted to get some answers. Was this fellow employee and acquaintance a serial killer or was he being accused unfairly? By then I knew that somehow, some way, I was going to write about the case.

Charlie didn't go to trial till almost a year later. In the interim I followed the intense rumor mill that revolved around the case, but it wasn't until I was drawn inevitably into the courtroom that I renewed my personal contact with Charlie. I knew I had to hear his testimony, because while so many others had prejudged him, I didn't want to come to any firm judgment until I had heard what he had to say from his lips.

I managed to wangle my way into the little crackerbox

courtroom, and one morning when he was on the witness stand ready to resume his testimony, he nodded at me in recognition and I nodded back. Contact established, I passed a note to him through his gentlemanly attorney, Mark Werksman, and so started a correspondence that has continued in fits and starts to this day. Perhaps when this book is published, it will end. I don't know.

I don't remember the first time I met Charlie. When he came onto the photographic staff at Petersen Publishing, I was the editor of the company's keystone title, *Motor Trend.* One day he just seemed to be there on a photo shoot, assisting his boss, Bob D'Olivo, who's a legend in the car magazine business. Though many of Charlie's photo mates took a dislike to him, I'll have to admit I kind of liked the guy. As much as I could tell, he seemed to try hard to do good work, and though he was quiet, he did have a sense of humor, a trait I appreciate.

In the course of our years together at Petersen Publishing, my relationship with Charlie was strictly business. We never hung around together. I never went to his house, and he never visited the boat where I was living in those days, but I think we developed a mutual respect for each other as guys who were trying to do the best job they could, sometimes without the support of others in the organization.

When he was suddenly accused of murder a couple of years after each of us had left Petersen, people who knew Charlie split two ways. One group couldn't believe that such a nice guy could be involved in anything as horrible as murder. The other group not only believed it, they also seemed immediately convinced he was responsible for a wide variety of other unmentionable acts as well. Me? I think I stood alone somewhere in the middle. Charlie had never done anything in my presence that would make me suspect he had murderous tendencies. On the other hand, I had learned enough about murder in my more than casual reading on the subject over the years to know that one can't tell a murderer by simply looking at him or her.

If you could, the cops' job would be much easier.

After his sentencing the correspondence between us grew more intense, though it has had its ups and downs. Sometimes the letters have come one after another, and at other times weeks have passed without a reply, but throughout our correspondence Charlie has been dignified, revealing if not open, and unremittingly insistent that he was unfairly convicted. He continues to maintain with all his might that what happened to Linda Sobek on the late afternoon in November, 1995, was nothing more than an accident, and after hearing him say that in person and in letters for more than a year, I'm convinced he believes it. Whether I believe it or not is another question to be answered in the concluding chapter.

In his letters to me Charlie wrote about two subjects— his life and the case. On the subject of his life he seemed thoughtful, open and at times insightful. He showed an uncommon ability to recall details of his childhood and appeared more introspective than most people. On the subject of the case, however, he was emotional, obsessive and impulsive. When it comes to the way he was prosecuted, he can barely contain his anger, even in print.

According to Charlie, the police and the prosecution were out to get him from the beginning, not because they harbored any vendetta against Charles Edgar Rathbun, Hollywood photographer, but because they desperately needed to win a high-profile case.

"It bothered me that he [Kay] went before the TV cameras and laughingly said, 'I had to show the DA's office could still take on the high-profile cases,' " Charlie wrote me in one of his early letters from prison. "But I knew all along that was his focus."

"Kay is a bully, exactly the kind I can't stand," he continued later. "He uses his power, not to find the truth, but to intimidate people into pleading guilty on higher charges than they deserve, by threatening them with even higher charges."

It is Rathbun's contention that the police and prosecution picked him out as the killer when he was arrested outside his house, then went to potential witnesses and forced or tricked them into testifying against him.

"The police were not just asking people, 'What do you know?' " he wrote me. "When you talk to Glenda she'll tell you how Robinson tried to tell her that she shouldn't try to protect me. The police could 'prove' I committed a number of other crimes. So people are put into the proper frame of mind that they must help put me away before I can strike again. I think almost every witness was given this treatment before testifying."

Because of what he claimed was police intimidation, he says, very little of the testimony presented at trial was an accurate reflection of events and his attitudes.

"It seemed to me that of all the witnesses presented by the prosecution only one seemed to give accurate, unembellished complete testimony," he wrote. "Most of them seemed to have been rehearsed or on a mission for the prosecution."

Very early on in my correspondence I endeavored to establish ground rules with Charlie, to let him know that I wasn't his friend or advocate; I was a reporter looking for the truth, and I was likely to ask some pretty tough questions.

"The fact is . . . I'm telling the truth about what happened," he replied. "I can answer any question you can put to me with absolute confidence because I was there. *I saw it happen.* I know I'm right. I know the DA is wrong. I know he knows he's wrong."

Even with my firm ground rules in place he welcomed my visits to him in prison.

"Come see me. Listen to me," he wrote. "Look at the police notes I have and when you think I'm full of it, let me know. If I can't convince you I'm telling the truth, then put it in your book. If I do convince you, put it in your book. Tell the world I'm a liar, a manipulator, or tell them I'm not. But be fair. Don't be on a crusade.

"If you do that then I am one hundred percent confident that you will have more questions about our justice system than about what really happened on November 16, 1995. Because to my mind my case stopped being about 'was there a murder?' and became 'how can the DA's office win a high-profile case and look good?' ''

Through his letters, it became apparent that Charlie found several aspects of the prosecution's case absolutely galling. One was the testimony of a female Kmart employee who claimed to have sold him the shovel he used to bury Linda Sobek. As he wrote me:

''I testified that on November 24, before I possibly could have known the police had a Kmart receipt, I quite specifically volunteered to Detective [Officer] Saldana, on tape, at South Bay Medical Center in the presence of a witness, that I purchased a shovel and gloves and that a young man 18-24 looking much like a young Jerry Mathers, let me onto the patio *for a couple of minutes*. Yet the prosecution established that I took twenty minutes of leisurely shopping and price checking to buy a shovel. They found a woman to testify that she was the only one with the key to the patio area, and that a tall man bought a shovel and gloves and only two people bought shovels that day.

''The police knew that lady didn't help me. They didn't care that she was wrong. They knew who did help me. But why find who actually did help me or that I only took two minutes or that I was panicked? It didn't help their case.''

Charlie raised an intriguing issue, but even if he had not known specifically that the police had the Kmart receipt, he still might have surmised it, since the authorities had recovered some of Sobek's personal effects, which had been deposited in the same trash can. Further, it's interesting that Charlie didn't dispute he was in Kmart and bought the shovel; he simply disputed who sold it to him.

Charlie is also absolutely obsessed with the testimony of the models, Cherie Michaels and Stella Henderson, who testified that he called Linda Sobek a bitch and implied that he hated her. Since both women testified that they barely knew Rathbun except on a professional basis, he has written me several letters that provide a vast array of personal details about them, attempting to prove that they knew him far better than they said at trial. It is very likely they knew Rathbun better than they admitted, although neither dated him or had any real personal relationship with him. But even if one completely disregards their testimony, it is my opinion that the absence of their statements would have no material effect on the prosecution's case. The point of their testimony was that Rathbun hated Sobek, yet later it became the prosecution's contention that he hated her so much he wanted to have sex with her. By the time Kay's summation rolled around, the prosecution scenario had evolved, putting forth the premise that Rathbun took Sobek to the dry lake "to see what he could get." His alleged hatred of the model was a tiny factor at best. Certainly, it wasn't the testimony of Michaels or Henderson that put him in prison.

Rathbun remains livid about the medical evidence the prosecution presented against him as well. In one letter he challenged me to use my reportorial skills to get answers to the forensic medical issues he felt were important. As he wrote:

"I want you to ask questions, like if Ribe was correct and Sobek was taken down in a restraint hold, why are there no abrasions on her knees? Even in court they slowed it way down so the 'model' wouldn't be injured. And if Linda was tied down on a hard surface which bruised her face, etc., etc., why was [*sic*] there again no marks on her knees, thighs, hips, stomach, elbows, shoulders or anywhere else, even though she was supposedly struggling so desperately to close her legs? And just what was that third ligature that would have been in the way of any conceivable purpose? And if Linda didn't die in the car, why was there blood soaked into the seat? Dead people don't have blood pressure so they don't bleed. And if the abrasions on her buttocks were caused by an object being forced between her cheeks, why isn't there as much or more damage from the same mechanism on the more delicate and sensitive *interior* tissue?

"Don't forget, Ribe abandoned his idea that hands gripping her butt cheeks caused the abrasions to her buttocks when he switched to Slaughter's 'forensic opinion' that it had to be an object, a hard object, held by the assailant. Thus one hand was occupied and *couldn't* have caused the dual abrasions to the exterior buttock."

The fact of the matter is the investigators don't have hard and fast answers to many of these questions. They have admitted they don't know exactly how Rathbun killed Linda Sobek, and they have admitted that they don't know exactly where he killed her. One of the most vexing questions to Robinson, Kay and Bowman is the matter of the ligatures. To what was Linda tied? And why was she tied? As to the wounds to Linda Sobek's anus, however, experts were more specific. Both Ribe and Slaughter testified that not only were there external abrasions, there was also severe interior damage.

Rathbun lays much of the blame for his "persecution" to timing and circumstances.

"Two *people*, not the characters created by the DA and the media, but two real people went out one day and the dynamics of each personality caused a tragedy," he wrote me. "The rest, the media build-up and speculation, the DA who sought publicity, the public reaction all was enhanced by the vacuum left by O.J. In short, I'm screwed because of O.J.'s sins."

The photographer is especially galled by the repeated contention of police and prosecutor Stephen Kay that he is a serial killer. As he wrote:

"I want to respond to your comment that Kay maintains he thinks I killed before and that I'm a sexual predator. All I can say is if he's right, why did it take five years after my parents' divorce to manifest? And why was I getting excellent grades in school if I was so devastated?

I'll go over why Kay is maintaining what he knows isn't true and how *his own investigators* uncovered the evidence to show that what some people said quite publicly isn't true.''

Just as he maintains his complete innocence in the Sobek case, he insists that he had nothing to do with the disappearance of Kimberley Pandelios.

''They knew from December 12, 1995, that I wasn't likely involved in Panderos [*sic*],'' he wrote. ''Everything pointed against it.''

He suggests that if he had access to more resources, the result in his case might have been different.

''I know what the answers are,'' he told me by mail. ''I know where the facts can be found. If I had O.J.'s cash I could have hired investigators to go out and prove it all.''

Despite his bad experiences with the authorities and the media, he still was more than willing to talk with me. I expect our prior relationship, as casual as it had been, had something to do with his feelings.

''So the police lied to me,'' he wrote. ''I trusted them, got burned. The same with *AJ* [*American Journal*, a magazine which interviewed Charlie but did not support him]. We'll see what happens with you. At least you're listening.''

Yes, I was listening, at least by mail, but I knew I had to speak with Charlie in person.

''Sorry I won't be home Friday,'' I told my wife one summer day. ''I'm going to prison.''

Chapter 45

IT WAS a bright August morning when I drove through the parched brown hills of Folsom, California, to the Sacramento State Prison, known by its guards and inmate population as New Folsom to distinguish it from Old Folsom, the notorious turn-of-the-century institution that stands rock-solid next door.

Unlike its limestone neighbor, the new prison is a recent structure of reinforced concrete that looks somewhat like a modern public library and somewhat like *Der Führer*'s bunker in Berlin. Its guards are no-nonsense men and women who look at all visitors with a jaundiced eye, perhaps wondering which one might be attempting to sneak in a shiv or plan a bank heist.

I wanted to do neither, but I did want to speak to Charlie Rathbun again. I had already been one of the first nonfamily members to visit him in North Kern State Prison in Delano, California, and after he was transferred to Sacramento State Prison in Folsom, California, a more considerable distance from the South Bay community I call home, I visited several times more.

On this as on other visits, I had no illusions that he would suddenly see the error of his ways and confess to the murder of Linda Sobek, nor did I think that he would trot out some amazing new evidence that would convince me of his innocence. After our lengthy correspondence, I had no expectation that he would tell me the truth about anything relating to the crime, but I felt I needed to ask some questions and get his direct answers to form my own conclusions about what did and didn't happen that day. I wasn't prepared to take his answers as fact, but I did intend to listen attentively.

After taking a school bus to the proper cellblock visiting area, I was escorted through a series of double steel and glass doors to a barnlike activity room to await Charlie's arrival. Moments later he ambled in. We settled down at our assigned table, where he cautioned me always to face the guards so they wouldn't suspect we were plotting against them.

I had no idea what to expect, but Charlie was in a reasonably good mood. He looked noticeably heavier than the last time I had see him at Delano, having added weight in the hips and thighs—not much exercise, I guessed. His hair was cut shorter than before. His baldness was advancing and most noticeable from the back.

With no prompting from me, he immediately began to rail about the prosecution's desire to "win a big one." It quickly became obvious that as always directing him into any kind of structured interview was going to be difficult, because he was overflowing with items he wanted to tell me, items he had been saving up for weeks. Sitting inches from me in a cheap institutional chair, he launched into a stream-of-consciousness litany of his travails at the hands of the justice system.

His first target was the way the case was tried in the media. He was particularly angry about what he described as Kay's habit of speaking out on the courthouse steps about things he had been forbidden to introduce in court.

Charlie brought up several recent notorious cases as examples of how the media manipulates and can be manipulated. In rapid succession he spoke about O.J., the Menendez brothers, the JonBenet Ramsey case and Andrew Cunanan, noting the glee with which the media dwelled on each. He told me he felt as much as anything that he was a victim of circumstances.

"I think the news media were just looking for another big case after O.J.," he said. "And my case happened to be it."

He told me his case and Cunanan's were examples of the media making more out of crimes than was really there. He noted that the media bestowed upon Cunanan superhuman criminal powers, particularly at disguise and escape, when in reality the gay spree killer was simply hiding on a Florida houseboat, waiting to kill himself. Of course, in his own case Charlie does not believe he even committed a crime.

What seems to anger Charlie the most is his feeling that the police and prosecution didn't play fair. In a low but very firm voice, he told me the police continually lied to him during his interrogation, especially Saldana of the Hermosa Beach police, whom he likened to Mark Fuhrman. In some ways a very naïve criminal, he said he thought the police were prohibited from lying by the Constitution [in fact they are not]. He said Saldana repeatedly lied about issues relating to his legal representation by Jim Nichols. Specifically he claimed the Hermosa Beach PD officer told Nichols that Charlie was unavailable to take a phone call about his legal rights after he had requested counsel when he should have been allowed to take the call. He also claimed Saldana handcuffed Nichols and kept the lawyer away from him at crucial points when he was making admissions about Sobek's body and its whereabouts.

"Saldana told me that Jim Nichols said I should co-operate with the police," Rathbun said. "But Jim never said that."

As I listened to the words spill out of him, I found it interesting that he was spending much more time protesting the way he had been convicted than protesting his innocence of the crime. But rather than confront him with that fact, I decided to keep my counsel, continuing to listen as his words flowed in an angry stream.

Gazing at me through his tortoiseshell glasses, he insisted the police had a single agenda in the case—find evidence to convict Charles Rathbun.

"The police have no duty to discover exonerating evidence," he asserted, sounding like a first-class jailhouse lawyer.

One piece of potentially exonerating evidence he claims the police either failed to produce or covered up was the record of the phone call he believes Sobek made during the Acton gas station stop. He says that the police notes he saw in discovery showed the existence of such records, something he pointed out to Mark Werksman for further investigation.

"But by the time he tried to get them it was too late," Charlie said. "Mark did a really crappy job. He didn't listen to me, and a lot of the time I wished I had defended myself."

When Charlie stopped to take a breath, I finally got a chance to throw in a question.

"What do you have to say about the prosecution's claim that you had a gun with you that day and that you inserted it into Linda's anus?" I asked.

"That was just more of their bullshit," he said. "You know, the test that the police lab uses to detect the presence of blood actually detects the presence of several organic substances. Human blood is one of those but [so are] some vegetable products and even human skin.

"I may have caused it myself by rubbing the barrel of the gun with my hand," he continued. "Or maybe it got some blood on it in the kitchen because I used to clean it near the place I kept the barbecue tools."

To Charlie the gun was just one of several inflammatory pieces of evidence the prosecution introduced that wasn't fit to go before the jury.

"I ask you, how did the abrasions get on both her buttocks when the prosecution claimed I must have had a gun in one hand when I assaulted her?" he said pointedly. He also asked me why Sobek's outer skin showed damage but her mucous membranes around the anal opening showed little or no damage, despite the prosecution's claim she was anally violated with the gun.

"If you wipe yourself with scratchy toilet tissue you injure yourself," he reminded me.

Calm, rational and at the same time very intense, Charlie was persuasive, so persuasive that someone not familiar with the facts of the case might have ended up believing him. But I kept reminding myself that he had every motivation to say and do anything that would put him in a favorable light. And I knew that there were some things he just couldn't explain away. One of them was his behavior after he realized Linda Sobek was dying. Rather than risk an end to the interview, I decided to slip the question to him sideways.

"Charlie," I asked, "have you ever thought to yourself that the outcome of all this would have been different if instead of buying a shovel and burying Linda, you had taken her to a hospital? Or to the police?"

He looked me straight in the eye and said, "The result would have been the same only quicker."

His reply stunned me, because I believe that if Charlie had gotten Linda medical help immediately after the incident, it would have been potent evidence that the death was accidental. It falls under the heading of commonsense behavior. If you have an accident, you seek medical attention; you dial 911. You don't drive around for hours with a body in your car and then bury it in the middle of the night.

Even if Charlie had raped and murdered Sobek exactly as the prosecution claimed, it undoubtedly would have looked better in the jury's eyes if he had taken her to a hospital rather than going off to Kmart to buy a shovel.

On this score, however, Charlie did not agree.

"I don't think it would have made any difference at all," he said. "After O.J. and Rodney King, the police were looking for a high-profile case that they could win, and this was the case."

According to him, they were much less interested in

getting at the truth than getting a conviction.

I couldn't let it go at that, so I said, ''Another thing that really looked bad was the fact you drove off with her body and then buried her. If it was an accident, why did you bury her?''

''I had to get out of there,'' he said. ''I was doing photography on National Forest land without a permit, and the last time I got caught without a permit it cost me more than five thousand bucks. Just think what they would have done to me if they discovered I had a dead woman in the car.''

He repeated his story about having been given a citation for doing photography without a permit, and he seemed nearly as irritated about the photo permit fine as he was about the Sobek murder conviction.

''Come on, Charlie,'' I said to him, ''even if you had to pay a fine, wouldn't it have been better than being here for the rest of your life?''

He ignored my bluntness and shook his head. For once he was speechless, and I got the impression he felt he had no choice but to try to hide the body and go on with his life as if nothing had happened—and you may well draw a conclusion from that.

One doesn't have to be a criminologist to suggest that an obvious reason to bury a victim is to conceal or destroy evidence that could lead to a murder conviction—evidence like semen or saliva on or in the victim's body. But if concealment was Charlie's reason to bury Linda Sobek, why would he then be the one to lead police to the grave-site?

That's just what I asked him.

''Because I didn't fear what the police would find,'' he replied coolly.

I found that a remarkable statement, since his story at the time the body was unearthed was that he had struck Linda Sobek with the Lexus LX 450. The autopsy quickly made it clear he hadn't collided with her, something he must certainly have known.

The police contend he led them to Sobek's body because he was convinced they would find it anyway and were getting close. Bowman told me that she believed Charlie's first search for the body, done by car with Bice, Saldana and Nichols, was a sham designed to waste time. She also suggested that Charlie might have believed that the body would be like soup after being so long in the ground and thus wouldn't give much evidence to the prosecution.

"Were you drinking or doing drugs? Something like that?" I asked him.

Self-imposed impairment isn't a legal excuse for what had transpired, but I thought it might be an explanation for his otherwise inexplicable behavior. He wouldn't take the out, however.

"I didn't have any drinks at all," he said. "Linda was the only one drinking. And I don't do drugs."

"Okay, Charlie," I continued, "what about those photos your brother claimed to have found in the Poppy Preserve?"

"I can't believe people think they are fake," he said. "Think of how difficult it would have been to find someone whose pubic hair color and pattern would have been a good match for Linda's. That would've been some audition."

In his opinion as an expert in photographic images, the differences the forensic witnesses (Robbins and Gausche) testified to could have been explained by different lighting conditions and the fact that in the autopsy photos Linda had been dead and buried for more than a week before the photos were taken.

"I asked Mark [Werksman] to ask about this, but he really didn't do much," Charlie told me.

Actually Werksman had put up a spirited bit of cross-examination centering on the lighting and the fact that one set of pictures showed a woman who was alive while the autopsy photos quite obviously showed a dead woman. But I was one of the few non-principals who examined the photos close up at trial, and to my untrained eyes they looked like the pubic areas of two different women. In spite of that, Charlie said the possibility of his brother or someone else finding a woman whose private parts looked so much like Linda's was minuscule.

"After all," he said, "[Dr. Marianne] Gausche only said that one portion of the anatomy [what she termed the clitoral hood] was different between the two photos."

Actually Gausche had also found differences in the hair patterns between the two women, while Heidi Robbins, the Sheriff's Department criminalist, had pointed out what she described as razor stubble on the woman in the "masturbation" photos, stubble not apparent on Linda Sobek's autopsy photos.

Despite this, in Charlie's opinion, it would be practically impossible to believe that his brother faked the photos, given what had to have taken place had he done so.

"Why didn't Werksman make these points more strongly during trial?" I asked him.

"Because Mark didn't listen to me a lot of the time," Charlie shot back. "He kept concentrating on the news reports that came in daily; he'd show me an article and say, 'We made some points there.' But I was more concerned about what was getting through to the jury."

In the trial controversy erupted over what Charlie testified was the Lexus insignia in the photos that his brother claimed to have recovered. When Heidi Robbins revealed that the insignia on the steering wheel in those photos was not the Lexus logo but the Oldsmobile logo, it was a blow to the defense. The implication was that the photos were fabricated by Robert Rathbun in a last-ditch effort to save his guilty brother. Charlie, on the other hand, said the mistake was a simple and honest one. He told me that when his brother described the photos to him by telephone and told them that one roll was filled with double exposures, he assumed that the roll was a half-shot roll of the Lexus interior.

Why he didn't shoot a whole roll of the Lexus interior

and where those Lexus interior shots are, if they ever existed, are questions that have never been answered. The police and prosecution don't believe that Charlie took interior photos of the Lexus. However, the day following Sobek's death, he took the sport utility vehicle to the Poppy Preserve and shot exteriors of it, photos that eventually appeared in *AutoWeek*. Since his photo assignment was to shoot both interiors and exteriors, one must presume he at least planned to photograph the interior.

In the visitors room in New Folsom, while other prisoners strolled the perimeter of the area hand in hand with their loved ones, Charlie tried to explain the photo mix-up. He said that after his brother had developed the film and looked at it, the two talked on the phone about what he saw.

"When my brother said he saw some sort of emblem on the steering wheel," Charlie told me, "I asked him to describe it to me."

Charlie, of course, had never seen the developed film, so he had no way of knowing exactly what it showed, but from his brother's description of the insignia, Charlie thought it sounded like a description of the Lexus logo, since the two have a similar right-to-left-to-right "whoosh."

"Of course, instead of the Lexus logo it was really the new Oldsmobile insignia that I had never seen [of course he *had* seen it when he photographed the Intrigue] but from his description it sounded like the Lexus logo," Charlie continued. "Why would I hide a roll of film that had absolutely nothing incriminating on it so the police couldn't find it, then tell my brother how to find it and have him do the double exposures and then age the film like it had been outside?

"When I first talked to my brother about the pictures, he said that they were hard to see," he added, excited to have someone listen to his side. "I thought it was because the emulsion had come off the film since it had been outside so long, but he said no, that wasn't it. It looked like there were double-exposures on it. And then he described the insignia to me, and I thought it sounded like the Lexus logo.''

Apparently between that time and the trial, the defense didn't bother to examine the photos well enough to determine the logo depicted in the double-exposed ''masturbation'' photos was not the Lexus logo, something Kay said the prosecution recognized about ten minutes after it received copies of the pictures.

That was bad enough, but Werksman's expert rebuttal witness on the photos, Norman I. Perle, was also a fiasco. Charlie acknowledged that, although he did try to defend Perle. Alluding to the portion of Perle's testimony when he identified the pictured woman's buttock as her thigh, Charlie said, ''He did correct himself, but Mark didn't make that as clear as he could have in his questioning.''

Charlie also said Werksman should have been better prepared for the prosecution's challenge of the photos.

''When my brother first sent the pictures, I told Mark that we needed to get some photo experts to authenticate them,'' he told me, ''but he never did.''

According to Charlie, he knew the prosecution would attack the photos because they were a key portion of the defense's case, but Werksman had seemed lackadaisical about authenticating them. Rathbun said he had told his attorney about the possible existence of the film canisters very early on in the case. He thought Werksman or someone who worked for him had gone out to the Poppy Preserve to look for the photos, but he wasn't sure that they had, and if they had, he wasn't sure they had taken the right road.

When I asked the defense attorney about the disputed photos, he told me he had never heard of the Poppy Preserve film canisters until Robert Rathbun called him, excited, with the news that he had developed them on the evening of March 14, 1996.

*   *   *

At trial the prosecution had asked Rathbun about a photograph he had taken that depicted a candy cane wedged between the buttocks of a female. Bowman referred to the picture as a bondage photo with the implication that Charlie was into bondage and thus likely to have bound Sobek's legs as evidenced by the ligature marks. The Sheriff's Department task force members had also found the photo very revealing.

Charlie shifted in his seat and moved closer to me as he gave me his explanation.

"During a long lead [press event] in Arizona, Van Tune [Editor of *Motor Trend*] and I were in a restaurant where there were no salt and pepper shakers, and over the course of the trip it became a running joke," he told me. "Where are the salt and pepper shakers? How about more salt and pepper shakers? That kind of thing."

A few weeks later, Charlie said, a woman came up to him on Sunset and asked, "Would you like a date?" He refused the hooker's advances, but suddenly he had an idea for a photo he could send to Van Tune. He asked her how much she would charge him to pose with a set of salt and pepper shakers. She told him, "Ten dollars or twenty dollars or something like that"; he agreed, and so they went to a place where they wouldn't be seen—a parking garage—and she posed with a pair of salt and pepper shakers in front of her bare breasts.

"But it turned out that I had bigger breasts than she did," Charlie said, "so we tried something else. She wanted to put them by her crotch, but I said that wasn't what I was looking for, so then we tried them with her butt, and that didn't seem to work either. I had some candy canes in the car, so I got those out and had her pose with one of them."

When he had the film developed, he thought the candy cane shot was the best, so he made up a Christmas card for Van Tune and then decided to make cards "for a few selected others."

"I sent out maybe about ten of them to people who I thought would appreciate them," he said.

Sergeant Mike Robinson found the photos during the second search of Rathbun's home soon after his arrest. The Sheriff's Department seized the proof sheet of the candy cane roll and hundreds of other photos, negatives and proof sheets, many of them depicting partially clothed women or portions of women's anatomy. Since their discovery Robinson has remained concerned that some of the women in the photos may have been other victims of Charlie Rathbun, a man he believes could well be a serial killer.

Charlie had an amusing explanation for at least some of the photos seized by police. He told me that after he was accused of rape in 1979, he always took sexually explicit pictures of the women with whom he had relationships "if they let me," because he believed that would help him defend himself against false rape or sexual molestation charges. He said he had such pictures of a number of women he had dated over the years.

That might explain some of the sexually explicit photos found in his home, but if this was Charlie's habit, one might well ask why the woman's face is never pictured in the "masturbation" photos.

He made no secret of photographing women in the nude.

"I just like taking pictures of females," he told me.

As the visiting hours wound to a close, I asked him about the Sheriff's Department suspicions that he was involved in the Kimberley Pandelios disappearance. "The police knew I didn't have anything to do with Panderos," he replied, heated by the accusation. "I was at work that day. There is no way I could have done it."

Repeatedly referring to the victim as Panderos, not Pandelios, he explained that because there had been complaints in the photo department about his irregular hours, he began to keep a log of his day-to-day activities. According to his log, he was at work during most of the day the attractive blond model disappeared. He did acknowledge that he had been out of the office for a few hours that afternoon, but, in his words, "that wouldn't have given me enough time to murder her and bury her." I thought it was odd that though he did not pronounce the model's name properly, he did seem to know the exact day that she disappeared and presumably was murdered.

I told him the police had an eyewitness who put him with Pandelios in a Hollywood Denny's restaurant a month or so before her disappearance. The witness said Charlie spoke to her while he went over Pandelios's portfolio during an interview of the neophyte model for a possible pictorial feature in a men's magazine.

He scoffed at that, saying an eyewitness claimed to have seen him with another California woman who disappeared in 1982, but that in 1982 he was living in Michigan and had a full beard. To further prove the unreliability of witnesses, he claimed eyewitnesses had put him and Linda together in Las Vegas on November 10, 1995, a day he could prove he was elsewhere.

"I thought Panderos met the guy who kidnapped her through an ad in the *Reader*," he said.

"The police told me she answered an ad for a model in the *Reader* or the *Recycler*, and the number turned out to be a phone number that you can rent by the week," I replied. "The phone number was rented by a guy named Edgar."

He looked at me blankly.

"They think you're connected, because your middle name is Edgar," I said.

"That seems pretty weak," he groaned.

During our hours upon hours together Charlie Rathbun did raise legitimate questions about the veracity of many prosecution witnesses, and he brought forward similar questions about the forensic evidence. But never did he offer substantive information that could have helped me clear his name.

Deep down I wish he could have, for the sake of his own family and for the Sobeks. But he didn't, and as I left Folsom in the sunset, I felt I had all the answers I was ever going to get.

Chapter 46

I DON'T know exactly what happened between Linda Sobek and Charlie Rathbun on November 16, 1995. Only one person does know, and he has spun several scenarios, to use his term, about the events. Since the trial that resulted in his conviction, he has clung quite closely to the story he told in court. It could be true, if for no other reason than that much of it is so illogical and irrational that it might just be real life. But after exhaustively examining both the evidence and the people who presented the evidence, I have to believe that Charlie's current story is just another in his series of scenarios designed to remove from his shoulders all culpability for the death of another human being.

The following is what I believe happened on Thursday, November 16, 1995. It is not gospel. In fact, it may vary as widely from the truth as any of the other stories that have been presented by Charlie himself and by those who prosecuted him for the crime. But it is based on the information gathered in more than a year spent talking to a wide variety of people who were connected to the case, who knew Charlie and who knew Linda. It might not be *the* answer, but it certainly is *an* answer.

When Charlie left his Canyon Drive home that Thursday morning, he was hoping to accomplish at least one simple thing. He wanted to pick up the Lexus LX 450 prototype vehicle from the Lexus headquarters and if possible to shoot some photos he needed to take for *AutoWeek* magazine. For a freelance photographer it would have looked like a light-duty day.

He knew that if he didn't shoot any frames at all on Thursday, he would be all right, because he had already planned a photo shoot for the following day with his girlfriend, Glenda Elam, as the driver. But the two of them had planned to do the shoot in Solvang, about two hours from Los Angeles. If he could get some of the photography out of the way, it would make their trip that much more leisurely.

When he arrived at the black marble and chrome Lexus headquarters on 190th Street, however, Joella Lamm, the public relations representative, told him she would like the vehicle back by end of business the following day. That news sent Charlie's plans into a cocked hat. To get to Solvang and back, do a full-on photo shoot and return by five o'clock seemed to him to be close to impossible. He groaned at the news, but then he had a brainstorm.

Linda Sobek, a model with whom he had renewed his acquaintance at the recent SEMA show, lived in nearby Hermosa Beach. As he stood in the lobby of the Lexus headquarters, he remembered the pleasant chat he'd had with her in Las Vegas, when she had written her home and pager numbers down for him so that he could contact her with work assignments. When they both had returned from Vegas, he had talked to her about a photography session for *Truckin'* magazine, but the shoot had fallen through. He knew he could hire her for the day for about three hundred bucks, and her pretty face behind the wheel would make the folks at *AutoWeek* happy. Why not give her a call?

He did, and he sighed when her answering machine picked up. But after dialing her pager, he was very pleased when she called right back. Like some other photographers, he had always considered her to be difficult at times and maybe a little bitchy, but she seemed to have softened a bit when he last spoke to her in Vegas, and she was attractive enough.

"It wouldn't be too bad to have *that* in the car for several hours," he said to himself.

Charlie made a deal with Linda for her modeling and driving services for the day. He didn't really need a model for *AutoWeek*, but since he planned to sell some of the photos elsewhere, having her in a few of the shots would give them a different look. Sure, she was going to be making considerably more than he would have paid a simple driver, but this was a last-minute deal. He figured he could afford it.

The two met at Denny's at 182nd and Crenshaw right around eleven o'clock, and even with her hair in curlers, Linda was stunning. She was as toned and fit as the freelance photographer was balding and pear-shaped.

On the drive north to the photo location, the pair of magazine photography veterans exchanged gossip and war stories. After years in the same business they had scores of mutual acquaintances, and they chit-chatted about several of them as they took the 405 freeway past the 101 to the 5 and finally to Highway 14, the Antelope Valley Freeway.

If Charlie had ever entertained thoughts of doing the photo session in Santa Barbara County, the coastal overcast drove it from his mind. Far better, he thought, to go to El Mirage, as he had told Oldsmobile's Pete Ternes he might do. That way the whole day would be considerably more relaxed, giving him more time to spend with Linda, who in his estimation seemed to be warming up to him a bit.

"Maybe she's not as bitchy as I thought she was," Charlie said to himself, as he drove the Lexus into an Acton gas station for a rest stop.

Linda walked to the phone to make a call or two, although whom she called or if she made a call at all remains a mystery. He went to the can and then bought himself some Doritos and a Diet Coke. Quickly they got back into the vehicle, heading north then east on Highway 14.

They arrived at El Mirage dry lake without incident at about one-fifteen, way too early to begin photographing the car because the vertical light from the overhead sun would throw all kinds of hotspots and shadows.

By this time Charlie's very active hormones were kicking in. He had become known at Petersen Publishing for his ''hound dog'' behavior and his seemingly omnivorous sexual appetite. Not only did he try to scam on nearly every woman who came on the scene, he also had been suspected by a few of being secretly bisexual.

Now, as they drove to the dry lake, a woman had reappeared on Charlie's radar screen, a beautiful young model who was making conversation with him, listening to what he had to say and seeming to enjoy his company. Whether Linda Sobek actually was enjoying his company is largely immaterial. The fact is he thought she was, and he began to think he should do something about it.

He tried to ply her with alcohol, using one of his favorite lines: ''I bet you twenty dollars you won't have a drink of [any liquor type here.]'' Charlie seems to have been particularly fascinated by this line, perhaps because it appears to reward drinking but actually promises the reward if the drink is refused.

Charlie rarely drank alcohol. He much preferred to stay in control while others were drinking. For Charlie it was much better to have the woman drink while he kept all his wits about him.

Responding to his bet, it is possible Linda Sobek might have taken a tiny drink or two. She was a businesswoman who was always looking for ways to squeeze more money out of a photo shoot. A couple of very short slugs of Scotch or tequila at twenty dollars a pop might have seemed like a good moneymaker for her. But I don't believe it is likely she had more than a taste or two of liquor on her own.

After Charlie tried his alcohol ploy, he started to work the other angle.

"Why don't we shoot some photos for your portfolio?" he said to her.

He knew the light wasn't optimum. He knew the wardrobe she had brought with her wasn't precisely the stuff of portfolio work, and she probably knew that as well. But there they were in the middle of nowhere with nothing to do for an hour or so. Why not burn some film?

From Linda's point of view, it would have seemed as if there was absolutely nothing to lose. Here was a high-quality professional photographer offering to take pictures of her for free. If it could enhance her portfolio, then she was all for it.

When she began to pose on the mottled clay under the hard light of the midday sun, she got into it. As a veteran professional, she knew how to light up for the camera, and under Charlie's direction she did. It became fun for her. For once she wasn't draped over a vehicle like a human car cover, and though parts of her clothing were left provocatively undone, she was wearing a great deal more clothing than she usually wore before the camera. She started to feel like a fashion model, not just hair and boobs brightening up some greasy idiot's '36 Chevrolet.

Several photographers who worked with Linda noted that she could instinctively look sexy, exude the essence of animal attraction, without actually being sexy. What she gave to the camera was craft, not emotion. But behind the camera, Charlie saw it another way. As the photo session went on and Linda teased him a bit with a hint of breast here, some inner thigh there, she was just delivering the kind of things she had seen higher-paid models deliver all their lives—the illusion of sexuality. It was a job to Linda, but to Charlie, seeing what he wanted to see, it was an invitation.

When another roll of film was exhausted and Linda returned to the Lexus to freshen up her makeup, leaving the rear door open, he came up on her from behind, and his closeness startled her.

"What are you doing?" she demanded, twisting around to look at him.

"What do you think I'm doing?" he replied, holding out the liquor bottle to her again.

"I don't know," she answered, both angry and a little frightened. "But I know I don't want another drink."

"I think you do," he said, moving a step closer, trapping her between his two-hundred-ten-pound frame and the Lexus. He brandished the bottle before her again, and he began to run his hand up the back of her thigh.

"Charlie, don't do this!" she said firmly, her voice somewhat below a scream.

She was a big girl now, and she had handled more than one guy who decided on his own to open the box and handle the merchandise without the proprietor's permission. She thought that a direct but firm approach that might leave the photographer some dignity was the best course of action.

Still his hand was on her leg.

"Charlie," she said with even more emphasis, "Don't do this! Don't do this!"

He started to wrap his other arm around her, and she jerked away.

"Look," she said, trying to stall him, "I'll have another drink."

She grabbed the bottle from his hand and tossed back a large quantity of the amber fluid.

He smiled at her.

"Yeah, good idea," he said. "In fact, I think you should have another one."

"Okay, okay," she said, trying to keep her distance from him, as inwardly she prayed, "God, please help me get through this. God, please help me now."

She took another drink, and the hulking photographer moved forward again. The prosecution claimed he was carrying a gun, but a gun wasn't necessary. He outweighed Linda Sobek by two to one. Fit as she was, she might have been able to put up a good fight, but Rathbun was much larger than she was, and they were isolated in the middle of the desert. Clearly, Linda recognized the sexual aggressor that stood before her had all the advantages he needed.

"Have another drink," he urged.

She swallowed some more liquid from the bottle. As usual, she had consumed virtually no food that day, and she was unaccustomed to drinking, so she could already feel its effects. She was growing more tired and dizzy by the second, and still Rathbun was leaning toward her, forcing her to drink, his body becoming a huge silhouette blocking out the sun.

She leaned back onto the warm leather of the Lexus's middle seat.

"Charlie, you don't want to do this!" she began to shout. "Charlie, this is the last thing you want to do!"

"No, it's not," he told her, and kneeling down into the clay, he started kissing her inner thigh.

She jerked away again in horror, but her quick movement didn't dissuade her attacker. He simply grabbed her legs and kept on.

"No, Charlie, no!" she screamed, trying to pull her legs away from him again, but the grip of his big hands and his body weight made it difficult for her to move.

"God damn it!" she screamed, "What are you trying to do?!"

He looked up from her crotch for a moment and said, "I'm trying to fuck. What are you trying to do?"

As tears of fury came to her eyes, she tried to rip her body away from him again.

"Like hell you are, you piece of shit!" she screamed. "Like hell you are!"

Her struggle to escape just seemed to make him stronger. Holding her down with his left arm, he began to open the front of his Levis.

"Touch yourself!" he ordered, pushing her hand down between her legs. "Touch yourself!"

She spat at him.

"Touch yourself!" he shouted again, "Do it!"

Screaming, "God damn you! God damn you!" she refused, and so he forced her hand to move.

"And now touch it!" he said, thrusting forth his penis. "Touch it!"

Again she refused, still screaming, and again he forced her hand to do what he wanted.

"Now, Linda, you're going to get the fuck of your life," he said, deliberately.

He moved to thrust his pelvis toward hers, but she scratched at him, refusing to let him enter her.

"No, no, no, no, no!" she screamed. "No! No!"

He fought to hold her down and thrust himself inside her, but she was strong and continued to fight back.

"No! No! No!" she screamed. "Not me!"

As he struggled with her, trying to enter her, he began to lose his erection. Realizing that his ability to enter her was going to be futile, he eased back from her for a moment.

"Touch it!" he commanded, trying to move her hand onto his deflating member. "Touch it!"

And when, forced by her attacker, she did, she felt its softness and laughed a sardonic laugh in his face.

"God, are you a loser!" she spit at him. "God, are you pathetic! You pathetic piece of shit, you hold me down, try to rape me and you can't even do it! God, are you shit!"

She kicked at him, sending his head crashing into the doorframe of the vehicle, and he reached down in a frenzy of curse words, grabbing her right ear. With a yank, he ripped her earring out of the lobe, blood spewing. Then he pulled her out of the car and dumped her onto the clay. The fall stunned her, and that blow, combined with the substantial amount of alcohol in her system, made it difficult for her to fight back.

"Oh, so I'm pathetic, huh?" he taunted her as she lay on the ground, the wind knocked from her lungs, near exhaustion. "I'm a pathetic piece of shit! I'll show you who's a piece of shit!"

Pulling a length of rope from his MacUser bag, he wound a quick loop around her left ankle and tied it through a gap in the Lexus's right rear alloy wheel. Then, running the rope back, he tied a loop around her other ankle and secured it to the other wheel. Her legs were spread apart, and no amount of her struggling could bring them back together.

"I'll show you who's a piece of shit!" he shouted, nearly incoherent in rage.

He grabbed the liquor bottle, and pushing her legs up so that her chest rolled back on her neck, he shoved the neck of the bottle into her anus again and again and again.

"I'll show you, who's a piece of shit!" he screamed.

She writhed in agony during the first few thrusts, but as he continued to bend her backward, her movement ceased, her cries ended.

By the time Charlie's brief flurry of perversion and rage ended, a stretch of less than three minutes, Linda Sobek was dead.

When Charlie came down from his murderous frenzy, at first he thought she was just playing opossum.

"She can't be dead!" his mind told him. "She can't be dead!"

He tried to determine if she was still breathing, if she had a pulse, but neither vital sign was present.

Like a punch to the solar plexus, it knocked the air out of him.

"I killed her!" he said to himself. "Jesus Fucking Christ, I killed her!"

His mind was racing, careening out of control.

"What should I do? What should I do?"

He thought of leaving her where she lay, but after a moment or two he realized that was foolhardy. In the openness of the dry lake, it wouldn't take long for someone to come across the body, even in this out of the way place. He quickly decided he would have to take the body elsewhere and make it disappear. As he said at trial, he wanted to make it somebody else's problem.

Charlie removed the rope from the wheels and looked down on the still body of the woman he had lusted for. Her injuries barely visible, she looked angelic, like one of the many sleeping women whose photos he had snapped over the years.

Shaking himself from his reverie, he lifted her body onto the middle seat of the Lexus and slammed the door. He gathered up his photo gear, packed it away in the rear cargo area and then climbed into the driver's seat.

His heart was pounding, adrenaline coursing through his veins, but a plan had already begun to mesh in his mind. He would carry the body into the Angeles National Forest, an area he knew like the f-stops on his Nikon from his days at Petersen, and hide it in the brush. It was too dangerous to have it in the vehicle for any longer than necessary. What if some cop stopped him just to look at the brand-new truck? That would be enough to send him to the chair.

Within minutes he had driven off the surface of the dry lake onto the cracked asphalt of the Pearblossom Highway, and twenty minutes after that he reentered the Angeles National Forest. Driving up a little-used dirt road, he came upon a short curve where some concrete surrounded a culvert pipe.

"This might be the spot," he said to himself.

But after he got out of the vehicle and looked around, he realized that it wasn't quite the place—at least not the place to stash her body until he could buy a shovel and come back and bury her. He drove back down the road a couple of hundred yards to a turnoff sheltered from the road by some trees.

"Better," he thought.

He parked the vehicle and peered down the road as far as he could in both directions. It was twilight, so visibility wasn't very good, but if some joker in a pickup truck saw him pulling the body out of the sport utility, he'd never be able to explain it. Calmer now, he examined her again. There were no obvious bruises on her corpse, little blood except that which had come from her torn ear, but he was wary of leaving his fingerprints, blood or DNA. Grabbing some Windex from his MacUser bag, he wiped her off and pulled her workout suit back onto her, demurely zipping up the top well past her cleavage. Carefully he pulled out the bundle that was now Linda Sobek's body and placed it in the shrubbery, covering it with the voluminous Lexus car cover.

He checked to see if any part of the car cover was visible from the road. It wasn't, so he climbed back into the vehicle, headed north and pulled onto the Antelope Valley Freeway. As he drove on, he kept his eye out for a store that could provide him with a shovel to make his logistical problem—Linda Sobek's body—go away. By the time he got to Avenue I, he realized he'd better find a store soon or he'd be back in the desert north of town, so he exited there, got a soft drink at the Arco station, perhaps asked someone where the nearest Kmart was, and then drove off to find it.

At the Kmart he bought a shovel, a pair of gloves and two Snapple iced teas. It doesn't really matter who waited on him. The fact is, Charlie was buying a shovel to dispose of a woman he had killed, not the typical behavior of someone who's been involved in an accident.

Leaving the store, Charlie called his girlfriend, Glenda, giving her the impression he was north of Santa Barbara, some sixty miles distant, and he also called his message machine. Perhaps he wanted to see if anyone had tried to reach Linda Sobek through him, having learned that she was going on a photo shoot with him. He was relieved to find nobody had.

With the shovel and gloves, he returned to the Angeles National Forest, drove directly to the site where he had deposited Sobek's body and put it back in the vehicle.

Then he motored up the road to the culvert pipe, pulled out the shovel and started digging, all the while wary of approaching cars. By this time it was well after dark, and the possibility of any traffic at all in the godforsaken location was slim.

He quickly dug a three-foot-deep rectangular hole and returned to the vehicle to look into Linda's face one last time. Her eyes were fixed and her skin was beginning to discolor. He shuddered, picked her up and carefully deposited her into the little excavation he'd dug. After shoveling the sandy soil over her, he placed some rocks atop the grave, then clambered back into the Lexus.

By eight o'clock that night he was in his own home, on the telephone with Glenda, planning the following day's activities. He tried to do some computer work that night, but he couldn't concentrate, and in bed he couldn't sleep. He kept wondering what he had done wrong, what mistake he had made that would connect him with Linda Sobek. And suddenly, about four o'clock in the morning, it hit him. He realized he still had some of Linda Sobek's stuff in the Lexus.

Running out of his house, he jumped into the LX 450 and looked around. Sure enough, there was Linda's leopard-print curler bag, her DayPlanner, her portfolio pictures—a bunch of things.

"I've gotta get rid of this crap," he told himself, and he fired up the Lexus and drove off. Again his instincts sent him to the Angeles National Forest, a place Park Rangers had told him was a prime dumping ground for bodies, often killed by Pomona street gangs.

As he drove along the Angeles Crest and Angeles Forest Highways he stopped at several different garbage cans. In each he deposited some of Sobek's personal effects. Soon, he knew, the refuse from those cans would be gathered up and disappear into a landfill somewhere. And even if they were discovered, how could they be connected to him?

Charlie made just one mistake. In his haste to shove

Linda Sobek's DayPlanner and portfolio pictures into the trashcan near the Oak Creek Ranger Station, he also threw in his Motor Press Guide Membership book and the borrower's agreement for the Lexus LX 450. Both bore his name. Bill Bartling's attentiveness the following Saturday would lead to the discovery of those two items by Hermosa Beach police, and that in turn would lead to Charlie's downfall.

But at that moment, leaving Angeles Crest, he felt positive that he could put the whole ugly incident behind him. He was too wired to sleep, and he didn't want to go back home, so he did what he did best—he took some photographs. Driving the big sport utility to the Poppy Preserve off Avenue I, he shot pictures of the vehicle as dawn bloomed over the desert. It was another day, and Charlie Rathbun was going on with his life.

He went on to spend a busy weekend with Glenda Elam. He traveled to Solvang and back, entertained a departing colleague and looked over his new house on Cheramoya. Despite the fact that he had murdered Linda Sobek in the commission of a felony, he was pretty much at ease.

He has insisted to me and others that all that weekend he was simply waiting for the other shoe to drop, for someone to come along asking him about Linda, but to those he was with that weekend, he gave no evidence of extreme stress. It wasn't till the news reports heralded Bartling's discovery and subsequent discoveries by police that he seemed to crack. And even then, the stress he exhibited seemed to be caused not by remorse for what he had done to Linda Sobek but by fear of what would happen to him.

He began to concoct various scenarios on the computer, made tentative contact with law enforcement and then, his resolve draining, he drank half a quart of Scotch, pulled out his gun and sent a suicide fax to Shannon Meyer. But though he was a member of a gun club, he couldn't quite find his temple with the muzzle of that .45.

Even when he was arrested, he still had one last chance to avoid the penalty he is now serving. If he had been able to hold his tongue during those first few interrogations and if he had not led police to the body of Linda Sobek on the day of the fateful helicopter search, he might still have been walking around among us. But by then Charlie was getting a new kind of attention, and he liked it.

In several of his letters to me he referred to "some poor kid who was different for some reason," and though he never specified who that kid was, I have to believe, on occasions at least, he was that kid. Ignored, too young, too small, on the outside looking in for most of his childhood and adult life, Charlie was suddenly the center of attention after his arrest. The police were very, very interested in everything he had to say, and so he dragged out the searches, first by car, then by helicopter to their last possible seconds. When he finally pointed out Linda's body to investigators, he must have held his breath and said to himself, "Let's roll the dice and see what they find." What they did find was a much better-preserved body than they ever expected, a body that revealed enough evidence to convict Charlie of rape and murder.

Charlie's last-ditch effort to maintain his freedom was the manufacture of the photos his brother eventually sent to defense attorney Mark Werksman, but that effort was so ill executed that it backfired, helping to assure his conviction. On the witness stand Charlie's highly choreographed testimony provided an answer for every single bit of forensic evidence against him, but in the end the jurors believed none of it. They felt his testimony was too contrived and its author, the man who buried the "accident victim," far too cold.

Charlie remains adamant in his contention that the death of Linda Sobek was an accident. I am convinced he believes it because in his mind her death *was* an accident. He didn't mean to kill her. He only meant to have sex with her. That she was utterly unwilling was nearly irrelevant to him.

As he wrote me in one of his first letters, ''There were so many points along the way where if any one had not been in place the chain would have been broken and life would have gone on essentially as before for everybody.''

Should Charlie ever admit the whole truth about that day, I'm convinced he would point to a half-dozen events that would qualify. If he hadn't picked up the Lexus that day. If Linda Sobek hadn't answered his page. If a third party had gone along on the shoot. If Linda hadn't resisted him. If he hadn't hit his head. If. If. If. If.

Some people think Charlie woke up that Thursday morning with murder on his mind. Maybe, but I believe too many things point away from that. If he was planning to murder her, why trust to chance that he could reach her on the spur of the moment? Why give her time to tell people about the photo shoot and the photographer? Why make a rest stop in Acton? And why not be well prepared to dispose of her body?

Cherie Michaels and Stella Henderson say Charlie hated Linda. I say quite the opposite. Charlie always seemed drawn to women who had strength and backbone—Shannon Meyer, Pam Downs, CeCe Berglund—women just like his mother. Linda Sobek certainly fit into that group, an attractive woman with steel in her spine, to Charlie a worthy partner. He was attracted to her and wanted her. His problem was she didn't want him.

A vexing question that remains in my mind: is Charlie Rathbun a serial killer? If he is—Stephen Kay is convinced he is—a woman who was most likely his victim was Kimberley Pandelios. Some detectives in the Sheriff's Homicide department think Charlie is the guy who killed her. To them, he matches the profile of a serial killer—a middle-aged white man with high intelligence whose job allows him mobility and contact with potential targets. Others within the same department cite statements Charlie made upon being arrested in the Sobek case as an indication he was not involved in the Pandelios disappearance.

In my mind a great deal hinges on whether he knew Pandelios prior to her disappearance. Because Charlie seemed to target women he knew for sexual assault rather than strangers, it is more likely to me that he was involved in Pandelios's death if he knew her prior to the day she vanished. And if he did kill her, my guess would be it was part of a rape that escalated into murder rather than a planned killing.

As to the other murders and disappearances to which his name has been connected, even those in law enforcement admit they are a long, long way from making a case against the Hollywood photographer. While some circumstances might point at Charlie in some cases, especially the murder of Kym Morgan, there is no hard evidence.

One of the first things Charlie Rathbun and I talked about during my most recent visit to Folsom was an issue he returned to in one of his latest letters. When we first settled down in that dreary, paper-strewn visitors room, the chipped plastic-covered table sitting in front of our knees like a rummage-sale coffee table, he said he wanted to show me something. He opened up a *National Geographic* magazine he had been thumbing through when I entered and gestured to a photo and caption. It was an artist's depiction of a prehistoric woman who had been buried and then discovered thousands of years later.

Charlie pointed out that the woman had been buried in a fetal position, just the way he had buried Linda Sobek. Paraphrasing the article, he said that burial in this position spoke of love for the deceased by the person who buried her.

"You know murderers often do strange things with the victim's body," he said.

"I know," I replied. "I've just read a book about some murders in the Seattle area, and that's just what the murderer did. In that case he didn't bury them, but he laid them out and posed them in a way that would degrade them.''

''That's interesting,'' he said.

We went on to other subjects, but I took a quick look to see the cover date on the magazine—July, 1987.

''How weird,'' I thought to myself. ''Did he bring this magazine so I could see this piece on burial or did a ten-year-old magazine with a burial story just happen to be in the visitors room on the day I came to interview an inmate who had been convicted of killing and then burying his victim?''

I didn't get the answer to my question that day, but I got a hint of the answer a couple of weeks later when a short letter from Charlie arrived in the mail, accompanied by a clipping about another burial, this time in Africa. The letter read:

Thought you might be interested in this piece from the new issue of National Geographic. *It's very similar to the piece you saw in the '87 issue. Two different cultures, millennia apart, yet one common way of doing things, both reverently and respectfully. A neolithic culture, some would argue not yet really human. Another culture, primitive but in our historic age. Clearly some things are so basic and fundamental in decency that they are done unconsciously, betraying one's true feeling. Did Neanderthal man really reason as he reacted the same way as the Venda people of S. Africa? Is Kay really credible in hoping things are a certain way? Or is it just wishful thinking on his part? C*

In all of our visits, Charlie never did give me the overwhelming evidence of his innocence that he had promised in his letters. He did give me reason to believe that some of the prosecution witnesses embellished their testimony to help get the verdict they thought he deserved, but that falls far short of proving he is not guilty.

After spending a great deal of time with him and reading a great many things he had written, including the letter above, I came away with the certain sense that he didn't hate Linda Sobek and didn't want to see her dead. What he wanted from her was her attention, maybe even her love. All his life he has been striving for attention, first from his parents and older siblings, then from classmates, then from coworkers and finally from just about any woman he ran into. Linda Sobek was just one of a long string.

Charlie Rathbun remains convinced her death, which he caused during the moments when he was raping her, was just a horrible accident—an accident far more horrible for him than for her.

He wrote me, "I did not murder Linda Sobek."

On that, as on so many things that have to do with humanity, kindness and love, Charlie is very miserably wrong. The poor little kid who was different from the others finally did become the center of attention. But at an outrageously tragic price—the price of another person's life.

Compelling True Crime Thrillers From Avon Books

FATAL MATCH
INSIDE THE MIND OF KILLER MILLIONAIRE JOHN DU PONT
by Bill Ordine and Ralph Vigoda
79105-6/ $6.99 US/ $8.99 Can

FREED TO KILL
by Gera-Lind Kolarik with Wayne Klatt
71546-5/ $5.50 US/ $6.50 Can

GOOMBATA:
THE IMPROBABLE RISE AND FALL OF JOHN GOTTI AND HIS GANG
by John Cummings and Ernest Volkman
71487-6/ $6.99 US/ $8.99 Can

CHARMER:
THE TRUE STORY OF A LADIES' MAN AND HIS VICTIMS
by Jack Olsen
71601-1/ $6.50 US/ $8.50 Can

DOUBLE JEOPARDY
by Bob Hill
72192-9/ $5.99 US/ $7.99 Can

FLOWERS FOR MRS. LUSKIN
by Arthur Jay Harris
78182-4/ $5.99 US/ $7.99 Can

AND THE BLOOD CRIED OUT
by Harlan Levy
73061-8/ $5.99 US/ $7.99 Can

The Best in Biographies from Avon Books

BLUES ALL AROUND ME: THE AUTOBIOGRAPHY OF B.B. KING
by B.B. King and David Ritz
                                    78781-4/$6.99 US/$8.99 Can

IT'S ALWAYS SOMETHING
by Gilda Radner   71072-2/ $6.99 US/ $8.99 Can

RUSH!
by Michael Arkush   77539-5/ $4.99 US/ $5.99 Can

I, TINA *by Tina Turner and Kurt Loder*
                                    70097-2/ $6.99 US/ $8.99 Can

OBSESSION: THE LIVES AND TIMES OF CALVIN KLEIN
by Steven Gaines and Sharon Churcher
                                    72500-2/$5.99 US/$7.99 Can

TIM ALLEN LAID BARE
by Michael Arkush   78260-X/ $5.99 US/ $7.99 Can

FERGIE: HER SECRET LIFE
by Allan Starkie   73080-4/ $5.99 US/ $7.99 Can

HER NAME, TITANIC
The Untold Story of the Sinking and Finding of the Unsinkable Ship
by Charles Pellegrino

On the evening of April 14, 1912, the awesome ocean liner *Titanic* struck an iceberg and vanished into the sea.

Seventy-three years later, a dedicated group of scientists set sail in search of the sunken behemoth—an incredible mission that uncovered shocking secrets buried two miles below the ocean's surface.

Author Charles Pellegrino combines two enthralling modern adventures in one— re-creating the terrible night the *Titanic* went down as well as providing a first-hand account of the remarkable expedition that found her final resting place.

70892-2/$6.50 US/$8.50 Can